With its tree-lined canals and snug brown cafés, Amsterdam is one of the most delightful cities to explore on foot. The climate of freedom and tolerance, and the flourishing of art and architecture, have created a remarkable city unlike anywhere else in the world.

Amsterdam Explored guides the visitor on nine walks that cover everything of interest from world-famous art galleries and national museums to secret almshouses and specialised shops. Each of the walks is accompanied by a detailed map and illustrated with paintings and historic maps - more than 80 in all - from collections around the world. For those with more time to spare, the author includes two cycling tours and a guide to suburban architecture. Comprehensive restaurant and hotel information is given in an appendix, together with a bibliography and full index.

Based on an intimate knowledge of the city, this affectionate guidebook is the ideal travelling companion.

ABOUT THE
past 16 yea
the art, archi
has lived in U
Brussels, and
of the Low (............ wnile living in Amsterdam for six years that he discovered the hidden delights and forgotten stories of the city. He now lives in Brussels with his wife and four children, but returns to Amsterdam whenever the opportunity arises, if only to browse in the bookshops on Spui and drink a Grolsch in De Jaren.

Also by Derek Blyth: *Flemish Cities Explored*
The best of all cultural city guides *The Times*
Superbly informative *RA Magazine*
An ideal companion for the serious art lover *Geographical Magazine*
Derek Blyth guides us expertly *TLS*
Well researched and informative *Aberdeen Press*
This pocket sized friend is just the companion you want *The Lady*

AMSTERDAM EXPLORED

DEREK BLYTH

PALLAS ATHENE

PUBLISHER'S ACKNOWLEDGEMENTS

*Many thanks Irene and Franz van Geen for their extended hospitality and help with this book,
to James Sutton, Amanda and Andrew Gardner, Jo Hedley, Julia Lloyd Williams
and to all the staff of the Amsterdam Historical Museum and other museums
who have been so generous with their assistance.*

All maps by Ted Hammond
Series editor: Alexander Fyjis-Walker
Editorial Assistant: Barbara Fyjis-Walker

Printed through World Print, Hong Kong for
Pallas Athene, 59 Linden Gardens, London W2 4HJ

ISBN 1 873429 63 0

First published 1998

CONTENTS

ILLUSTRATIONS

Zandhoek, photograph by Jacob Olie. Gemeentearchief Amsterdam, p. 271
Windmill on the Blauwhoofd Bastion, Rembrandt. Museum Boymans-van Beuningen, Rotterdam, p. 273
Doorway on Zaanstraat, author's photograph, p. 275
Window of the Spaarndammerplantsoen post office, author's photograph, p. 276
The Jewish Cemetery, Jacob van Ruisdael. Gemäldegalerie, Dresden, p. 280
Still-life, Abraham van Beyeren, Rijksmuseum, Amsterdam, p. 293
Titus in 1655, Rembrandt. Museum Boymans-van Beuningen, Rotterdam, p. 299
Portrait of Rembrandt's mother, Gerrit Dou. Rijksmuseum, p. 308

Cover: *View of the Westerkerk* (detail), Jan van der Heyden. National Gallery, London.
   This was painted for the governors of the Westerkerk, probably in 1660, and hung in their meeting room until 1864. At 90 x 114 cm. it is three times larger than most of Van der Heyden's paintings

Plates on pages 54, 67, 77, 135, 186 and 202 by permission of the Amsterdams Historisch Museum, Amsterdam; plates on pages 17, 21, 23, 33, 42, 70, 89, 91, 96, 106, 109, 115, 127, 143, 227, 262 and 271 by permission of the Historisch-topografische Atlas van het Gemeentearchief van Amsterdam; plates on pages 45, 57, 105, 146, 160, 165, 189, 191, 213, 244, 245, 247, 249, 293 and 308 by permission of the Rijksmuseum-Stichting, Amsterdam; plate on page 49 by permission of the Kupferstichkabinett, Staatliche Museen zu Berlin Preussischer Kulturbesitz; plates on pages 273 and 299 by permission of the Museum Boymans-van Beuningen, Rotterdam; plates on pages 55 and 118 by permission of the British Museum, London; plate on page 124 by permission of the Instituut Royal du Patrimoine Artistique, Brussels; plate on page 125 by permission of H.M. the Queen, © The Royal Collection; plate on page 174 by permission of the New York Public Library, the I.N. Phelps Stokes Collection; plate on page 183 by permission of the Cleveland Museum of Art, gift of Harry D. Kendrick; plate on page 231 by permission of the Teylers Museum, Haarlem; plate on page 280 by permission of the Gemäldegalerie, Dresden; plate on page 177 by permission of the Louvre, Paris; plate on page 204 by permission of the Mauritshuis, The Hague; plate on page 220 by permission of the Anne Frank Foundation, Amsterdam. Cover by permission of the National Gallery.

ACKNOWLEDGEMENTS

I am particularly grateful to Yvette Rosenberg for keeping me informed about the latest developments in Amsterdam, and, moreover, for lending us her apartment during our visits to the city. Thanks, too, to John Chalker for the Baedeker, Helen Bannatyne for her insights into Dutch history, Doug Hutchinson for a rare book on Dutch urban paintings, Jane Hedley-Prôle and Menno Spiering for allowing me to plunder their library, and Andrew Johnson for taking care of Anna for the day. I would also like to thank Marc Hameleers of the Gemeentearchief Amsterdam for providing the excellent photographs of the 1625 Florisz. map used in the book, and Marijke Kunst of the Rijksmuseum-stichting for helping to locate elusive paintings in the Rijksmuseum. My gratitude, also, to Esther Pierre at the Dutch tourist office in Brussels, for answering my many requests for information with friendly enthusiasm. I am deeply grateful to Alexander Fyjis-Walker for proposing the book and suggesting many improvements to the text. My wife, Mary Maclure, has been a constant source of encouragement since I first began to write about Amsterdam. This book is dedicated to her.

TO THE READER

't kan verkeren (things can change). This notion, coined by the 17th-century playwright Bredero, should be remembered when we go to Amsterdam. Though I have visited every sight mentioned in this book, and checked every detail, it can sometimes happen that a museum closes, a shop goes out of business, or a restaurant changes hands. It is enormously helpful, therefore, when readers who discover such changes take the time to note down their observations on a postcard and send them to the publisher.

Preface

It is now ten years since I first wrote a book about Amsterdam, while living in a warehouse apartment in the old Jewish district. The city has changed considerably since then, as old districts such as the Nieuwmarkt have been restored, and new buildings, often striking examples of modern Dutch architecture, have sprung up in Zuid and the eastern docklands. Yet the Dutch genius for conservation has preserved the best features of Amsterdam intact. The Molenpad café is as genial as ever; the Athenaeum bookshop remains one of the best in Europe, and the view looking down Oude Waal to the Montel-baanstoren is still among the finest urban prospects in Europe.

My one regret is that I no longer live in Amsterdam. We left a few years after the birth of our first daughter, when the warehouse apartment finally became too cramped. When I went to the town hall to deal with the official paperwork, I told the city clerk we were leaving Amsterdam. He looked surprised, as if this had never happened before. *Waarom?* he asked.

Why indeed?

Derek Blyth
Ixelles, 1998

Introduction

I. My Amsterdam. It was a rainy afternoon in 1979 when I first fell under the spell of Amsterdam. I had lost my way on the canals, as everyone does in the begining, and happened to come upon a brown café near the old harbour. The name was painted on the window pane in an old-fashioned calligraphy and the interior felt like the cabin of an old ship, with brown walls and mellow golden light, creaking wooden floorboards and cramped alcoves. Looking out of the café window, I could see a sailing boat tied up on the quay, its wet brown sail flapping in the rain.

That was my first impression of Amsterdam. It felt old, damp and slightly mysterious. I went back again many times, captivated by the dark rambling bookshops, the Vermeers and Van Goghs, the red brick canal houses, and the strange little electric cars that used to putter along the canals in search of a battery-recharge point. Amsterdam was still something of a hippy city in those days (it is, even now). Where the new town hall now stands, there was a grafitti-daubed squat with a flock of wooden birds on the roof. An eccentric American artist named Victor Bulgar (or King Victor IV as he preferred to be called) lived on a houseboat nearby, sometimes bumping along the canals in a van covered with fur. He constructed bizarre clocks that ran backwards, and occasionally tried to smuggle one into the Stedelijk Museum to hang on the walls. The houseboat next to the Blauwbrug was slowly transformed into a floating island, complete with sheep grazing on the deck and chickens clucking in the bilges. Guides on canal boat tours would cheerfully point him out as 'the king of the hippies'.

Amsterdam changed over the years. The hippies grew old and moved out to the suburbs with their Eric Clapton records and brown bean-bags. The electric cars, too, disappeared from the streets, another abandoned experiment, leaving just the rusting metal shelters covered in dead leaves. And then one day King Victor IV drowned in the Amstel. At his funeral, a procession of boats sailed down the river while a woman sang a lament. It felt like the end of the hippy age.

Looking at old maps of Amsterdam, at old paintings or prints like the view of the Spinhuis opposite, made in about 1780 by Hermanus Schouten, we have the comforting impression that the city has barely altered over the last three centuries. The half-ring of 17th-century canals remains more or less intact, and the houses still have baroque gable roofs and projecting beams for hoisting pianos into the living rooms. This is an illusion, though. Look behind the cheery red brick gables and you will find that the city has changed enormously since the days when Rembrandt painted anatomy lessons. The old churches, for example, are rarely used for religion these days. The Nieuwe Kerk on the Dam allows its whitewashed interior to be used for art shows, photography competitions and, on one memorable occasion, an exhibition of poisonous snakes. The Zuiderkerk, where three of Rembrandt's children were buried, now contains a permanent exhibition on urban planning, and though the Oude Kerk, where his wife Saskia was interred, is still used as a church, it lies in the middle of the red light district, which reduces the congregation to perhaps a few elderly women and a drunk tourist snoring in the corner.

After we have seen a few churches, we may come to the conclusion that nothing is sacred in Amsterdam. We are not the first to think thus of the Dutch. 'They are not so much upon the punctilio of honour, as the other Nations, but are rather given to Trade and getting,' wrote William Aglionby in 1669. A pragmatic nature leads to everything being reused; old warehouses near the harbour were turned into apartments long before other ports discovered their abandoned

docklands, and the city canals are lined with disused Rhine barges converted into houseboats. The former stock exchange on Damrak is now a concert hall; the baroque town hall, seen in Berckheyde's painting on page 42, became a royal palace (the chimney cowls in the painting are crowns), and another town hall, occupied after the first became a royal palace, is now an hotel. Meanwhile, the old police station on Leidseplein has been turned into a drugs café.

This restlessness, this constant change, perhaps spring from the fact that Amsterdam, like most of the Netherlands, is built on land reclaimed from the sea. 'You see it all below the level of the water, soppy, hideous, and artificial,' grumbled Matthew Arnold on a visit to Holland in 1859. Amsterdammers enjoy pointing out to visitors that all the buildings in their city stand on wooden piles to stop them sinking into the soggy brine. They are equally proud to inform travellers that Schiphol airport, fifteen kilometres out in the suburbs, lies well below sea level, built on reclaimed polder that was once an inland lake. Indeed, Dutch and Spanish galleons fought a naval battle there in 1573, on the spot where Boeings now touch down.

You can live for years in Amsterdam without ever realising that most of the streets lie below sea level. The city officials recently decided that this ignorance was not to be encouraged, and they constructed a hydraulic model in the new town hall (the one that hasn't been turned into something else) which features three acrylic tubes filled with water tinted blue. One column indicates the height of the sea at the North Sea coast. Another one fills up every so often with a gurgling rush of water to show the level reached during the great flood in 1953, when much of Zeeland was awash with sea water. It is enough to make you catch the next plane home, though perhaps not from that airport built on the drained lake.

Whenever the streets are dug up, you became suddenly aware that the houses are built on sand. Each building is supported on long wooden piles (or concrete columns in the case of modern buildings), which are hammered into the damp sand until they reach a fairly firm layer. You can remain blissfully unaware of this disturbing fact until you happen to come upon a heap of sand, looking like a small beach, where the paving bricks have been dug up, or glimpse a building site where ancient gnarled tree trunks poke above the ground.

The peculiar nature of Amsterdam's situation leads to endless practical problems, such as pile rot (the parasite that eats away at the wooden foundations of houses), rising damp and sinking pavements, not to forget leaking houseboats and cars that occasionally roll into the canals. Erasmus, that connoisseur of human folly, found the Amsterdammers particularly ridiculous, and coined a joke about them being the only people he knew who lived at the tops of trees. The 17th-century Amsterdam playwright Bredero provided an equally pithy phrase to sum up this ethereal city, when he wrote: *'t kan verkeren* (things can change). This motto can be seen on a brass plaque attached to a wall in Nes (unless, of course, things have changed there too).

Bredero was right. I thought I knew Amsterdam, with its 1,000 bridges, 7,000 protected monuments and 2,500 houseboats (one a refuge

for stray cats and another decorated with plastic replicas of the Manneken-Pis statue in Brussels). When I lived here, I had my favourite corners, such as the Spaarndammerbuurt, the old Jewish cemetery in Oudekerk, the room of Amsterdam Impressionists in the Rijksmuseum, and the smaller, more quirky markets like the one held on the Noordermarkt. I enjoyed the availability of almost anything a person might need, be it a copy of the *New York Times* or a foundation for the improvement of false teeth. 'Where else in the world could one find all life's commodities and curiosities?' Descartes observed in 1634, when ships of the East and West India Companies were returning to Amsterdam laden with unknown spices, rare plants, coffee beans, bales of tobacco, Chinese porcelain and precious furs. The warehouses are still standing on Brouwersgracht, Oude Schans and Prinseneiland where these goods were stored, in buildings that bear evocative names such as the Greenland Warehouses on Keizersgracht and the Rhineland Warehouses on Nieuwe Uilenburgerstraat.

Even now, when most cities can supply everything we might desire, we can still hunt in Amsterdam for elusive books long out of print, beers brewed in remote Czech villages, paintings by forgotten Swedish artists, replacement buttons for an old coat, or stamps issued by countries that have disappeared from the map. Amsterdam is also a city where curious sights abound, such as a floating flower market, a doll doctor, three pet crematoria and a museum of piggy banks.

Yet for all its exotic allure, Amsterdam still retains an unmistakable Dutch flavour. The lifestyle is relaxed and peaceful, the streets are filled with rattling bicycles, and the apartment interiors sometimes recall paintings by Vermeer and De Hoogh. This quiet mood, tinged with a certain nostalgia, can be felt most strongly in brown cafés on rainy Sunday afternoons, when the only sound to break the silence is the clunk of a chess piece or the rustle of a newspaper.

Things *can* change, though. Returning to Amsterdam to write this book, the first thing I noticed was a man on a bicycle talking into a mobile phone. That was new, as were the many tattoo shops, and indeed the tattoo museum, which has now joined the cannabis museum and the two sex museums as proof of Amsterdam's limitless indulgence. I was back to being an innocent tourist and, on one visit, I even stepped in front of a bicycle, which is virtually the only sin you can commit in Amsterdam.

They tolerate everything else here. They admitted Jews when countries such as Spain and Germany made their lives a misery. The great jurist Hugo Grotius provided a sober rationale for doing so in his *Remonstratie* of 1614, where he argued: 'Plainly God desires them to live somewhere. Why not here rather than elsewhere? The scholars among them may even be of service to us by teaching us the Hebrew language.' Encouraged by this welcoming attitude, Jews flocked to Amsterdam in the 17th century, settling in the unfashionable eastern quarters where they took up the diamond trade or ran the market stalls. Other refugees followed - Protestant Flemings, French Huguenots, Walloon Protestants, Scottish Presbyterians, Armenians and the occasional political exile such as Descartes. 'In what other country can one enjoy such complete liberty?' he wrote in 1631 to his friend Jean-Louis Guez de Balzac.

Amsterdam is still seen as a city where anything is possible. It is famous for its tolerance of gays, buskers, squatters, marijuana smokers and prostitutes, and remains a haven for artists, writers, poets and even the occasional fraudulent king. This tolerance is partly habit and perhaps partly a lingering belief that these outsiders may bring something useful to the city. Plainly God desires them to live somewhere, so why not here?

The one reason they may not live here is the shortage of accommodation. Even with warehouses converted to apartments, and old barges turned into houseboats, the city suffers from a chronic lack of living space. Those looking for an apartment have to resort to ingenious ploys, as in the case of one unhappy student who stuck a plaintive notice to a lamp-post: 'Help! My landlord has found the love of his life and I am now homeless. Can anyone help?' Even when an apartment is found, it is likely to be cramped, or noisy, or in a house propped up by wooden poles. Yet people still flock to Amsterdam from all over the world, lured by its endless vitality.

Not everyone, however, has been seduced by the city's charms. 'Amsterdam did not answer our expectations,' Hazlitt grumbled in 1826. 'It is a kind of paltry, rubbishy Venice.' Maybe it sometimes seems that way, but we should never forget Bredero's words. Things can change. This brief history proves the point.

II. A brief history. You come across two different stories on the origin of Amsterdam. The more picturesque is that Amsterdam was born on the spot where a seasick dog threw up after jumping ashore from a fishing boat caught in a storm in the Zuider Zee. The city fathers clearly relished this legend, for they adopted a coat of arms showing a fishing boat with two fishermen and a dog on board, all looking glum. This image can be spotted on the old stock exchange, the 1928 town hall, and even, if we look closely, on the mantelpiece in the burgomaster's chamber in the 17th-century town hall.

Another theory, rather more plausible, is that Amsterdam began as a fishing village on the River Amstel. This alternative story has led the city in recent years to prefer the more prosaic emblem of three black Saint Andrew's crosses, one above the other, on a red background (the presumed coat of arms of the Counts of Amstel). This symbol is the one we see most often nowadays, decorating the city's flag, lamp-posts and even the distinctive maroon bollards known affectionately as *Amsterdammertjes*, designed to prevent cars from parking on the pavements.

Whatever theory we choose to believe, we know that Amsterdam's name comes from the dam across the River Amstel built in about 1270. The first official document to refer to 'Amstelledamme' was an exemption from tolls signed by Count Floris V in 1275. This dammed river was not an obvious site for a city, as Thomas Macaulay, among others, observed. 'On a desolate marsh overhung by fogs and exhaling diseases, a marsh where there was neither wood nor stone, neither firm earth nor drinkable water, a marsh from which the ocean on one side and the Rhine on the other were with difficulty kept out by art, was to be found the most prosperous

Verus Oppidi Sigillum

Sigillum secretum opi. amstelredamensis 1387

community in Europe.'

This prosperous community began to develop in the 14th century, when ships brought grain and beer here from Hamburg, Riga and other northern ports. By the turn of the 15th century, democracy, of a sort, had been established, with the construction of the first town hall (seen in the painting by Saenredam on page 57) and the election of burgomasters. The influence of the burgomasters, though, did not last long. When Philip the Good, Duke of Burgundy, gained control of the Low Countries in 1428, he moved the court from Dijon to Brussels, and pursued a policy of centralisation that eroded most of the mediaeval privileges enjoyed by the great cities of Flanders and Holland.

We may be surprised to discover that Amsterdam, which is now so radical, was a rather conservative city in the middle ages. The marriage of Mary of Burgundy, the grand-daughter of Philip the Good, to Maximilian of Austria, caused widespread revolt in the Low Countries, but Amsterdam remained relatively calm. Maximilian rewarded this loyalty by granting

INTRODUCTION

Amsterdam the right to add the imperial crown to its coat of arms. More than a century later, long after the Dutch Republic had broken all ties with the Austrian Hapsburgs, the city was still proud enough of this honour to add a bright blue Hapsburg imperial crown to the tower of the Westerkerk.

The son of Mary and Maximilian, Philip the Fair, married Joan the Mad in 1496. Four years later, in Ghent, a son was born, the future Charles V, who at the age of fifteen gained control of a vast empire which included the Low Countries, the Hapsburg lands, Castile and Aragon. It was under Charles V that the first rumblings of the Reformation reached the Low Countries. Even conservative Amsterdam witnessed a brief uprising in 1535 when a group of radical Anabaptists, inspired by a revolt in Münster, stormed the old town hall. Amsterdam's first squatters were evicted the next day and promptly executed on the Dam.

The abdication of Charles V in 1555 marked a turning point in Dutch history. His morose son, Philip II, took a hard line with the Protestants, sending in Spanish troops to quell the rebellious cities. Philip's attitude toughened after the eruption of iconoclasm known as the Beeldenstorm (literally, picture-storm), when Catholic statues and altars were smashed in a frenzy of religious zeal. War with Spain finally broke out in 1568, and William of Orange (also known as William the Silent) took command of the Dutch rebel forces in the northern Netherlands.

As we might have expected, Amsterdam was slow to join the rebels, hedging its bets until it was confident that the north was winning. The city finally threw its lot in with William of Orange in 1578 in a peaceful revolution known as the Alteratie. The city obviously made the right choice, for Amsterdam was flooded with Flemish Protestants fleeing the reign of terror unleashed in Antwerp after its capture by the Spanish in 1585. The refugees boosted Amsterdam's economy by bringing new wealth as well as skills such as publishing, cartography and diamond cutting.

As Antwerp declined, Amsterdam seized the opportunity to become the main port in Europe. The Compagnie van Verre - founded in 1594 by

25

nine Amsterdam merchants - began to develop the profitable spice trade in the Far East. Five years later, investors in the company reaped a 400 per cent profit when four ships returned from the East Indies laden with spices. It was during this period of rapid expansion that Amsterdam began to assume the shape we know today. Most of the canals we walk along as tourists were laid out under the Plan of the Three Canals, drawn up in 1609 by Hendrick Staets, the city carpenter. Eventually executed in two phases, this vast urban planning project created the great semi-circle of canals - Herengracht, Keizersgracht, Prinsengracht and the Jordaan - known as the *Grachtengordel* (canal ring).

Hendrick de Keyser (1565-1621) was city architect at just the moment when the economy began to boom. He built new Protestant churches such as the Westerkerk and the Noorderkerk, added ornate spires to the brick towers left behind when the old city wall was demolished (such as the Munttoren) and created one of the most flamboyant private houses in the city for the brewer Guillielmo Bartolotti. De Keyser's mannerism

fell out of fashion in the second quarter of the 17th century, when style-conscious merchants began to adopt the more sober classicism of Jacob van Campen. Constantijn Huygens, the powerful secretary to Prince Frederik Hendrik, gave his stamp of approval to Van Campen (as he had done to Rembrandt), arguing that he 'admonished Gothic curly foolery with the stately Roman'. The Coymans House at Keizersgracht 177 was one of the first houses built in this new style.

A different type of classicism was developed in the mid-17th century by Philips Vingboons, who invented the neck gable, a simplification of De Keyser's step gable. If we turn to the painting of Herengracht on page 177, we can see the step-gabled Bartolotti house on the left and a Vingboons neck gable on the right. Another type of gable, the bell gable, was popular in the 18th century; two fine examples can be seen in the print by Schouten on page 109, to the right of the church tower.

The signing of the Treaty of Münster, which ended the Eighty Years' War with Spain, was one of the supreme moments in Dutch history.

Those who know the Dutch rooms in the National Gallery in London may be familiar with a painting showing the Dutch and Spanish delegates signing the treaty in 1648. The Rijksmuseum has a painting by Bartholomeus van der Helst illlustrating the splendid banquet held soon afterwards in the guild house of the Amsterdam crossbowmen (reproduced on page 165). It was in this jubilant year that an architect was chosen to build the new Amsterdam town hall. The job went to Van Campen, whose 'stately Roman' style was favoured by the Calvinist city council. The town hall was dubbed the eighth wonder of the world, at least by the Dutch.

This was the Golden Age in Amsterdam's (and Holland's) history, when the city built its model prisons and orphanages, Rembrandt painted Amsterdam's wealthy merchants (and sketched the hungry beggars), and Admiral Michiel de Ruyter caused panic in London by sailing the Dutch fleet up the River Medway. There were some setbacks, of course, such as tulip fever - tulipomania - which swept through the country as the price of rare tulip bulbs soared, and left many families destitute when prices suddenly slumped in 1637. Yet the general mood of the Golden Age was one of quiet contentment, as we see in the paintings of Vermeer, De Hoogh, Van der Heyden and Cuyp.

So it came as a great shock when the country was invaded on all sides in 1672. Known as 'the year of disasters', this saw the armies of Louis XIV invading by land while the English fleet (with whom the Medway episode still rankled) attacked from the sea. The Dutch managed to fight off the attacks (though Maastricht was lost to the French), but the confident mood of the Golden Age never quite returned. By the end of the 18th century, Amsterdam merchants were content to imitate the architecture and fashions of Paris, as is reflected in the engraved views of Amsterdam published in Fouquet's *Atlas* from 1760 to 1783, one of which we saw on page 17. When the French revolutionary army marched into Amsterdam in 1795, the people put up very little resistance. They did not even complain when Napoleon's brother Louis Napoléon became King of the Netherlands in 1806, and turned the baroque town hall on the Dam into a royal palace.

After Napoleon's defeat at Leipzig in 1813, Louis was forced to flee, leaving behind a fine collection of Empire style furniture that can still be seen in the royal palace. The economy of Amsterdam remained depressed for many years, until the construction of the North Sea Canal, opened in 1876, brought new prosperity to the port. Historians talk about a second Golden Age in the late 19th century, when the old fortifications were torn down and new residential districts built around the edge of the city. This was the period when Cuypers designed the Rijksmuseum, wealthy families such as Heineken built grand eclectic villas near the Vondelpark, and Breitner painted Impressionist views of the crowded Amsterdam streets.

This mood of confidence lasted until the German invasion of 1940. As we wander through the streets of Amsterdam, we come across countless reminders of the war years, such as the Dokwerker statue near the Jewish Museum which commemorates the dockers' strike of 1941, and the roofless shell of the Hollands Schouwburg where thousands of Jews awaited deportation. For many visitors, the most haunting spot is the house on Prinsengracht where Anne Frank and her family went into hiding in the summer of 1942. Almost nothing in the cramped annnexe has changed since the morning of 4 August 1944, when the police burst in and arrested the eight people in hiding.

Half a century on, Amsterdam has recovered its reputation as a haven of tolerance and enlightened city government. Despite some ill-fated experiments in the 1960's - such as the white bicycle scheme, which flopped after thieves spirited away the entire stock of free public bicycles - the city continues to press ahead with utopian solutions to the problems of urban living. Amsterdammers, too, take enormous pride in the physical beauty of their city, setting up foundations to protect historic houses, nurturing clematis in the sandy soil outside their houses, and furnishing their front rooms like an interior design magazine (and leaving the curtains open so that their good taste does not go unobserved).

Nor do they ever stop building. We can take

bus 32 out to the KNSM island, an abandoned area of docklands in the eastern harbour. It's a long trip that takes us through the old maritime district, past sailing ships, party boats, potato warehouses and the occasional cruise ship. Finally, the bus crosses a stretch of empty wasteland to reach the remote island in the IJ where buildings are rising out of the ground. Gusts of sand blow across the pavement as we walk along the old waterfront, past barges with evocative names like *Nooit Volmaakt* (Never Completed). The place seems strangely isolated, like a 17th-century trading post might have felt. It may come as no surprise to learn that this is known as the new Manhattan.

III. Arriving in Amsterdam. Whether we travel by plane to Schiphol, or cross the North Sea by ferry, or take the Eurostar through the Channel Tunnel, we will probably arrive at Centraal Station, built on an island in the inlet of the IJ (pronounced 'eye'). Here, we will have to struggle through the crowds, past flower stalls, sock shops and posters put up by the League Against Bad Language. On leaving the station, we are immediately engulfed by clanking bicycles, screeching trams, Russian buskers and perhaps the distant sound of a barrel organ. We should head for the tourist office on the other side of the square, located in a curious white wooden structure originally built in 1911 as a tram station.

If we need to book a hotel, we can do so here, though the queue may be forbidding. We may have a long wait even in February, when we might have thought that nobody with any sense would visit Amsterdam. In the summer, it is impossible. We may have to wait an hour or more while the staff ring around in search of vacant rooms. If we already have a hotel room, we need not bother with the tourist office, unless it is to pick up a free copy of *Uitkrant* magazine, which lists the most important cultural events in town, and some of the odd things too, such as rare films that are shown nowhere else in the world and plays staged in the most unlikely locations. The magazine is entirely in Dutch, but we can probably figure out that *Kinderen* means children and that *Muziek* covers music.

The real reason we are here is to visit Smits Koffiehuis, on the floor below the tourist office. This café gives us a first impression of traditional Dutch style, with its fondness for solid wooden tables and elaborate iron lamps. In the summer, when the rain holds off, we can sit outside on the waterfront terrace. This is a good spot to get our bearings before we set off.

We are now on an artificial island built in the 19th century in the middle of the old harbour. An enterprising photographer climbed onto the roof of Centraal Station soon after it was built, in

1889, to take this panoramic photograph of the old harbour front. From where we are sitting (just to the left of the bridge in the photograph), we can probably recognise some of the buildings, such as the St Nicolaaskerk to the left of the bridge, the Oude Kerk in the middle and the round Lutheran Church on the right.

The road running straight ahead is the Damrak, which in 1889 was lined with elegant shops shaded by canvas awnings. One of the few remaining signs of grandeur today is the Victoria Hotel on the corner. This had only recently opened when the photograph was taken; its solid pompous style, reminiscent of Imperial Germany, was designed by the German owner, and architect, a Herr Henkenhaf. Looking more closely, however, we can see that his hotel does not occupy the entire block. Two local residents stubbornly refused to sell their houses at Prins Hendrikkade 46 and 47, and Henkenhaf had no option but to modify his grandiose plans, leaving us with the strange sight of the two 17th-century houses embedded in the fabric of the hotel.

IV. Looking at a map. We must now look at a map of Amsterdam to understand the city. Any map will do, as long as it includes the Jordaan to the west and the Plantage to the east. The map on the inside front cover shows the main area we will be exploring, but it is rewarding to pore over old maps of Amsterdam, such as the 1544 bird's eye view by Cornelis Anthonisz. reproduced opposite. Not that we can rely on Anthonisz. to navigate around the city; too much has changed since he looked down on it from above.

The main use of Anthonisz.'s map is to show us the original shape of the city, with the broad river Amstel dividing Amsterdam into two virtually identical halves. To the left of the river as we look at it lies the Oude Zijde, the old side; to the right, the Nieuwe Zijde, the new side. This simple logic continues in the naming of the churches: the Oude Kerk on the left side, the Nieuwe Kerk on the right side. Furthermore, each side is drained by two parallel canals, whose names reveal their location on the Oude Zijde or Nieuwe Zijde. Thus, with just a few words of Dutch, we can begin to navigate around the old quarters.

Yet things have changed. Many of the waterways were filled in during the 19th century to create broad streets for trams, the Amstel was covered over to make the streets Rokin and Damrak, and the two canals to the west of the Amstel were also turned into streets, leaving only the east side looking as it does on the map. A more useful map to use on our walks is the one published by Balthasar Florisz. in the 17th century. Two editions were printed of this map, in 1625 and 1650. I have used the earlier version, which shows Amsterdam as it was when Rembrandt was

AMSTERDAM

a young artist and Manhattan was still owned by the Manhattoes (it was bought by the Dutch in 1626). The later version is similar, but it shows the new town hall on the Dam. Florisz.'s map is too minutely engraved to reproduce it in its entirety here, but we will be enjoying details throughout our walks. His general view, on page 2, shows a city dominated by churches and spires, but above all by hundreds of ships bringing all the riches of the world to what one traveller called 'this modern Tyre, the mistress of commerce, the warehouse of the world, and one of the finest, greatest and most wealthy cities in Europe'.

In the period between the two maps, Amsterdam had grown enormously, from a fortified trading place into the modern shape of town we see today. The main development was the grachtengordel, the three vast residential canals curving round the western half of the old town. Florisz.'s map shows us the great ring of canals - or at least the part of it that had been built in the early 17th century. When the plan was completed towards the end of the century, it gave Amsterdam

a structure that remained virtually intact until 19th-century developers filled in the canals and widened the streets. The baroque girdle is sometimes compared to the rings of a tree or a spider's web, though Albert Camus more gloomily saw it as a representation of the circles of Hell.

The clearest picture of the city plan at its most perfect extent is perhaps the map opposite, which was produced by a third artist through whose eyes we will be looking at Amsterdam. Pierre Fouquet, a French art dealer living in Amsterdam, signed this map in around 1780, as part of a great collection of views of Amsterdam that he published. We have already seen one of them, on page 17, based on a drawing by Hermanus Schouten, and we shall be looking at many more. Perhaps Fouquet might be considered more of an entrepreneur than an artist, since all his prints bar the map are taken from drawings by other men; but as we will see, it was his vision that made the series. What his map shows is how the old town drawn by Anthonisz. has survived, but entirely surrounded by the grachtengordel on the west and south, and vast dock areas to the east, all protected by

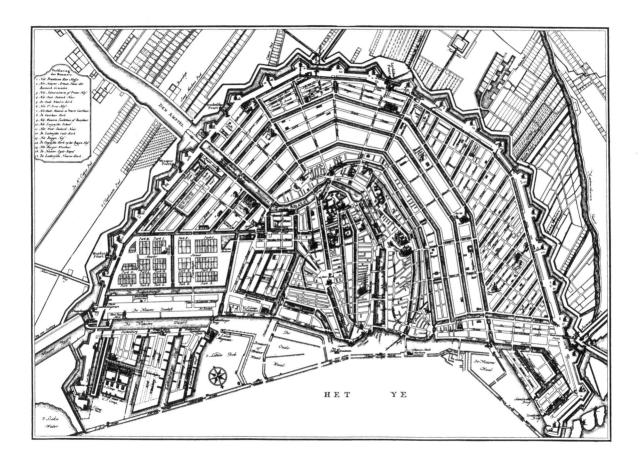

DEN AMSTEL

HET   YE

a fortified wall with windmill-topped bastions (the windmills helped drain the waterlogged land) and by a palisade on the port side.

It is time to come down to earth and think about our walks. Opposite is our first detail from Florisz.'s map of Amsterdam at the height of its glory. His view of the harbour, with the great ocean-going ships moored by the palisades while smaller lighters load and unload the goods, shows Amsterdam as the great mart of Europe. The wooden building we are sitting in now (if we are still happily in Smits café) was modelled on the Paalhuis, built in 1561 as a toll house at the end of the Amstel. We can see the Paalhuis on the map, surrounded by rowing boats, to the right of the bridge named Nieuwe brugh.

Turning back to the photograph from the station roof, we can identify most of the areas we will be exploring on our walks. The first walk takes us through the old centre, straight ahead of us, where most of the canals have vanished, but many 17th-century public buildings are still standing, such as the town hall whose cupola we see rising above the Victoria Hotel. Our second walk delves into a beautiful, somewhat forgotten area to the east, behind the Oude Kerk, whose single spire can be seen to the left of the Damrak. On our third walk, we go beyond the mediaeval city into the eastern area of Amsterdam where Rembrandt lived and worked, to explore the streets around the Zuiderkerk, the spire of which rises to the left of the Oude Kerk. Our fourth walk takes us along the waterfront on the left of the photograph, to wander through the historic harbour quarter where 17th-century Dutch mariners set off on voyages of discovery, while our fifth walk takes us down Singel, past the Round Lutheran Church that rises above the roofs seen on the far right.

We then turn our attention to the great ring of canals built beyond the western limits of the mediaeval city. We begin with the majestic Herengracht in walk 6, followed by Keizersgracht on walk 7. Walk 8 takes us along Prinsengracht and into the lively Jordaan district, past the Westerkerk whose spire we see to the left of the Lutheran Church. Our final walk goes beyond the 17th-century city, into the museum district built in the

op 't Water

Nieuwe brugh

Oude-syds Kolck

Warmoes straet

Warmoes straet

Wacht

Camper-hooft

Kraen

late 19th century, where we visit the three great art museums, the Rijksmuseum, the Stedelijk, and the Van Gogh museum. Before we do anything else, though, let us look at the Dam.

The Dam and its Neighbourhood

THE BEURS *to* THE BEGIJNHOF

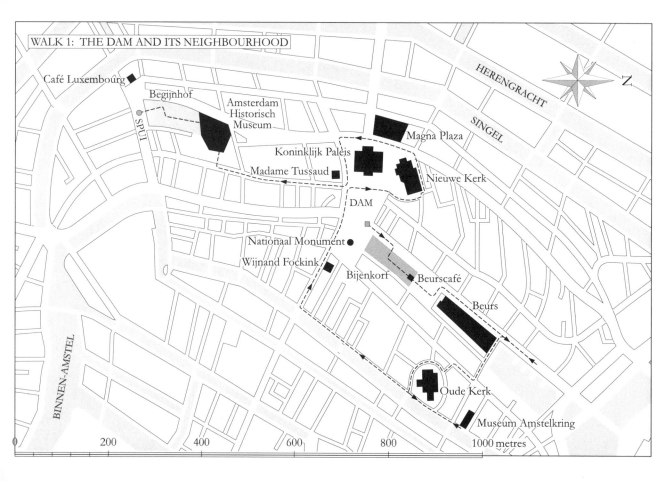

WALK 1: THE DAM AND ITS NEIGHBOURHOOD

Café Luxembourg

SPUI

Begijnhof

Amsterdam
Historisch
Museum

Koninklijk Paleis

Madame Tussaud

Magna Plaza

Nieuwe Kerk

DAM

Nationaal Monument

Wijnand Fockink

Bijenkorf

Beurscafé

Beurs

Oude Kerk

Museum Amstelkring

HERENGRACHT

SINGEL

Z

BINNEN-AMSTEL

0   200   400   600   800   1000 metres

The Dam and its neighbourhood

THE BEURS *to* THE BEGIJNHOF

The Dam is a fitting place to begin our exploration, as it was here, in the early 13th century, that Gijsbrecht II dammed the River Amstel and built a castle nearby. Not that we will find any dam now, nor indeed any sign of the Amstel, which was buried below ground many years ago. Yet the Dam still remains the heart of the city, as it was in the 17th century, when Dutch and foreign merchants - including the occasional exotic figure in a turban - gathered here to do business, as we see in the painting overleaf, painted in 1658 by Gerrit Berckheyde. The big building straight ahead is the town hall, and the church to the right is the national church; we will visit both during this walk, as well as the stock exchange and the city orphanage, though not one of these buildings is still used for its original purpose. The town hall is now a royal palace, the stock exchange a concert hall, the orphanage a historical museum, and the national church, though still used for the occasional royal wedding, is far more likely to be the setting for an art exhibition or antique fair. As well as these historic monuments, we will spot several curiosities along the way, including a secret chapel in an attic, a giant tooth, a mechanical model of Goliath and a street hung with paintings. This is a fairly long walk, which will take us at least four hours, so it is perhaps wise to begin with a coffee.

I. The Beurs. A century ago, travellers arriving

on the Dam would have consulted their red-covered Baedeker's guides to find a suitable café. Some would have headed straight to the Krasnapolsky Hotel, built in 1883, and described by Baedeker as having 'one of the largest cafés in Europe, with summer and winter gardens and numerous billiard tables'. The Krasnapolsky is still standing today, and the famous winter garden, designed by G. B. Salm, has been restored to its original splendour, though it is now reserved for hotel guests. There is a small café open to the public, but this has little to commend it apart from the view, so we should perhaps think about somewhere else.

There were once several grand cafés in Kalverstraat and Warmoesstraat, which run south and north respectively from the Dam, but they have all closed down. The one grand building remaining is the Bijenkorf, on the corner of Dam, a department store built in 1915 where we find everything we might need, including the latest newspapers, a good selection of novels in several languages and a kitchen department stocked with fashionable Italian espresso machines and German gadgets for uncorking wine. There is a literary café on the third foor, next to the bookshop, and an espresso bar on the ground floor. I suggest the ground-floor Beurscafé, which serves good coffee and, moreover, enjoys a splendid view of the Beursplein, where Hendrik Petrus Berlage built the Beurs (exchange) between 1899 and 1903.

This is not the original exchange. Financial trading was done at the Beurs on the Dam (see page 59), and other merchants in the 17th century traded in a renaissance building which stood just north of here, under the far corner of the present Beurs. On the detail overleaf from Florisz.'s 1625 map it is an open arcade, marked Corenbeurse - corn exchange. The map was drawn at a time when lighters sailed all the way up to the Dam to unload their cargoes. Most of Berlage's new exchange was built on the site of the old harbour, and gave Amsterdammers their first glimpse of modern architecture. They were not all impressed; one person complained bitterly: 'It's as plain as a mill.'

This was hardly fair. Looked at closely,

43

Berlage's building incorporates a wonderful variety of sculpture, such as the tiled clock in the tower with the motto 'bide your time,' which we might just be able to see through the foliage, together with a relief on the gable opposite us, near the top, depicting the foundation of Amsterdam (a boat with two fishermen and a sick dog). The interior of the Beurs is even more splendid, with gleaming tile pictures, ironwork and wood panelling. After the stockbrokers moved out of the building a few years ago, the main hall was converted to a concert hall, and the Berlage Museum was opened in the south section. If we have time, we should visit the museum to admire Berlage's brickwork and the painted tiles by Dutch artists. As an added bonus, we can climb Berlage's clock tower to look down on the old city.

The square we can see from our café is decorated with enormous 19th-century iron lampposts and a curious granite fountain. The Amsterdam authorities take a commendable interest in street furniture, commissioning designs like these by the best architects and sculptors of the day.

The latest project, which we can admire as we sip our coffee, is on Damrak, where Tom Potsma and Alexander Schabracq have created a remarkable series of turquoise street lamps, benches, bike racks and rubbish bins. Those who know their modern sculpture might spot familiar motifs on the lamp-posts, borrowed from famous modern works.

Damrak has been a busy street since the 17th century, when it was known as op 't Water. At about the time Florisz. made his map, the street was lined with shops selling atlases, compasses, maps of the East Indies and provisions for the long sea voyages that started from the harbour only a few yards away. The printer Johannes Janssonius ran a shop at No. 48, Willem Blaeu and his son Johannes sold their famous world atlases at No. 46 and the publisher Louis Elsevier lived at No. 81. Visiting Amsterdam in 1641, John Evelyn found a curious tavern called the Bruiloft in the Oudebrugsteeg, a lane just off Damrak indicated by the number 12 on Florisz.'s map. 'In the upper rooms of the house were divers pretty Water workes rising 108 foote from the ground, which seem'd very rare, till the Engine was discovered: here were many quaint devices, fountaines, artificiall musique, noyses of beasts and chirping of birds etc.'

Evelyn's tavern has gone, as have Blaeu's shop, which now sells photographic equipment, and Elsevier's house, now a French bakery. The only bookshop left hereabouts is Allert de Lange at No. 62, which stocks literary Dutch novels and guidebooks to the city. Damrak today may be a disappointment, but we can still spot the occasional splendid relic of the past, such as the Art Nouveau buildings at Nos. 37 and 79 (No. 79 is signed at the base, to the right of the entrance, by the architect Gerrit van Arkel), and the tall office building at No. 28 decorated with statues by Joseph Mendes da Costa representing Love, Wisdom and that very Dutch virtue of Thrift.

Given the changes that have occurred, it is remarkable that we can still track down the view of Damrak that George Hendrick Breitner painted one day in 1900. This sombre realist, sometimes called the Zola of Amsterdam, was famous for painting out of doors, and we can locate the exact spot where he stood on this occasion by leaving the café and walking down Damrak past the Beurs, pausing at the corner below the tower only to admire the statue of Gijsbrecht II van Amstel, the 13th-century noble who founded Amsterdam - unless, of course, we prefer to believe the legend of the sick dog. Beyond the exchange, we find the last stretch of water on Damrak. If we stand next to pier 4, where the Meyers Rondvaart boats tie up, we can see some of the buildings painted by Breitner, including the spire of the Oude Kerk and the dark brick warehouse to the left. The houses rise directly out of the water, as they do in Venice, though there are no gondolas here, only glass-topped tour boats driven by skippers in jaunty nautical caps, who will try and cajole us into taking a one-hour trip.

II. The Oude Kerk. We retrace our steps to the Beurs and turn left along Oudebrugsteeg. This lane leads into the the red light district, though we can avoid this by turning right along Warmoesstraat. If we had gone straight ahead

instead, we would have found ourselves in Lange Niezel, which was a highly desirable address in the 17th century, but is now a dingy lane lined with peep shows and sex shops. Even Bredero would scarcely have believed that things could change so much.

Yet it is not all seedy. We might catch a whiff of roasted coffee beans coming from Geels coffee shop at Warmoesstraat 67, which has a tiny museum on the first floor filled with antique coffee grinders. Soon after that, we turn left down Enge Kerksteeg, where pails of yellow tulips and pots of basil are set out in front of a florist's shop. This lane leads to the oldest church in Amsterdam, which is now surrounded on all sides by brothels. Milan Kundera described the alluring scene in his novel *The Unbearable Lightness of Being*: 'There are houses running along one side of the street, and behind the large ground-floor shop-front windows all the whores have little rooms and plushly pillowed armchairs in which they sit up close to the glass wearing bras and panties. They look like big bored cats.'

Occasionally, one of the big bored cats will tap frantically on the glass to catch the attention of the passing men, few of whom have come here in search of Rembrandt's Saskia. That is our purpose, though, and we achieve it by entering the Oude Kerk by the south door, to the right of the tower. After buying a ticket (churches in Amsterdam are rarely free) we enter a vast gothic church whose rough stone floor is paved with ancient cracked gravestones. Some of the tombs have names carved on them, or coats of arms, or guild symbols, but others bear nothing except a number. No. 29K lies in the north aisle, in a chapel that once belonged to the guild of wheat merchants. Only the number distinguished it, until recently an inscription was added: 'Saskia, 19 Juni 1642'.

Nine years earlier, Rembrandt made the drawing oposite. Under it he pencilled a few lines at the bottom that help us to understand Saskia's vivacious looks: 'This is drawn after my wife, when she was 21 years old, on the third day of our betrothal, the 8th of June 1633.' Saskia is wearing a straw hat and holding a small flower, perhaps a rose. But all the freshness and the vigour of the new bride faded very quickly. Only a few years later, his portraits showed her looking pale, or lying sick in bed. Soon after the birth of their son, Titus, she died.

Rembrandt is often accused of showing no grief after Saskia's death. This rather harsh judgment is based on the self-portraits done in the 1640's, where there is indeed little sign of sadness. Yet this was the period when Rembrandt took to wandering out of Amsterdam, following the winding Amstel river or the deserted dikes to the east of the city. He took along his sketch book and produced drawings of empty flat landscapes and solitary buildings such as the windmill reproduced on page 273. It is these works, perhaps, that reveal the depths of Rembrandt's grief.

Another 17th-century woman, Maria Tesselschade, is buried somewhere in the Oude Kerk. I have occasionally looked for the grave, but without success. It may be just a number on a stone, like Saskia's, for the Dutch have a tendency to neglect their dead writers. Maria's father was the poet Pieter Cornelis Hooft, a friend of Bredero. On the day his daughter was born,

Hooft was caught in a furious storm off the Texel coast in which 44 ships sank and 1,000 seamen drowned. He miraculously survived the storm, and celebrated his good fortune by saddling his daughter with the name Tesselschade - Texel Wreck. Undaunted by her odd name, Maria Tesselschade became a famous poet and musician, with a flair for foreign languages. When she died at Muiden Castle in 1649, the diplomat Constantijn Huygens wrote her epitaph:

This is Tesselschade's grave.
Let no one presume
To measure her immeasurable quality in words:
Everything that can be said of the sun is true of her.

If we have trouble finding Tesselschade's tomb, there will be no missing that of Admiral Willem van der Zaan in the corner chapel next to the organ. Designed by Rombout Verhulst, it celebrates a Dutch admiral who died in 1669 fighting the Barbary pirates. The monument is laden with cannon, anchors, skulls and a relief showing the sea battle in which he perished. Even more swaggering is the memorial in the opposite chapel to Admiral van der Hulst, who was killed in a ferocious four-day battle fought against the English in 1666. We see the admiral lying on the ground, his sword still in his hand, while cherubs and angels blast out a fanfare on gilded trumpets. Clearly, the Dutch thought highly of their dead admirals.

The organ in the Oude Kerk was built in 1724, and remodelled soon after by Johannes Caspar Müller. It is worth going along to one of the concerts, though it should be pointed out that this church is the coldest as well as the oldest in Amsterdam. The spire, which was added by Joost Jansz. Bilhamer in 1565, can be climbed in the summer for an interesting view of the red-light district. The carillon hung in the spire is played every Saturday afternoon between four and five o'clock to entertain Amsterdammers as they rush to buy a last bottle of Beaujolais before the shops close.

There is one more - and very special - place to visit before we leave this neighbourhood. On leaving the church, we turn left, and on reaching the canal left again. A flight of steps leads to the front door of the Amstelkring Museum at Oude Zijds Voorburgwal 40. This handsome 17th-century merchant's house was once owned by Jan Hartman, a Catholic merchant from Westphalia who made his fortune selling stockings. The interior is now furnished in the style of the Dutch Golden Age, with black and white tiled floors, heavy oak cabinets and 17th-century Dutch paintings. To add to the atmosphere, the rooms are dotted with little domestic touches, such as bowls of fresh fruit, vases of flowers and casually discarded clay pipes, as if Hartman had just stepped out to take the air.

Thie is an intriguing place to explore, with its creaking staircases, windows in odd places and a concealed priest's room right in the middle of the house. We begin in the front room, where Hartman once sold his stockings, then go through to the tiled kitchen, where enormous windows shed light into the darkest corners. One floor above, we enter the main living room where Hartman built a splendid fireplace bearing the coats of arms of himself and his wife.

The most extraordinary feature, though, is the chapel of Onze Lieve Heer op Zolder - Our Lord in the Attic - hidden in the roof. We perhaps imagine this as a cramped little room under the rafters, but it is in fact a full-size baroque church built on top of three adjoining houses. Clearly, this was not a particularly secret church, nor were any of the other Catholic chapels which we see pinpointed on the 17th-century map of Amsterdam in one of the upper rooms. These chapels, though officially illegal, were quietly tolerated, like the cafés that now sell illegal soft drugs, or the prostitutes we can see from Hartman's living room window.

Hartman died in 1668 and the house was bought three years later by a Protestant merchant called Jan Reynst. He originally intended to rent out the attic as storage space, but changed his mind on realising that he could earn considerably more if he let it out to Catholics as a chapel. The house was eventually acquired in 1739 by a Catholic priest who rebuilt it in flamboyant baroque style. A large altar was squeezed into the chapel, incorporating an ingenious hinged pulpit that could be folded away, and a system of removable paintings so that the congregation could look on a Resurrection at Easter, an Assumption on August 15th and an Annunciation on Lady Day.

Looking north from the upper windows of the chapel, we can see the neo-baroque domes of the St Nicolaaskerk on Prins Hendrikkade, where the congregation of Onze Lieve Heer op Zolder decamped after the ban on Catholic worship was officially lifted in 1887. The empty chapel in the attic was then almost demolished, but a group of Catholics known as the Amstelkring bought the house to preserve it as a museum.

On leaving the house, we might pause at the top of the outside steps to look across the canal at the handsome 1656 neck gabled house opposite, at No. 19. The top is adorned with splendid dolphins draped with strings of pearls, though few people in this part of Amsterdam show much interest in such details. If we turn right along Oudezijds Voorburgwal, past the Oude Kerk, we will see that most are lured here by the claims of sex shops to offer '100% guaranteed porn'.

What would Maarten Tromp make of all this? We see the great admiral on a curious painted wooden relief above the door of No. 136, standing in front of a sinking Dutch ship. The ship is the *Gouden Leeuw*, copied from a marine painting by Willem van de Velde the Younger now in the Rijksmuseum. Van de Velde was famous for his accurate rendering of sea battles, though in this case he seems to have allowed his imagination to run wild, for the *Gouden Leeuw* never did sink. Perhaps it was wishful thinking: at the time the painter was working for the English, who would have been more than happy to see Tromp's flagship at the bottom.

We now turn right on Damstraat, a busy street that leads us back to the Dam, but first we might make a brief detour down a passage on the right, next to Wout Arxhoek's cheese shop. This leads to a mediaeval alley called Pijlsteeg, where we discover Wijnand Fockink at No. 31, a 17th-century *proeflokaal* - a tasting-shop - with painted wooden shutters, the name in florid calligraphy and a collection of rotund liqueur jars hand-painted by impoverished art students with caricatures of Amsterdam burgomasters.

Wijnand Fockink closed down a few years ago, and was much lamented, but it has now reopened. It was originally a gin distillers' shop where customers could sample a glass of jenever before making a purchase. Only a few such places still survive in Amsterdam, often hidden down dark alleys where tourists rarely venture. The proper etiquette in these places is to go up to the bar and ask for a *jenever - jonge* or *oude*, young or old - or even , if we are in a mood to experiment, one flavoured with berries, such as a *bessen jenever* or a *Korenwijn.* The barman takes a tiny tulip glass and fills it to the rim. We do not pick up the glass - this is frowned upon - but follow Dutch etiquette, and bend over, hands held behind the back, to take the first sip.

III. The Dam. We might return later in the day to practise our jenever drinking technique, but for now we are going to explore the buildings on the Dam. The first thing to do is to get our bearings by locating Madame Tussaud's, which occupies a former department store on the south side of the Dam. This waxworks museum is modelled on the famous Victorian institution on Marylebone Road in London, founded by the Madame in 1835. If we wanted to go into Amsterdam's version, which has recently been revamped, we would find several unusual features, such as a mock Amsterdam canal paved with genuine red bricks, and a reconstruction of a Vermeer interior. It would also treat us to the curious experience of entering a murky Dutch tavern permeated with realistic cooking smells, and looking upon a skating scene made that bit more authentic by the occasional blast of cold air. John Evelyn would no doubt have loved the 'many quaint devices', including a giant mechanical figure called Amsterdam Man, who descends out of the ceiling amid a cloud of smoke.

But these diversions should perhaps be left for another day. Our present aim is to locate the spot where Jan van der Heyden painted the view illustrated overleaf, now in the Amsterdam Historical Museum. Van der Heyden specialised in townscapes, painting various picturesque scenes such as the view of Herengracht on page

177. He is sometimes called the Dutch Canaletto, though it might be more fitting to call him the Dutch Leonardo da Vinci, for he was a technological wizard too: one of his achievements was to invent the fire hose. He often set off with his sketchbook to draw detailed views of the smouldering ruins of canal houses. Of course, Rembrandt did the same once, drawing the charred rafters of the old town hall, but Van der Heyden had a more professional interest, and eventually published a book in 1680 titled *Brandspuitenboek* - 'The Fire-Engine Book' - in which he outlined the merits of tackling fires using hoses rather than buckets of water. The city eventually adopted his recommendations and put the artist in charge of the fire department. He was also the city's first inspector of street lighting, having persuaded the city fathers in 1669 to introduce oil lamps to light the streets at night. Van der Heyden even devised his own method of filling the lamps with different quantities of oil depending on the season. By the end of the 1680's, more than 2,000 of Van der Heyden's oil lamps were flickering along the canals.

The artist had not yet invented his lamps and hoses when he painted this scene on a summer afternoon in about 1665. The Dam seems unusually quiet compared with other views, such as the one on page 42. Apart from a boy pushing a hoop, the only activity is a horse dragging a sledge laden with three barrels. Perhaps this was because the Dutch were fighting the English at the time, though hardly a year went by when they weren't fighting the English.

If we also feel that the Dam seems unusually spacious compared to today, this is because van der Heyden has cheated and used two different viewpoints. The church is seen in full splendour, and the Royal Palace has been pushed almost out of the frame. We have to turn back to the Berckheyde view on page 42 to see the entire building. This was originally the town hall, and was formally opened ten years before Van der Heyden started his painting, in 1655. It replaced the old town hall, which appears in a painting by Pieter Saenredam in the Rijksmuseum, reproduced opposite, and on the maps of Anthonisz. and Florisz. The gothic fabric looks reasonably

sound on the 1625 map on page 59, but it had evidently become derelict and overgrown with weeds by the time Saenredam painted it. The chimney is tied precariously to the roof, the roof has a shaggy tin flashing, the stonework is dilapidated and no doubt every niche has had a statue torn out of it. Even the whale's jawbone hanging from a window seems a little sad. Why did Saenredam paint this down-at-heel building with such gentle affection? If we look at the signature we may get a clue. In the building to the right of the tower, we can see a row of little shops on the ground floor, one of which appears to be stacked to the ceiling with books. Over the canopy that shelters the shops appear to be carved the words: 'Pieter Saenredam first drew this from life, with all its colours in the year 1641, and painted it in the year 1657.' The gap of sixteen years is what counts: this is a painting about nostalgia, for the old town hall was no longer standing by 1657. In 1640 the council had decided to pull the building down (as if it needed any help), and Saenredam drew it the following year, perhaps as a memorial. In fact the council did not get

round to the job, but the drawing still served its purpose, for in 1652 a fire gutted the whole picturesque muddle. Saenredam recorded the date as another carved inscription, along the first step of the building, and we know it independently from a melancholy sketch of the charred ruins made by Rembrandt two days after the blaze.

How could any new building live up to this charming ancient structure that managed to captivate two such different artists? We may still regret the decision when we compare the new town hall, which was already being built when its predecessor burnt down. Its architect was named in 1648 - the year the Treaty of Münster was signed, marking the end of the Eighty Years' War. The city had to choose between the two leading Amsterdam architects of the day - Philips Vingboons and Jacob van Campen. Vingboons proposed a flamboyant building adorned with a dome, whereas Van Campen offered a more sober classical design. The job went to Van Campen, possibly because Vingboons was Catholic. The Calvinists were prepared to toler-ate hidden Catholic chapels, but they were perhaps unwilling to pay a Catholic to design their town hall.

How enormous the project was can be seen from the detail of the whole area from Florisz., opposite. The old town hall, labelled 't Stadhuys on the detail, was small beer compared to the Nieuwe Kerk and even to the Beurs, the commercial heart of Amsterdam; something grander and more fitting really was required. The new town hall takes up not only the site of its predecessor but also of all the buildings behind it and to the right on the detail. Every Dutch school child is meant to know the exact number of wooden piles sunk into the ground to support the town hall. The answer, should you ever want to test a Dutch child, is 13,659. The construction proceeded rapidly; by the time Saenredam's painting was finished the new building was already occupied. At the opening ceremony in the summer of 1655, Constantijn Huygens read a sixteen-verse poem he had written, and the great poet Vondel, never one for brevity, recited an ode that ran to 1,500 lines. A feast was held

in the new building, at which Jacob van Campen was conspicuously absent, having resigned his post six months earlier.

The painting by Gerrit Berckheyde on page 42 shows the town hall in 1658. Berckheyde stood near the same spot - or spots - that Van der Heyden would later choose, but facing the town hall rather than the Nieuwe Kerk. The square seems far more bustling, as a horse pulls a sledge carrying a large wooden barrel, and foreign merchants stand around discussing business. The view we see now is slightly different, as the old weigh house on the right was demolished on the orders of Louis Napoléon, who claimed that it spoilt his view. What poor taste he had is clear from the Florisz. detail, where it looks charming. We also glimpse it to the right in Berckheyde's painting; the houses to the left have also gone. Only the town hall survives - and that only after a fashion, for it is now a royal palace.

The entrance is deliberately small, for the city fathers feared a repeat of the riots in 1535, when a group of Anabaptists stormed the old town hall. The new one was therefore designed with small ground-floor windows protected by solid iron bars. We enter through a door on the far right of the middle section, where a small notice informs visitors of the opening times. If the palace is closed, as it often is, we will have to return another day.

The interior is more flamboyant than we would imagine. It was decorated by Artus Quellien, a Catholic sculptor from Antwerp. As with the choice of an architect, the city fathers would probably have preferred a Calvinist Dutchman, but there were few sculptors left in the Netherlands after the Beeldenstorm of the previous century, whereas Catholic Flanders could offer a plentiful supply of flamboyant baroque sculptors. Quellien, or Quellinus as he preferred to be called, was born in Antwerp in 1609 and travelled to Rome to study classical statuary. He lived in Amsterdam from 1650 to 1665, working alongside his cousin Artus Quellien the Younger and another Flemish sculptor called Rombout Verhulst.

Quellien and his assistants faced an enormous task, for they had to carve two pediments for the front and back of the town hall, six statues to stand on the roof, twelve gods, 88 capitals, 184 garlands and 250 foot of frieze. The first we see of Quellien's work is in the pediment overlooking the Dam, where a tangle of bodies illustrates the oceans paying homage to Amsterdam. The three figures on the skyline represent the virtues of Prudence, on the left, Justice, on the right, and Peace on top.

We discover some of Quellien's work again in the Vierschaar, a room on the ground floor where magistrates once pronounced the death sentence. The public could peer through the windows to watch the grim proceedings as the condemned prisoner was led into the room through a bronze door decorated with thunderbolts, skulls and a coiled serpent. The magistrates sat on the left, on a long marble bench beneath Quellien's four voluptuous caryatids, representing captive women in various states of remorse and anguish.

The panels between the caryatids are decorated with elaborate scenes representing Biblical justice. The left panel shows the Judgement of Zaleucus, in which a Greek judge was forced to sentence his own son for adultery, while the centre panel illustrates the Wisdom of Solomon, when he cannily settled a dispute between two mothers claiming a single child. The last scene illustrates the story of Brutus, who ordered his two sons to be executed for treason. All this was intended to remind the judges of their task, as was the figure of Justice, wearing a blindfold and carrying a sword in her right hand, though she has lost the scales she once held in her left hand.

We now climb the marble staircase and enter the Burgerzaal, a vast and echoing hall where the city fathers once ruminated on municipal matters, such as the advantages of fire hoses over buckets. The figure on the far wall is Atlas struggling to hold up an enormous globe, just as the Dutch were struggling to control their far-flung empire. We have to cross the hall to look at what is underneath Atlas, steering ourselves around three maps inlaid in the floor, which represent the known world in the 1660's. Everything is as it should be until we look at Australia, or Nova Hollandia, as it was called by the Dutch, where the cartographer has had to make a wild guess about the land south of the Tropic of Capricorn.

The figures on the far wall eventually become more distinct, as we see a woman, Justice, trampling two figures sprawled at her feet. The glum bearded man represents Greed, while the withered woman with snakes entwined in her head symbolises Envy. Another woman perched on the corner looks as if she might be a dreamy poetess, but she is in fact Punishment. A gentler allegory is illustrated on the opposite side of the hall, where the Maid of Amsterdam is holding an olive branch in her right hand to symbolize Peace. The two women at her side represent Strength and Wisdom, and the plump little cherubs on the right denote Trade and Wealth.

We need to look closely at the doors off the main hall to discover the quirky details carved by Quellien. Debtors who had been summoned to appear before the bankruptcy court were reminded of their folly by a relief above the door showing the fall of Icarus. If that failed to impress, they might have been stirred to remorse by the festoon above the lintel, in which rats are gnawing at broken safes and poking inside empty purses. Other city departments had similar decorative flourishes. Thus, quarrelling couples summoned to the court of matrimonial affairs were confronted with the figures of Venus and Mars on either side of the door, and a turtle dove nesting in a garland. Again, the insurance room has the figure of Arion riding on the back of a dolphin, while the town clerk's office reveals its function with the figure of a faithful dog standing guard over his dead master.

All this solemn symbolism rather lost its point when the town hall was turned into a royal palace. The queen's bed was moved into the burgomaster's chamber and a throne was placed in the former sheriff's room. The town council room became a dining room, and showy chandeliers were installed in the great hall for official receptions. The palace is still occasionally used by the Dutch royal family, but most of the year it stands dark and empty, waiting perhaps to be turned into something else.

On leaving here, we cross the road and enter the Nieuwe Kerk, which has been the national church of the Netherlands since the 19th century, though we might wonder if it is still a church at all, for the outside is often hung with banners announcing exhibitions of photography or antique fairs. Yet it is still a church, and one with an interesting history that dates back to the early 15th century. If we can get inside without paying too hefty a charge, we can sit down in the nave to read its history.

The original church was funded by wealthy citizens such as Willem Eggert, a banker who looked after the Count of Holland's finances, but this building was still unfinished when fire swept through the mediaeval city in 1521 and destroyed it. The city was rich enough to rebuild the church, changing from the original plain gothic to the more flamboyant late gothic style that was creeping slowly northwards from Flanders. Various guilds paid for the construction of an arc of chapels at the east end of the church, and other buildings were later tacked on to the outside in an early renaissance style.

Much of the lavish decoration was prompted by the fierce rivalry between the Nieuwe Kerk and Oude Kerk. The Oude Kerk had the blessing of the Bishop of Utrecht, but the Nieuwe Kerk had the support of the wealthy merchant class. When the Oude Kerk installed its new organ, the Nieuwe Kerk responded by adding a splendid pulpit. And whenever one church added an altar, the other did the same, so that eventually the Oude Kerk could boast of 38 altars, just beating the Nieuwe Kerk at 36.

The Oude Kerk then added its elegant, late gothic spire in 1565. Not to be outdone, the Nieuwe Kerk began work on a soaring spire. Massive stone foundations were laid at the west end of the church and a carilloneur was appointed to play the bells that would soon hang high above the Dam. Artists occasionally included the tower in views of the Dam, though it was never built, and the carilloneur never played a note. Three years after the work begun, Amsterdam converted to Protestantism. The Nieuwe Kerk was stripped of statues and furnishings, and each of its 36 altars was destroyed. Building a tower in such circumstances was clearly out of the question.

As if that was not enough, the roof caught fire in 1645 and the church burnt down. The council, having resolved in 1641 to build a new town hall, decided to construct a new church at the same time. But what about the tower? Willem Backer, a strict Calvinist burgomaster, argued in favour, since it would look bad if the city spent more money on the town hall than the church. 'God's wrath must surely fall on a city that spends such treasure on the outward appearance of a worldly building,' he warned darkly. Some progress was made on the tower, but then Backer died, another war broke out with England, and the plan was quietly shelved, leaving just a blackened stone stump at the west end of the church.

Obviously, there will not be many relics of the middle ages to be seen inside the church. Willem Eggert's chapel is now a bookshop, and the other chapels are rather bare, apart from the late gothic screen of the Drapers' Chapel and a renaissance screen on the Boelens Chapel. Yet we should pause to consider the pulpit carved by Albert Vinckenbrinck, which took the sculptor nineteen years to complete. It is an extraordinary renaissance work, featuring a six-sided base carved with buildings shown in deep perspective. On closer inspection, we can see little scenes illustrating the seven works of charity, such as tending the sick and burying the dead.

The flat wooden tester above the pulpit was designed to direct the preacher's words to the congregation. It is surmounted by a tower decorated with florid pinnacles and small figures looking out of windows or peering over parapets. It is an odd, whimsical relic of the gothic age, whereas the new organ, built at the same time, has a splendid casing designed by Jacob van Campen in a soaring classical style that almost looks like an Amsterdam canal house. Artus Quellien was called in to carve the marble panels at the base, and the shutters were painted in 1653 by Jan van Bronchorst with scenes from the life of David.

As this is not our first church in Amsterdam, we will perhaps not be surprised to find, where the high altar once stood, the tomb of an admiral - this time, Michiel de Ruyter. Rombout Verhulst worked for five years on the monument, which shows the marble admiral laid out on a cannon, surrounded by crabs, dolphins and sea creatures blowing on shells. The panel above shows the sea battle off the coast of Syracuse in Sicily, when De Ruyter was killed fighting the French in 1676. Other panels on either side are carved with female figures representing Steadfastness and Prudence, though we might wonder if prudence is the right word to describe the admiral who sailed a Dutch fleet up the River Medway and set fire to several English ships. De Ruyter's many other deeds are inscribed in gilt capitals on three black marble panels at the base of the monument.

It is worth walking to the north side of the nave to find the tomb of yet another admiral, Jan van Galen. Van Galen died twenty-three years before De Ruyter, fighting the English at the battle of Leghorn. Artus Quellien designed the tomb, and Rombout Verhulst and Willem de Keyser carved the marble. We see Van Galen surrounded by cannon, arrows and flags. The tomb on which he lies is illustrated with a sea battle; but the iron railing prevents us getting

close enough to see the ornate sterns of the warships, one of which is decorated with an elephant. Joost van den Vondel was buried in the Nieuwe Kerk three years after De Ruyter, but he was a mere poet and his grave, like Saskia's, was unmarked. A small memorial urn was attached to a pillar in the south transept in 1771.

Enough of tombs. On leaving the church, we should turn left, steering around a café terrace that stands on the site of the mediaeval churchyard. We follow the lane that curves around the east end of the church. It used to be called Ellendigesteeg - Wretched Alley - after the small churchyard here where suicides and hanged criminals were buried, but the residents finally persuaded the city council in 1865 to change the street name to the less morbid Eggertstraat.

The lane leads to Gravenstraat, where a low building in Dutch classical style was added to the church in 1642. The bell gable house at No. 16 is occupied by De Drie Fleschjes, a traditional proeflokaal furnished with dark green wood, old brass lamps and rows of padlocked kegs inscribed with the names of local companies who entertain their customers here. On reaching Nieuwezijds Voorburgwal, we should cross the road and stand in front of Harold's Hairstudio, if Harold is still in business. This is where Jan de Beijer stood in the 18th century to paint the view opposite, now in the Amsterdam Historical Museum. The main structure in the foreground is the massive stone base of the aborted tower, which was still standing then; it was later demolished, leaving just the small stump we now see attached to the church. The tiny shops once built against the church walls have almost all gone, but one survives in which Christmas World sells Yuletide decorations all year round. We might indeed be approached by someone wearing a Santa Claus costume while we stand here. I last saw him on a sweltering July afternoon, ringing his bell forlornly in the hope that someone might buy an advent calendar, a pack of Christmas cards or perhaps a silver fairy.

Where De Beijer saw tall merchants' houses and trees opposite the church, we now find a shopping centre, housed in what was the main post office, a 19th-century building decorated with so many florid turrets that it became known as the pear mountain. It is now named Magna Plaza for no particular reason except that Latin is currently fashionable. The arcaded interior where Amsterdammers once queued for stamps and fishing licences is now filled with elegant shops that try to persuade the thrifty Dutch to spend extravagant sums on designer baby clothes and Calvin Klein underwear.

The pavement in front of Magna Plaza is the best place to study the back of the royal palace. The figure perched on the town hall's roof is Atlas, holding up an enormous globe. The pediment below his feet is decorated with an elaborate sculpture depicting the continents of the world paying homage to Amsterdam, much as the seas do in the front pediment. We need to look hard to pick out the details, such as the two men on the far left pushing bales of tobacco, the elephant to their right, and the figure of Asia carrying a tulip to Amsterdam. (It's worth comparing the similar motifs in the Frontispiece.)

We now return to the Dam, and follow the crowds down Kalverstraat. We possibly have to

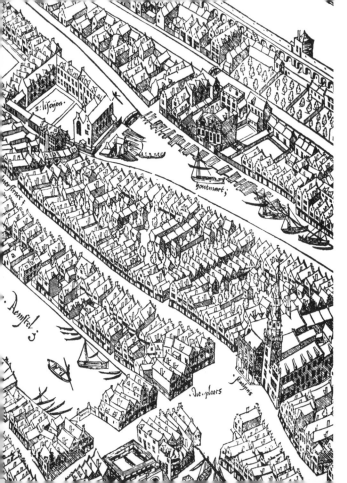

be Dutch to enjoy this crowded shopping lane filled with the smells of patat and perfume, though it can be fun searching for an elusive second-hand book in De Slegte at Nos. 48-52, or briefly savouring the old-fashioned elegance of the Maison de Bonneterie department store at No. 183. We are ultimately bound for the lane at No. 92, which leads into one of the most seductive corners of the city.

IV. The Amsterdam Historical Museum. The building we are about to enter was once the St Lucienklooster, a convent established in 1414 which we can see on the detail from the Anthonisz. map here, where it is marked S. Liserijen. Anthonisz. seems so much less polished than Florisz. but he does make up for it with unexpected details. It may not be so surprising to see somone punting down the Amstel at the bottom of this detail - but is that an oarsman sculling past S. Liserijen? And it is well worth examining the town hall, which still has its tall spire - just a memory when Florisz. and Saenredam were working.

After Amsterdam converted to Protestantism, the S. Lucienklooster was taken over by the city to use as the city orphanage. The gate through which we are about to go was added in 1581 by Joost Jansz. Bilhamer, the sculptor whose Oude Kerk spire we saw, and perhaps even climbed, earlier on this walk. The gate is encrusted with renaissance motifs - the latest fad in the 1580's - such as imitation iron rings and horned lions' heads. A carved relief shows a a dove surrounded by orphans, some of them missing limbs. The verse on the panel below was penned by the prolific Vondel.

We are growing fast in number and need;
Our second fathers lament.
Please do not pass by this gate
Without contributing a cent.

There was once a collecting box in the lane to collect the cents, but it has gone, as have the orphans, who moved out in the 1960's to a new building designed by Aldo van Eyck.

In through Bilhamer's gate, we find a hidden courtyard where the orphan boys once played, strictly segregated from the girls in the adjoining courtyard. The drawing overleaf, by Hermanus Schouten, shows the scene here in about 1797, as observed from the far side of the courtyard, next to the pump. The building on the right with the open arcade was fitted with wooden lockers where the boys kept their clothes. The arcaded wing straight ahead (under which we came in), originally the convent's cow shed, was rebuilt by Pieter de Keyser, complete with a splendid colonnade in Tuscan Renaissance style. It became the carpenter's workshop, which perhaps explains the man dragging a plank along the corridor in Schouten's drawing.

The lockers are still there, some of them now used to display objects from the museum's collection; and the carpenters' workshop is now the museum café. The main change is that the courtyard is now shaded by a lime tree, planted in 1898 for the coronation of Queen Wilhelmina. When the sun shines, we can sit at a café table under the tree, and enjoy a scene that has hardly changed since Pierre Fouquet, a French art dealer,

WALK 1: THE DAM AND ITS NEIGHBOURHOOD

made his fortune publishing prints after idyllic views of Amsterdam drawn by artists like Schouten. He collected the views in what he called his *Atlas*, which sold in large numbers in Paris and Amsterdam. We still come across loose sheets from the *Atlas* in Amsterdam's antiquarian bookshops, reminding us of the halcyon days before cars invaded the canals.

The museum café is called David en Goliath after two splendid wooden figures that stand next to the kitchen, alongside a third figure representing a bearer. These curiosities were constructed in about 1650 for the owner of the Oude Doolhof, a pleasure garden on Prinsengracht which survived until well into the 19th century (the entrance can still be seen between Nos. 338 and 340). The Oude Doolhof contained diversions such as a maze, a fountain, and several mechanical figures, among them a king of France and William of Orange. The figures of David and Goliath were probably carved by Albert Vinckenbrinck, the sculptor we met in the Nieuwe Kerk toiling for nineteen years on the pulpit. It is worth trying to look behind Goliath at the complicated system of secret wires and pulleys which, when tugged, made him blink his eyes and roll his head.

On leaving the restaurant, we turn right along the arcade and then immediately right again under an archway to reach a little courtyard where a brick wall is covered with old stone tablets rescued by the Association for the Preservation of Gable Stones. One delightful specimen shows a view of the Oude Schans with the Montelbaanstoren on the right and the spire of the Oude Kerk in the middle. This must have been carved after 1565, when the Oude Kerk's spire was added, but before 1606, when the Montelbaanstoren was altered by Hendrick de Keyser. Another stone shows a glum Corendrager, a corn porter, carrying a heavy sack of grain on his head; but perhaps the most delightful specimens are 'The Three Black Moles' and 'The Giant Tooth', the latter presumably once a dentist's shop sign.

We now go back under the archway into the old orphanage, though not without pausing to admire what is a renaissance gate. This once formed the entrance to the city carpenters' yard on Oude Turfmarkt, before it was moved here in 1634. The gate was originally decorated with snakes, flowers and stars, but these have worn away over the years. The strange variety of rustication imitates traditional wood carving patterns. Back inside the orphanage, the curious Schuttersgalerie is straight ahead of us, through an automatic glass door. This was once a narrow canal, which provided a useful boundary between the girls' and boys' quarters; it then became a lane, and finally, in the 1970's, a picture gallery. We can walk through it like any normal street, though only when the museum is open. It is used to hang the museum's collection of civic guard group portraits, one of which (the second on the left) is by Govert Flinck, one of Rembrandt's pupils, and shows *Joan Huydecoper's Militia Celebrating the Peace of Münster* in 1648. We see Huydecoper in the foreground carrying a banner and wearing a handsome silver-embroidered jacket with a white sash. Flinck is behind him, looking out at us. One of the richest merchants of the 17th century, Huydecoper served several times as burgomaster.

In 1639, he commissioned the fashionable Philips Vingboons to build him a magnificent classical mansion, which once stood at Singel 544, near the floating flower market. We can see part of the building in the painting, just behind Huydecoper. It was destroyed when a bomber crashed on the building in 1943, though an intriguing plan now exists to rebuild the mansion on Bloemgracht using fragments salvaged from the rubble.

We now go back through the automatic door, and turn left into the girls' courtyard, designed in 1634 by Jacob van Campen. This is Dutch classicism at its barest - no lions' heads or iron rings, just white doves and girls' heads above the doors. The door straight ahead leads into the Amsterdam Historical Museum, which opened on 27 October 1975, exactly 700 years after Count Floris V signed a document exempting Amsterdam from tolls. Some historians prefer to take this as the foundation date of Amsterdam. The museum occupies most of the rooms of the former orphanage with a fascinating collection of maps, models, paintings and other relics. We need at least an hour to see everything, and much longer if we read all the text in the red information folders that can be borrowed at the cash desk.

The painting reproduced on page 135 hangs in room 1. Willem van de Velde the Younger's *The River IJ at Amsterdam* shows the river in 1686 crowded with all types of ships. The largest vessel is the *Gouden Leeuw*, which we saw earlier today on the house in the red light district, though it was sinking when we last saw it. This had been Admiral Tromp's flagship, but Tromp was long dead by the time the painting was done. He was killed in action (like any decent Dutch admiral) fighting the English and was commemorated by a suitably pompous memorial tomb in Delft's Oude Kerk. This painting was commissioned by the Amsterdam harbour masters to hang in their office in the Schreierstoren. We can see the squat brick tower in the painting, near the familiar spire of the Oude Kerk.

Willem van de Velde the Younger, like his father, devoted himself single-mindedly to marine painting. He would often bob about in a little boat in the thick of a sea battle, carefully sketching the shattered masts and sinking ships. The Dutch greatly admired his skill at depicting ships' rigging and other nautical details, but so did the English, who persuaded father and son to move to England in 1672, and turn their attention to glorifying King Charles II's fleet (or what was left of it after De Ruyter's raid). Willem the Younger must have returned to Amsterdam, though, to paint this view in 1686.

We find Cornelis Anthonisz.'s bird's eye view of Amsterdam of 1544 in this room (reproduced on page 33). He climbed the mediaeval towers to produce this extraordinary view, which shows the Oude Kerk with its choir still unfinished (it was finally completed fourteen years later with money raised in a lottery), the orchard that once stood on Kloveniersburgwal, and cattle grazing in the meadows east of the Montelbaanstoren. The map is so detailed that we can even count the windows on the old town hall. In the bottom right hand corner is the grisly island where the bodies of criminals were left to rot on gallows as a warning to foreign visitors.

Anthonisz. produced the woodcut, and a

version painted on wood which we see later, during the rule of Emperor Charles V, when Amsterdam was still a loyal Catholic city. The map shows numerous convents and monasteries that would disappear after 1578. It also reveals the extensive timber yards along the quays, including the one marked *houtmarkt* near the St Lucienklooster. If we look carefullly we will see the great tree trunks laid out carefully side by side on the quay edge. The need for all this timber is evident when we turn to look at the model of a mediaeval Amsterdam house nearby. The builders required a constant supply of good timber not only to build the houses but to sink the wooden piles on which each house rests.

What looks like Saenredam's painting on page 57 is in fact a copy by Jacob van der Ulft. This version has more people in the streets, and a different inscription on the canopies above the shops: 'Painted by J. van der Ulft from a vivid picture; burnt on 7 July 1651,' it says, though this is not quite accurate, as the town hall was burnt down in 1652, as we know from Rembrandt's sketch.

A curious painting in the same room was done by Anthonisz. eleven years before the bird's eye view. The banquet of seventeen civic guards shows the members of the Guild of St George, one of the military guilds formed to defend the city. These were the crossbowmen, who armed themselves with the sort of weapon we see hanging on the wall beside the painting. When they weren't doing target practise in their guild house on Singel, the crossbowmen clearly enjoyed a good banquet. One man is playing the pipes, and next to him, fourth from the right, another man is holding a page of music. A Dutch scholar set himself the task of finding out the exact score. As a result of this diligent research, we can now push a button to listen to a recording of the song that was being sung as the crossbowmen sat down to their meal of roast waterfowl and knotted herring in 1533.

A few rooms further on is a similar painting of *The Fourteen Archers of the Red G*. Fashions have changed in the twenty-nine years since Anthonisz. painted the crossbowmen - as have tastes in entertainment. We can see one of the company holding a sheet of paper, on which the motto reads: *In vino veritas*. Now we move on to room 5, which recalls the heady atmosphere of the early Dutch voyages of discovery. A splendid painting by Hendrick Cornelisz. Vroom shows *The Return to Amsterdam of the Second Expedition to the East Indies*. This was a turning point for Amsterdam, as the gilt inscription around the frame explains. A fleet of eight ships had sailed for the East Indies on 1 May 1598 and, though four were lost, the others returned on 26 July 1599, loaded with valuable spices. We see the four ships here moored off the coast of Texel, where the cargoes - and, it would seem, some East Indies men - are being unloaded onto smaller vessels.

The same room contains several globes, including one made by Johannes Blaeu, who ran a shop on the Damrak. John Evelyn did some shopping there in 1641, though he had some trouble with the spelling of Blaeu, noting in his diary: 'Mr Bleaw, the setter-forth of the Atlas's and other Workes of that kind is worth seeing.'

Room 6 contains paintings of the Dam, among them a view by Johannes Lingelbach showing the town hall under construction in 1656. Room 7 has a painting by Gerard de Lairesse that depicts *The Continents Paying Homage to the Maid of Amsterdam*. We have already met this theme in the pediment of the town hall, but we can see the symbolism more easily in this painting. The Maid seems rather aloof as foreigners from various continents lay exotic products at her feet. One man in a turban is bringing a camel; another is carrying bales of tobacco. There is even an American Indian lurking in the background.

Another painting in this room shows *The Battle in the Sont in 1658*. It is by Willem van de Velde the Elder, whose son we met in room 1. The painting here shows a fleet sent from Amsterdam to break Swedish control of the channel leading to the Baltic. Hundreds of men are leaping panic-stricken into the sea. We then climb the stairs to room 8, where a painting by Job Berckheyde shows the courtyard of the old exchange in about 1660. Room 9 sometimes contains Berchem's elaborate *Allegory of the Plan of the Three Canals*, painted in 1663, a small detail of which is shown opposite. This painting celebrates the construction of the 17th-century ring of canals. The Maid of Amsterdam holds a map of the city on which the baroque canal ring is clearly marked. About half of the final project is shaded in, indicating how far the construction work had reached by 1663. The rich symbolism is sometimes quite difficult to decipher. We may have no problem identifying the figure representing Mercury, god of trade, who is reclining on a nearby cloud to the right of the Maid, but how should we interpret the young girl holding an hour glass and offering Mercury a ripe peach?

We should find Rembrandt's *Anatomy Lesson of Dr Deyman* in the same room. Or rather what is left of it. The painting originally hung in the anatomy theatre in the Waag - not the one so cavalierly destroyed by Louis Napoléon, but another that we pass in walk 3 - next to *The Anatomy Lesson of Dr Tulp*, but it was badly damaged by a fire in the 18th century, and all that now survives is the corpse - that of a famous Flemish baker and criminal known as Black Jack - and a servant holding the top of the skull.

Rembrandt's signature can still be read - but only just - at the bottom of the painting, and all we have of Dr Deyman is a pair of hands.

The little end room (No. 10) dwells briefly on religion. Jan de Beijer's view of the Nieuwe Kerk, which showed us the sad foundations of the spire, may still be hanging here. Two wooden models show how the spire might have looked if the city hadn't frittered away its wealth on the new town hall and the wars against the English.

A wooden staircase in this room leads to a little bell-room in the attic where we can bang our fists on a model carillon keyboard. On a visit to Amsterdam in 1641, John Evelyn was taken up the tower of the Oude Kerk to watch the carillon-player at work. 'He struck on the keys, and playd to admiration,' he wrote. 'All this while, through the clattering of the Wyres, dinn of the too neerely sounding bells, and noise that his wooden gloves made, the confusion was so greate, that it was impossible for the Musitian to heare any thing himself; or any that stoode neere him; Yet to those, who were at a distance, and especially in the streetes, the harmony, and the

time were most exact and agreeable.'

The next few rooms have many small gems that might hold us up, though it is worth looking out for Govert Flinck's sad portrait of Vondel (who called the painter 'the Apelles of Cleves') and Breitner's painting of the *Widening of Raadhuisstraat* (reproduced on page 202) if they are on show. Perhaps we should also look at the Van Speykkamer just beyond the Regentkamer, where a few relics of Jan van Speyk are displayed. Van Speyk was once an orphan here, running around the boys' courtyard in the early 19th century. He joined the Dutch navy and found himself in command of a munitions ship moored in Antwerp harbour during the Belgian Revolt. Van Speyk decided to blow up the ship rather than allow it to fall into rebel hands. We can see a painting showing him about to ignite the gunpowder with a cigar, while the Belgian boarders look on in horror. The explosion killed Van Speyk and twenty-four of his crew, earning the former orphanage boy a memorial in the Nieuwe Kerk alongside De Ruyter and other Dutch heroes.

That completes our tour. All that remains to do is to buy a few postcards and perhaps a reproduction of the Anthonisz. map. On leaving the museum, we turn right, past an iron pump decorated with a lion head. A door leads through to the rear courtyard, where we might glance inside the museum workshop, to see craftsmen working amid a clutter of drills, broken statues, old paintings and toothbrushes. Just beyond the workshop, a little gate on the right offers a glimpse, unexpectedly, as so often in Amsterdam, into one of the most peaceful spots in the city. Îf this gateway is locked, there are two more around the corner that we can try.

Amsterdam was just a small town when the walled Begijnhof was established here in the 14th century. The origins of this Low Countries institution date back to the Crusades, when thousands of young men perished in the Holy Land, leaving behind a surplus of single women. Some joined a nunnery, but others, who preferred a less austere life, moved into a Begijnhof, where the rules - no hens, dogs or men - were more easily borne.

The first Begijnhof, or Béguinage, was probably founded in Liège by Lambert le Bègue. The order rapidly spread through Flanders, the Rhineland and Holland, creating secure enclaves for women in the heart of the great northern cities such as Bruges and Ghent. Enclosed within strong gates, these communities have the seductive charm of a village in a city.

Amsterdam's Begijnhof is one of the most attractive of all. We might have expected it to have been turned into a bank, or a museum, or something different from its original purpose, but it is still occupied by single women, each enjoying her own private garden as seen in the Florisz. detail here, though they no longer have the use of the neat little church built for them in 1419. This has been known since at least Florisz.'s time as the English Church, to the fury of many Scots as it is in fact a Scottish Presbyterian church. Presented by the city to the exiled Scots in 1607, the church is still used for religious services, and concerts on Saturday afternoons. After losing this church, the Beguines built the clandestine Mirakelkapel opposite in 1671, though it can

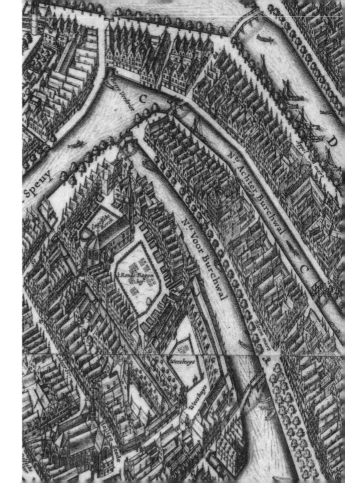

hardly have been a secret church given that the architect included gothic windows.

Most of the houses in the Begijnhof date from the 18th century, but the Houten Huis at No. 34 is a wooden house built in the middle ages. Many of the dwellings are identified by stone tablets with the name of a saint; a little courtyard to the left of the wooden house contains a collection of gable stones salvaged from other houses.

A narrow passage leads us out onto Spui. This was a broad stretch of water when the Begijnhof was built, providing the women with a useful moat, but in the 19th century it was filled in to create a small square. Planted with trees and dotted with benches, Spui is one of the most pleasant spots in the city, particularly on Friday afternoons in the summer when the cafés spill onto the street, and on Saturday afternoons when Amsterdammers flock to the bookshops in the neighbourhood. Even on Sunday mornings, when the rest of the city is still in bed, Spui is enlivened by a trickle of people picking up Sunday newspapers or browsing among the market stalls selling crafts and paintings.

The Athenaeum Boekhandel at No. 14 occupies an Art Nouveau shop built in 1904. The interior was cleverly redesigned in 1966 to create a warren of tiny dens devoted to English novels, films, psychology and Latin. The Athenaeum Nieuwshandel next door stocks *The New Yorker*, *Vrij Nederland* and *Vogue* in most languages, and can occasionally even supply a copy of *The Phnom Penh Post* to those who need it.

A little bronze statue called Het Lieverdje stands opposite the bookshop. It represents a young urchin and was presented to the city by a tobacco company. In the heady days of student revolt, this was a focus of protests and happenings. Things are a lot quieter now, but we might still see the Lieverdje daubed pink, in support of gay rights, or wrapped in toilet paper, for no obvious reason.

We have now reached the end of our walk. If we want to try a typical brown café, we need look no further than Hoppe, an old bar dating back to 1670 whose two cramped and smoky rooms are packed with university teachers, students and stockbrokers. Like a British pub of yore,

Hoppe has a basic bar in one room and a slightly more comfortable lounge next door. The floors are strewn with sawdust, and the only decoration is a grimy oil painting, yet Hoppe remains a cherished institution. On summer evenings, the crowd spills out into the street, chatting loudly in several languages while irritated cyclists try to squeeze past.

Café Esprit at Spui 10 is another possibility, though here the customers tend to look like fashion models. The menu obligingly lists chic Californian salads guaranteed to add not a gramme or blemish to the perfect figure. One last place to consider is Café Luxembourg at Spuistraat 22. This may look like a typical brown café, but remember Bredero's warning. Things can change, and in this case the building recently changed from the German tourist office to a brown café. It looks as if it has been here for decades, with its solid wooden furniture, waiters in long aprons and reading table piled high with copies of *Le Monde*, *De Standaard* from Belgium and perhaps even a copy of the *Herald Tribune* with the crossword puzzle left untouched. If we

are lucky, we will find a plump armchair in the back room, where we sit down and watch the tour boats chugging past.

We are now in a good neighbourhood for eating out. Café Luxembourg itself serves good food, or we can walk down Spuistraat to eat an Indonesian meal at Kantijl & De Tijger (at No. 291). Following a formula that first proved successful in The Hague, this spacious brasserie has polished wooden tables and waiters dressed in fashionable black costumes. The menu is entirely Indonesian, but the waiters can explain anything we need to know. Most of the dishes are lightly spiced, such as grilled goat on skewers or satay. We can sample a single dish for lunch or eat an entire rijsttafel, sitting alone at a small table or banqueting with friends at a big table.

Luden is in the same street at No. 306. This brasserie is also based on a successful restaurant in The Hague, but the style here is Mediterranean. You can sit on a hard, uncomfortable bench in the brasserie section for a simple pasta or a fashionable carpaccio, or opt for the more comfortable restaurant section where new French food is served.

A few doors down, Lucius at No. 247 is a chic fish restaurant with, again, hard wooden benches. A wide range of seafood is chalked up on the blackboard, though you might need a Dutch-English dictionary to decipher some of the rare species of fish that are being cooked.

The Oude Zijds

MUNTPLEIN *to* THE OUDE MANNENHUISPOORT

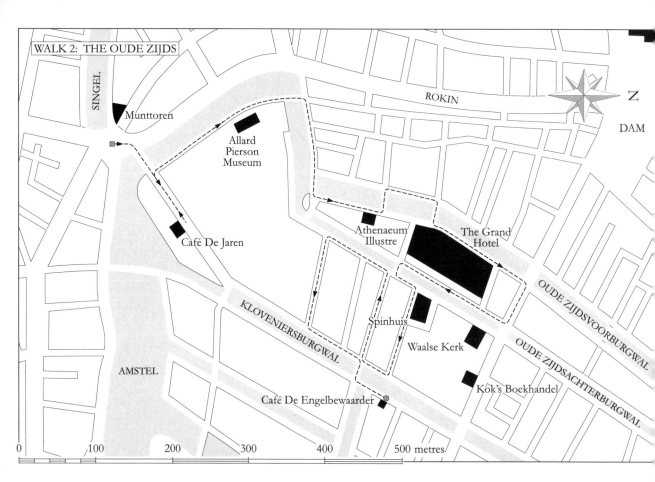

WALK 2: THE OUDE ZIJDS

SINGEL

Munttoren

ROKIN

Z

DAM

Allard
Pierson
Museum

Café De Jaren

Atheneaum
Illustre

The Grand
Hotel

OUDE ZIJDSVOORBURGWAL

KLOVENIERSBURGWAL

Spinhuis

Waalse Kerk

OUDE ZIJDSACHTERBURGWAL

AMSTEL

Café De Engelbewaarder

Kok's Boekhandel

0   100   200   300   400   500 metres

The Oude Zijds

MUNTPLEIN *to* THE OUDE MANNENHUISPOORT

Our next walk is a gentle stroll in one of the oldest quarters of Amsterdam. This walk can be done in an hour, ideally on a Thursday between noon and one when the bells of the Zuiderkerk are played. The route takes us down two narrow canals shaded by elm trees where we will pass tall 17th-century houses, curious little corner shops and the occasional lank heron perched on a houseboat. We will see the old Admiralty, the city pawn bank and an 18th-century passage lined with bookshops. During term time, this quarter of Amsterdam is mobbed with students cycling to lectures on rattling black bicycles. Some of them will no doubt stop off for a coffee on the way, and we might be inspired to do the same.

My favourite café in this quarter is De Jaren at Oude Doelenstraat 22. If we begin on Muntplein, we will find it in the street that runs down by the Hôtel de l'Europe. It occupies a solid stone building which was once a bank. The spacious interior has been skilfully converted to create an airy café on several levels with little hidden back rooms and a broad waterfront terrace overlooking the Amstel. The staff are young and friendly, and speak German, French, English and perhaps even a few words of Japanese. In the morning, we should be able to find an empty table with a view of the river, but by lunchtime we will probably have to hunt in one of the little back rooms for a place to sit, for this has quickly become one of the most popular cafés in the city.

The land opposite De Jaren was the site of a mediaeval convent called Nieuwe Nonnen (The New Nuns). We can see the building on the 1544 Anthonisz. map here, near a half-moon bastion, but it had disappeared by the time Balthasar Florisz. was working in 1625 (opposite). The intervening years marked the decisive change from a Catholic city shaped by churches, convents and a proper enclosing wall (the cannon can be seen poking through) to a merchant town crowded with boats and new buildings - but also planting trees where the walls once stood.

The New Nuns belonged to the Third Order of St Francis, as did most of the monks and nuns in mediaeval Amsterdam. This order was less strict than the other two Franciscan orders, which is perhaps the reason for its appeal in this laid-back city. The Nieuwe Nonnen convent was closed down during the Reformation, as were all the convents and monasteries, no matter how laid-back their religion. This sweeping change was referred to in Amsterdam simply as the Alteratie (the Conversion). The convents and monasteries we see on the 1544 map were seized by the city and torn down, or put to new uses as orphanages, lending banks and naval warehouses. Yet there was little violence in Amsterdam. Even the Franciscans, who had played a key role in the Inquisition, were simply escorted out of the city and left on a dike. As a result of the Alteratie, not much now remains of Amsterdam's mediaeval monasteries, apart from two small chapels and an alley called Gebed Zonder Ende (Prayer Without End). Let us now look at what has been built on the sites of the monasteries.

I. Grimburgwal. On leaving De Jaren, we turn left, retracing our steps to the Hotel de l'Europe, then right down Oude Turfmarkt, where the two splendid gates once stood at the entrance to the city stonemasons' yard (we saw one of them on our first walk, outside the Amsterdam Historical Museum; the other is coming soon, the first of a whole series of grand gates on this walk). The stern neoclassical building at No. 127 was once a bank. It is now the Allard-Pierson Museum, which contains a collection of classical relics amassed by Dutch archaeologists. It is not a

large collection, but it has some interesting finds from Greece and Crete.

We now reach a little hump-backed bridge, where we can pause to enjoy an unexpected view of a canal before turning right past a souvenir shop to reach Grimburgwal. If we stand near (but not too near) the canal, opposite the shop at No. 7, we will see a view of Grimburgwal that has not changed much since Hermanus Schouten sketched the scene that we see opposite, on a summer afternoon in 1796. An elm tree casts dappled shadows on the red-brick houses, a mother is strolling in the sun with her children, and a group of boys are playing a game that looks like marbles. Altogether this is one of the most delightful illustrations in Fouquet's *Atlas*, a collection of prints of Amsterdam views published by a French art dealer, Pierre Fouquet, during the second half of the 18th century. Many of his most popular views were drawn in the Oude Zijds by Schouten; three others are reproduced later in this walk.

The house with the neck gable and the washing hanging outside to dry (No. 15) has scarcely changed since Schouten stood here. Even the wooden shop canopy over the hatter's, inscribed with an old Dutch proverb, has survived intact (though it seems to have moved along from No. 13, which has lost its renaissance step gable).

The splendid building Schouten shows on the other side of the canal has gone. It was designed by Philips Vingboons in 1647 as the Oudezijds Herenlogement - the Old Side Gentlemen's Residence - where famous visitors such as Tsar Peter the Great of Russia once stayed. After spending a night here in 1653, the English traveller Robert Bargrave praised it as: 'the noblest taverne in the world; every room is furnished with brave pictures and paved with black and white marble, especially the chiefest room, which is likewise hanged with the richest guilded leather I have ever seen and furnished with a glorious organ.' The noblest tavern in the world was demolished in 1876 and a not very noble hospital was built in its place. The only detail spared was the old gateway, which now provides a grand entrance to a house at Keizersgracht 365.

If we continue now to the next bridge, we will

see the building with the step gable in Schouten's view. Situated on a corner where three canals meet, the Huis aan de Drie Grachten was built in 1609 in a jaunty Dutch Renaissance style. The 'House on the Three Canals' had 18th-century sash windows when Schouten drew it, but these were replaced by leaded glass windows and red shutters during a fastidious 19th-century restoration.

II. Oudezijds Voorburgwal. Once across the bridge, we turn left down the narrow canal Oudezijds Voorburgwal where we might bene-fit from a brief Dutch lesson. Oudezijds Voorburgwal means, literally, the canal on the old side in front of the city wall. This is to distinguish it from Oudezijds Achterburgwal (the canal on the old side behind the city wall), and also from Nieuwezijds Voorburgwal, which is, as you might have guessed, the canal on the new side in front of the city wall. Just to make things that bit more confusing, there is no longer any Nieuwezijds Achterburgwal, which became Spuistraat in the 19th century.

Now that we have the name sorted out, we might be surprised to notice a stone tablet on the wall of the House on the Three Canals, which gives the canal's name as Fluwelen Burgwal - Velvet Canal. This is an old name dating from the period in the 18th century when this was a highly desirable stretch of canal. A few houses on the canal have kept up appearances, such as the white house with the plump cherub at the top (No. 239), built in 1634, possibly by Philips Ving-boons. This house is decorated with an early neck gable, or a late step gable, depending on how we look at it. It was once the home of Magdalena Stockmans, a wealthy widow who was wooed, but with little success, by the rois-terous Bredero, who lived on the same canal at No. 244. The tall house next door (No. 237) was built in 1736. Its splendid top decorated in Louis XIV style with the owner's coat of arms, still has a wooden hoist beam, with the rope attached.

We now reach the spot where Schouten drew the splendid gate opposite, in about 1750. Again, little has changed, though we no longer have to step over carpenters working in the street. The

18th-century twins to the right of the gate (Nos. 233 and 235) have lost the ornate tops just visible in the 18th century through the trees, the sash windows at No. 233 have gone, and an extra house has crept in, but the gothic chapel and renaissance gate still look as they did when Schouten passed this way. This gate stood until 1632 on the Oude Turfmarkt, where it was built in 1571 as one of the entrances to the city carpenters' yard, along with a second gate which we saw at the entrance to the city orphanage in St Luciensteeg. The gate we see here is the more elaborate of the two, carved with what is already a familiar panoply of lions' heads, rings and other Dutch renaissance motifs.

The chapel beyond once belonged to the convent of St Agnes, whose nuns opted for the easy life style of the Third Order of St Francis. After the Alteratie, the empty chapel was used for a time by the Admiralty for storing cannons and ropes. The Admiralty eventually moved elsewhere, and the Athenaeum Illustre, the first university in Amsterdam, moved here in 1632. The 1571 carpenters' gate was rebuilt here, and the date above the entrance changed to 1631, the year the Athenaeum was founded.

We now cross a little iron footbridge called the Makelaarsbruggetje and turn right down the canal until we come to a doorway with a lengthy inscription above it (at No. 300). This massive brick building with solid wooden shutters was the Amsterdam Pawn Bank in the 17th century (it still is a bank). The pawn bank was established in 1614 in the warehouse to our right, which was built by Hendrick de Keyser. The building we are looking at now was added in 1669 and decorated with a gilded inscription written by Vondel, who, when he was not writing lengthy poems, worked here as a book-keeper until he retired at the age of 81.

Vondel's poem explained the principles of the pawn bank to those who could read it. Others could turn into Enge Lombardsteeg, the narrow lane on the right beyond the old warehouse. Over the doorway is a very worn relief of a woman trying to pawn her property; and above her four twisting cornucopias show the transformation of goods of all kinds into cascades of money. This pictorial definition of the pawn was designed by Hendrick de Keyser.

If we now return to the canal, we will see a curious mannerist gateway near the bridge. It looks as if it might be another work by Hendrick de Keyser, but cannot be, if the date on it (1624) is to be trusted, for De Keyser died in 1621. It is carved with the name of a former inn called De Brakke Grond (Brackish Ground) - a name poetic enough to have been adopted by a Flemish theatre company based nearby.

We cross the canal again by an iron footbridge called the Lommertbrug and turn left. This brings us to a gate with the name The Grand (No. 197), through which we go to reach a cobbled courtyard with an old stone pump. We are now on the site of the St Cecilia Convent, which stood here until 1578. The building on the left with the clock was once the convent chapel. After the Alteratie, the city used the old convent buildings as lodgings for 'princes and noble gentlemen', renaming it the Prinsenhof. We can see it marked on the detail from Florisz.'s map overleaf. William of Orange in 1581, Elizabeth's favourite, the Earl of Leicester during his ill-fated intervention in 1586 and 1587, and Maria de' Medici in 1638 all stayed here. Nine years later, the Gentlemen's Residence was built on Grimburgwal and the Prinsenhof was handed over to the Admiralty.

The Admiralty built the handsome classical wing we see facing the chapel in 1662, adding gilded ships on the chimneys and a pediment carved with sea gods, sailors and ship's equipment. We should be able to spot Neptune with his trident, a Roman soldier, and a cock symbolising wakefulness. The fence around the rampant lion in the middle represents the garden of Holland. After Louis Napoléon took up residence in the town hall on the Dam in 1808, the burgomaster and aldermen had to move their desks into the Prinsenhof. Here they stayed, even after the French had left, adding a new wing in the 1920's in Amsterdam School style, and later, in the 1950's, commissioning Karel Appel to decorate the staff canteen with an abstract mural, though this so upset the staff that it had to be painted over. After the new town hall opened on Waterlooplein, the city was left with

an empty building, which has now been turned into a luxury hotel. The Grand, as it is called, takes great pride in informing its guests that it is once again the residence of princes and noble gentlemen.

On leaving the courtyard, we can sit on a convenient bench next to the canal to compare Florisz. with what we have seen, and to look at the former meat hall on the opposite side, with three ox's heads on the gable top. The shop to the right, at No. 272, was once occupied by a butcher with a sense of humour, who painted a couplet on the wooden canopy aimed at the city officials based in the town hall:

> *Of this the council of Amsterdam is sure*
> *You are best to come to me for a cure.*

The tar-black house a little farther on, No. 187, has a different message to tell. If we look up at the top, we can see that the step gable is decorated with figures of African slaves and American Indians sitting on bales of tobacco. In 1663, when this house was built, the Dutch West India

Company was shipping a yearly average of 4,000 slaves to work in the Caribbean sugar cane plantations. As many as a quarter of them died during the voyage.

We now turn right down Oude Doelenstraat. Ahead of us, across the next canal, is Kok's bookshop at Nos. 14-18. This huge, rambling bookshop is crammed with old volumes on history, painting and literature. It has gradually become more cluttered over the years; the aisles blocked by tottering piles of books, the walls covered with old postcards, scraps of poems and faded calendars. Yet Kok's remains one of the best places in town to hunt for elusive art books, rare postcards of Amsterdam, and perhaps the occasional copy of a 1958 Ellery Queen Murder Mystery.

III. Oudezijds Achterburgwal. The narrow canal we have come to is Oudezijds Achterburgwal, which, as its name says, was once behind the city wall but is now, we may have noticed, on the edge of the red light district. We can avoid the seamier end of the canal by turn-

ing right down the side with the even numbers. If we stop at No. 164, we can see on the far side of the canal the square drawn by Schouten in 1780, reproduced overleaf. The church has hardly changed but, more surprisingly, neither have the houses on either side. The long building on the left with the classical cornice (Nos. 151 to 155) has merely lost one of its hoist beams. The two neck gable houses to the right have also survived (Nos. 167 and 169), though they have grown rather differently over the years, with all the minor alterations of window frames and glazing that happen when different owners go their own way. The only other significant alteration is that the railings beside the canal have been removed, which may explain the ladder now attached to the wall, in case someone should tumble into the water. Not that many people do. In an average year, only one or two people drown in the Amsterdam canals, though hundreds of bicycles are lost, along with old television sets, shopping trolleys and the occasional car.

If we look carefully at Schouten's print, we will see something that was once typically Dutch.

The carriage to the right could come from more or less anywhere in Europe. But the one to the left? There is something low-slung about it, even sporty: it is in fact a sled, dragged along the street on runners, and no doubt terrifyingly fast in the winter.

A sign on the side wall of No. 167 points to the Eglise Wallonne - the Walloon Church - where services are held in French every Sunday. This modest building is all that is left of a monastery that belonged to the Brothers of Paul. Only the chapel survived demolition, and it was given in 1587 to French-speaking Protestants who had fled from the Spanish in the Southern Netherlands. A new classical door was added in 1661, but otherwise this quiet cobbled square has remained undisturbed.

We find another building drawn by Schouten further down the canal (the print is reproduced on page 17). The Spinhuis (just beyond No. 185) was built as a house of correction; hence the iron bars on the ground floor windows. It stands on the site of an abandoned mediaeval convent with the rather inappropriate name of the Eleven Thousand Virgins. The inmates of the Spinhuis were mostly prostitutes, beggars and petty thieves,who were set to work spinning wool in an attempt to turn their minds from crime.

One young inmate we know something about was Jacomijntje de Witte, the daughter of Emanuelle de Witte, an irascible Dutch painter famed for his church interiors. Jacomijnte seems to have been led astray by her step-mother, who taught her to break into houses while the families were at church. She cannot have been a very good burglar, for she was eventually arrested after breaking into her neighbour's house by smashing a hole in the wall.

By the time Schouten drew the scene, the Spinhuis was almost at the end of its life. It finally closed in 1782, but the building is still there (though without the jokey stork chimney cowl), as are the three houses to the right. The one next to the alley (No. 187), where three men are idly talking, has lost its neck gable, but is otherwise intact. A carved stone tablet above the door is dated 1727, though it is perhaps hidden by the foliage. It shows a *huysman* (a gentleman

97

farmer) standing in front of a country house. The next house (No. 189) has lost its 18th-century windows, but gained Empire lights above the doors, added in the 19th century by an owner keen to keep in touch with the latest French fashions, but probably unable to afford any major alterations. No. 191 on the far right, where a man is staggering in under a sack, is still standing, but only just. The last time I passed this way, I noticed a sign on the door that said: 'Knock hard three times,' though three hard knocks might be all it would take to demolish this tottering house.

We now cross the bridge just beyond here, then turn back down the canal, past the Kinderkoekcafé at No. 193, where local children bake cakes and toss pancakes in a tiny tiled kitchen. We then turn right down Spinhuissteeg, pausing to look at the gateway designed by Hendrick de Keyser. The relief in the arch, now blackened with soot, shows one of the inmates receiving a sharp slap with a cat o' nine tails. The poet Pieter Cornelis Hooft composed the couplet below to reassure passers-by who might have

been worried. 'Be not alarmed,' it says, 'For I am not seeking revenge but forcing out good/My hand may be stern but my motive is love.'

We continue down the Spinhuissteeg, which brings us out on Kloveniersburgwal, a broad canal that follows the course of the city's mediaeval moat. If we turn right, we come to The Book Exchange at No. 58. This orderly second-hand English bookshop is a wonderful place to browse. We may even find a discarded copy of *Boswell in Holland*, not that Boswell has much to say about Amsterdam, which he visited only for 'whoring'. He is hardly any more illuminating on Utrecht, where he spent a miserable year studying law, for his attention during the stay was almost entirely focused on the beautiful and elusive Belle de Zuylen.

Beyond the bookshop we turn right down Rusland, where the remarkable SAS Hotel occupies buildings on both sides of the street. An old bible publishing works on the left side called Het Wapen van Amsterdam and several 18th-century shops on the right now belong to the hotel. One of the buildings has a wooden canopy bearing an old inscription informing us that this is the shop of a Bible bookseller.

No longer. The traditional houses conceal an atrium filled with rampant tropical vegetation and a gurgling waterfall. A church once stood here, but all that survives is the former vicarage, which is now a hotel bar called Pastorie, furnished in a comfortable Old Dutch style with heavy wooden cabinets, gilt-framed mirrors and ornate chandeliers. Guests can now sit by the fireplace where the local pastor once toasted his toes, and listen to the house pianist play old favourites.

We might be tempted to stop here for lunch. The Palmboom, which occupies a former tobacconist with an Empire frontage dated 1767, serves excellent Scandinavian open sandwiches and pastrami rolls made with seasoned smoked beef. The Laxenoxen restaurant offers more sophisticated dishes, including fresh Norwegian salmon landed in Nordic waters only a few hours ago.

At the end of Rusland, we turn left along the final stretch of Oudezijds Achterburgwal. After passing the unpoetic Slijkstraat (Slime Street) we come to a gate which is just visible in the view of Grimburgwal on page 89. This is the Gasthuispoort, built in 1603, but reconstructed in 1736, when the figures of two old people were added by Jan van Logteren.

We have walked past another gate, which has a pair of spectacles above the entrance, put there to symbolise old age. This gate, the Oudemanhuispoort, was once the entrance of the Old Men's Home, but is now, as we may have guessed from the heaps of bicycles lying around, part of the university. Once through the gate, we come to an 18th-century covered passage occupied by a row of tiny shops with red wooden shutters. These were originally let to raise funds for the old men's home; most are now occupied by antiquarian booksellers who spread out piles of dusty books and magazines on folding wooden tables. We can hunt here for old postcards of Amsterdam, or sift through stacks of dog-eared Fouquet prints for a view to take home and frame. The passage emerges on Kloveniersburgwal, under a sculpture carved by Anthonie Ziesenis in 1786, which shows a plump Maid of Amsterdam comforting two elderly inmates of the home.

Our walk is near an end. All that remains is to find a café, if we have not already stopped for lunch. The Engelbewaarder is just across the canal, at Kloveniersburgwal 59. The interior is dark and brown, though perhaps too brown for younger Amsterdammers, who now prefer their cafés to have white walls and waiters to have long aprons. The Engelbewaarder tends to attract older bohemians who have hung on in Amsterdam, eking out a living as artists or musicians. Jazz bands play here on Sunday afternoons, but Saturday morning is my favourite time, when the café is almost empty, apart from a cat dozing on the piano and a solitary customer reading the *Volkskrant* while a Tom Waites tape plays quietly in the background.

We can eat here, or go around the corner to the Thai restaurant Klaas Compaen at Raamgracht 9 (closed on Sunday). Named, appropriately enough, after a 17th-century Dutch seaman, this inexpensive basement restaurant is as cramped as a ship's galley. There are only a couple of tables, but if these are taken we can perch on a bar stool and watch the Thai cooks conjure up delicious dishes full of spices and coconut.

In search of Rembrandt

THE DOELEN HOTEL *to* REMBRANDTSPLEIN

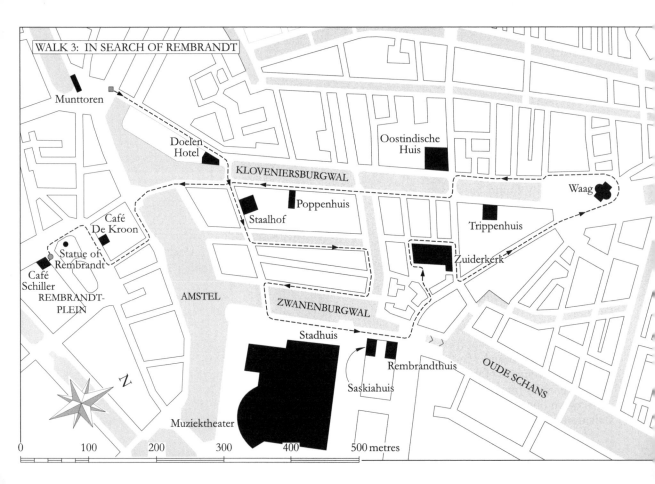

WALK 3: IN SEARCH OF REMBRANDT

Munttoren

Doelen
Hotel

KLOVENIERSBURGWAL

Oostindische
Huis

Waag

Poppenhuis

Staalhof

Trippenhuis

Café
De Kroon

Statue of
Rembrandt

Zuiderkerk

Café
Schiller

ZWANENBURGWAL

REMBRANDT-
PLEIN

AMSTEL

Stadhuis

Rembrandthuis

OUDE SCHANS

Saskiahuis

Muziektheater

0   100   200   300   400   500 metres

In search of Rembrandt

THE DOELEN HOTEL *to* REMBRANDTSPLEIN

Having already found Saskia's grave and one damaged painting by Rembrandt, let us now look around the quarter of Amsterdam where he spent most of his life. This walk is best done on a Thursday morning, when the Zuiderkerk carillon is played from noon to one, but it can be done at any time during our stay, apart from Sunday mornings when the Rembrandt House is closed. During the walk, we will see the house Rembrandt bought in 1639, the church where three of his children were buried, the weigh house where he painted *The Anatomy Lesson of Dr Tulp*, and the remains of the wall where *The Night Watch* originally hung.

We begin once again on the Muntplein. If we walk down Nieuwe Doelenstraat, we can admire De Jaren café once more. It was at a house that once stood on the same site (No. 20), that Rembrandt lived with Saskia for two years, moving here in 1635 soon after they married. While living in Nieuwe Doelenstraat, Rembrandt painted a woman, perhaps his pregnant wife, dressed as *Flora* (now in the National Gallery in London). Their first son was born here in December, but died the following spring.

I. The Doelen Hotel and the Saaihal. A few doors down, the Doelen Hotel stands on the site of the Kloveniersdoelen. We see it clearly marked (though spelt differently) on the detail overleaf from Florisz. It was here that Rembrandt painted *The Night Watch* in 1642. This large painting (now

103

in the Rijksmuseum) showed a company of civic guards led by Captain Frans Banning Cocq and Lieutenant Willem van Ruytenburch. The remains of the brick wall on which the painting once hung were recently discovered in the hotel. If we are curious to see it, though it is only a bare brick wall, the hotel receptionist will point in the right direction.

Another painting by Rembrandt, also in the Rijksmuseum, that once hung near here is *The Syndics of the Cloth Guild*, reproduced opposite. Reynolds did not care for it, but other critics have agreed that it is (in the words of the great German art historian Alois Riegl) 'the final development of Dutch national art'. Rembrandt certainly took enormous care over the picture, changing the placement of the figures several times; but it has been suggested that he was willing for once to make alterations at the sitters' request, as he was at the time exceptionally short of money. Certainly there is a vivid focus on the money bag being gripped by a syndic on the right; and more than one commentator points out that the group is seen from the viewpoint of a

petitioner. The setting is the Saaihal, which we reach by crossing the bridge and going straight ahead down Staalstraat. On our right is a cluttered cinema bookshop called Ciné Qua Non (at Staalstraat 14), its cramped interior overflowing with Hollywoodiana. The building where the Syndics met is No. 7b opposite. The Florisz. map shows an institution called the Staalhof on this spot, but this was replaced in 1641 by a classical building designed by Pieter de Keyser, and decorated appropriately with swags knotted up as a kind of silken ball. It was here that Rembrandt painted the five officials of the cloth guild in 1661-2. The building now houses the university pensions office.

The city mason's yard - marked Stadts Steenhouwery on the Florisz. map - once stood here too. It was here that Pieter de Keyser's father Hendrick worked, carving the flamboyant mannerist ornaments we have seen decorating the city's gateways and spires. If we stand on the wooden drawbridge just beyond here, we can see one of De Keyser's distinctive spires - this one belonging to the Zuiderkerk. Rembrandt never

met the elder De Keyser (who died in 1621), but he may have run into his son, who lived near here in a house provided by the city. As well as the Staalhof, Pieter built the Westerkerk tower, which Rembrandt sketched several times.

Opposite is a drawing of this little wooden bridge as it was in 1817. We can find the exact spot where Gerrit Lamberts stood if we cross the bridge and turn left down Groenburgwal, stopping outside No. 47. Looking back down the canal, we can see that as well as the bridge, the two houses nearby are still standing, though the classical building on the right has lost almost all its trappings. Only the windows show that it is the same structure. The Church of England church next door was where Hendrick de Keyser lived; it is said to be modelled on (of all things) Dublin Cathedral.

Gerrit Lamberts' drawings give us an impression of Amsterdam in the aftermath of the Napoleonic Wars. The autumnal streets are strangely deserted compared to the bustling scenes recorded by Schouten a couple of decades earlier. There are no carpenters working in the streets, no barges unloading on the quayside. Only the occasional solitary hunched figure appears, like the man pushing a barrow across the bridge. Hardly any houses were built in this period; all we find from the early 19th century are a few fanlight windows decorated with palm trees and other Empire motifs in fashion when the Netherlands were under Napoleonic rule.

If we walk to the end of Groenburgwal, where it joins Raamgracht, we can stand on the spot where Schouten drew the more cheery view opposite in the 1780's. The Zuiderkerk tower looks the same, as do the houses to the right of the lane (Raamgracht 17 and 19). The house at No. 21 has lost its bell gable, but otherwise remains recognisable. This building was bought by the architect Philips Vingboons in 1668 when he was 61 years old. If he looked out of his front window, he would have seen the tall wooden frames similar to those in Schouten's print. The Raamgracht was named after these frames, *ramen* in Dutch, used to dry linen.

We now turn right along Raamgracht. The new town hall is straight ahead, but we can only reach it by turning right down Zwanenburgwal, and then left over the next bridge. This leads us to an island that was once the heart of the Jewish quarter, where Rembrandt and Saskia rented a house called the Suyckerbackerij after leaving the Nieuwe Doelenstraat in 1637. The house has gone, along with every other old building on this island. Most of the properties lay empty at the end of the last war, after the mass deportation of the Jews; they were stripped for firewood during the desperate winter of 1945, and then left in ruins. To make matters worse, the city built a highway through the heart of the district, and then tore down the last remaining houses to build the metro, leaving just one squatted factory on Waterlooplein with curious wooden birds on the roof. That, too, was eventually demolished to build the new town hall-opera house complex.

The only feature of the Jewish quarter that has survived is the Waterlooplein flea market, which is held every day next to the town hall. It was once larger and more lively, but the loss of the Jewish community robbed it of much of its charm. Multatuli, one of the classic Dutch writers,

described the market as it was in the 19th century in his novel *Max Havelaar*: 'Lying there were headless nails, toothless saws, bladeless chisels, locks without springs, keys without locks, hooks without eyes and eyes without hooks.' The stalls around the town hall can now be counted on to sell battered leather jackets, bicycle parts, scratched Grateful Dead albums, bakelite telephones, defunct radios, broken toys and perhaps, when things get really desperate, old copies of the free *Uitkrant* magazine.

After a brief browse among the stalls, we can enter the Stopera. This building was designed in the 1980's by Cees Dam and Wilhelm Holzbauer as a combined town hall and opera house. The Dutch critic Gerrit Komrij saw the Stopera as an example of 'that cut-price philosophy of two for the price of one that is so dear to the Dutch commercial soul'. There is not much to admire inside the town hall, but one feature seems to hark back to the stern moralising tone of the old Stadhuis on the Dam. Near the porter's lodge, we can observe three perspex tubes which slowly fill up with gurgling water. One of the tubes shows the water level in Amsterdam, a second indicates the tidal level at IJmuiden on the North Sea and the third, most worrying of all, shows the level the waters reached during the floods in 1953. The message is as clear as the rats gnawing banknotes in the old town hall. Beware of disaster!

Putting these worries to one side, let us look for a café. There are two inside the Stopera, one opposite the opera house ticket office, and the other, Dantzig, overlooking the Amstel. I suggest we try Dantzig (if it is still called that).When it opened in the late 1980's, Dantzig had a different name and a quite different post-modern decor. The style didn't work, though, so the café was redesigned in the style of a private club, complete with plump armchairs, a grand piano and a library. This seemed to catch the Zeitgeist perfectly and Dantzig is now very popular, though with luck not so popular that we cannot find a table. So let us settle down, after picking up a newspaper, or perhaps even a book from the library, though most of these turn out to be dusty 19th-century medical textbooks.

On leaving Dantzig, perhaps having learnt something useful about the diseases of the liver, we turn right along Zwanenburgwal. If we squeeze past the market stalls on the left, we should be able to reach the ancient lock visible on this detail from Florisz. (sadly, the drawbridge has gone). Across the water is the elaborate tower of the Zuiderkerk; to the right the attractive modern Pentagon apartment complex designed by Theo Bosch.

II. The Rembrandt House. We now climb the steps next to the Saskiahuis, where a new entertainment complex was being constructed the last time I passed by. Once we reach Jodenbreestraat, we turn right to the Rembrandthuis Museum at Nos. 2-4. This house was built on a former country road, Breestraat, which had become a city street by Florisz.'s time. Rembrandt's house is the left-hand of the two step-gabled houses next to the St Anthonis Sluys (left of the letter E). He lived here for nineteen years, from 1639 until his debts caught up with him in 1658.

The house was built in 1606 - the year Rembrandt was born. It was originally a large red-brick house with a step gable. In 1625, it was still one of the largest houses in the neighbourhood, much grander than the home of Pieter Lastman, Rembrandt's teacher, which stood nearby on the Sint Antoniesbreestraat opposite the Kerckhof. Rembrandt paid 13,000 guilders for the property, which was a sizeable sum for a young artist to raise. Let us take a look at what he got for his money.

This is not all that easy, as the house has gone through many changes since Rembrandt lived here. Two years after he moved out, in 1660, the building was split in two and the step gable replaced by a more fashionable classical pediment. By the end of the 19th century, the house was barely recognisable. Van Gogh had trouble locating it in 1877, and the old Baedeker guides were not much help, simply mentioning a small plaque on a wall. The house was eventually restored by Karel Petrus de Bazel in 1906 on the 300th anniversary of Rembrandt's birth (and of the house). He removed one of the doors that had been added, but retained the pediment put up after Rembrandt had moved out, so that it is still not quite the house Rembrandt knew.

Nor is it likely that Rembrandt would recognise the interior. Not one chair has survived from Rembrandt's day; everything was seized by the bailiffs in 1658 after the artist was declared bankrupt. As we wander through the dark, shuttered rooms, and climb the narrow creaking staircase, we will find it hard to picture Saskia lying ill in bed, or Titus leaning pensively on his desk (see page 299), or Hendrickje posing for Rembrandt's *Bathsheba*. Gone are all the Japanese swords, antique props and exotic shells that Rembrandt once owned. The only traces we find of the artist are a few hundred engravings and drawings.

They are enough. One engraving in the Agterkamer (back room) shows Rembrandt and Saskia in 1636, when they were living in Nieuwe Doelenstraat. Even in this early print, poor Saskia looks pale and tired. She had recently lost her first child. Three children later Saskia herself died, just after Titus was born in 1642, and only three years after they had moved to this house.

The Tussenkamer (mezzanine) contains some of Rembrandt's most popular engraved works, including a wonderful portrait from 1632 of a hunched rat-catcher calling at a country house. Rembrandt did other etchings of organ-grinders, street musicians and beggars, which he sold in large numbers, though obviously not large enough: his debts were beginning to mount up.

The landscapes are hung in a dark room called the Schildercaemer (picture room) at the top of the house. These works were done soon after Saskia died, when Rembrandt, never one for travelling, went on long walks through the flat landscape around Amsterdam, drawing languid views of the Amstel which have an almost Japanese lightness. We may find here a curious sketch of the Montelbaanstoren, though we are unlikely to recognise this as the tower that stands near here on Oude Schans. Rembrandt drew it without the delicate wooden spire designed by Hendrick de Keyser, even though this feature had been added many years before. In fact, the spire was added in the year Rembrandt was born, so he could never have seen the tower in this ruined,

overgrown state.

On leaving the Rembrandthuis, we cross the road and turn left, where we can pause on the bridge to look at the spire of the Montelbaanstoren, and perhaps ponder Rembrandt's curious decision to omit it in his drawing. The little black building to the right of the bridge was once the lock-keeper's house, and an old gateway on the opposite side of the bridge came from the Lepers' House, which in Rembrandt's day stood at the end of the Breestraat, next to the city wall. Paulus Potter, famous for his paintings of cows (including the splendid lifesize beast now in the Mauritshuis in the Hague), died here in 1654.

We now turn left and walk down Sint Antoniesbreestraat (marked 84 on the Florisz. map). Not many old houses have survived on this street, which was rebuilt by Aldo van Eyck and Theo Bosch after the metro was dug out along the route. One splendid 17th-century house still standing, however, is the Pintohuis at No. 69. Rembrandt was still living nearby when Isaac de Pinto, a Portuguese Jew, bought this building, which was then a simple gable house. In 1680, long after Rembrandt had died, De Pinto converted it into a classical mansion rivalling the buildings that were then being erected on Herengracht. With its six columns and elegant wrought iron fence, De Pinto's home was the most splendid house in the Jewish quarter. Something of this grandeur, and the bustle of the area at the height of the Golden Age is obvious from the engraving opposite. Even now, the interior rooms have kept their handsome 17th-century gilded beams and painted ceilings.

Opposite this house, a renaissance gateway decorated with skulls, the work of Hendrick de Keyser, of course, leads into the former Zuiderkerk churchyard. Rembrandt would probably have passed through this gloomy gateway when his children were buried in the churchyard - two-month-old Rombertus in 1636, one-month-old Cornelia in 1638, and another Cornelia, even younger, in 1640. Their last son, Titus, lived long enough to allow Rembrandt to paint the tender portrait that now hangs in the Boymans-Van Beuningen Museum in Rotterdam.

The churchyard has been paved over, and the old gable houses replaced by the attractive modern apartments we glanced at earlier. The only building to have survived is the Zuiderkerk itself, built by Hendrick de Keyser a few years after the spire of the Montelbaanstoren. It was completed in 1614 - the date given above the clock faces on the tower. This was the first Protestant church built in Amsterdam, but the Protestants have no further use for it, and the building is now given over to a fascinating permanent exhibition on Amsterdam town planning. The space where the congregation once gathered is now filled with detailed maps of the city, scale models of 20th-century housing projects and photographs of Amsterdam School apartment blocks.

On leaving the church, we turn right and then right again into Zandstraat, where we may find the church tower open. If so, we can climb up to the balcony below the clocks, led by a local guide. From this vantage point, we get an interesting view of this attractive quarter, with its secret roof gardens and quirky modern buildings;

HOF VAN DE E: HEER DE PINTO

Nieuwelyks uytgegeven door Pieter Persoy met Privil.

it is worth comparing with the details from Florisz. Back on the street, we turn right along Zand-straat, then right down Zanddwarsstraat and again right down Nieuwe Hoogstraat; this should bring us back to Sint Antoniesbreestraat, where we turn left and walk towards the Nieuwmarkt.

In the 17th century Sint Antoniesbreestraat was popular with artists and architects. We mentioned Rembrandt's teacher Lastman, who lived at No. 59; another name we have come across is that of the Vingboons family, who lived at No. 64 in one of the few old houses left standing. David Vingboons, a painter, bought the house in 1611, when it probably looked as it does on the Florisz. map (to the right of an alley called the Salamandersteeg, at 82 on the map). The house now has a different façade, which was added in the 18th century, but the structure remains the same as it was when David Ving-boons lived here with his wife, seven sons and three daughters.

We do not know for sure if Rembrandt knew the Vingboons, but they certainly moved in the same circles. One of the sons, Philips Vingboons,

built a house near here for Nicholas van Bambeeck, whose portrait Rembrandt painted in 1641. Philips' younger brother Justus designed the Trippenhuis, which we will see in a few minutes. Another brother, Johan, was a cartographer employed by Blaeu.

III. The Waag. Ahead of us the looming brick hulk in the middle of the Nieuwmarkt is the Waag. This was originally one of the mediaeval city gates, and on Anthonisz.' map opposite it is still a proud entrance to the town on one of only two land roads. This side are farmhouses, orchards, wasteland, polders and a few houses by the sluice, including the predecessor of Rem-brandt's house. The contrast with the teeming streets of Florisz.'s Amsterdam sums up all the energy of the Golden Age.

By then the Waag had outlived its usefulness - it looks somewhat forlorn in the speedy sketch made about 1610 by Claes Jansz. Visscher (on page 118). The gate had by then become a weigh house (or Waag), and the moat filled in to create a market square. Yet the building can still be

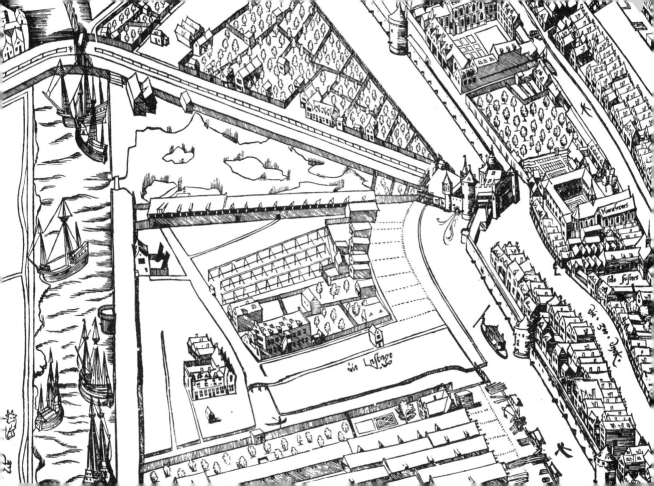

d'Oude S. Antonis poort

recognised as the one drawn by Visscher, who sketched it from the north, near the present taxi rank. If we stand in front of the iron railings (designed by the same team as the quirky lamp-posts on Damrak), we will see the building from the spot he chose. The little wooden turret next to the moat was rebuilt soon after the drawing was done, to match the one on the other side and an ancient stone tablet was added to the new brick tower, bearing a gothic inscription: 'On the 28th day of April in 1488, the first stone of this gate was laid.'

Rather than demolish the old gate after it had ceased to serve its purpose, the city council rented out the upstairs rooms to three guilds. The masons, surgeons and artists each had their own entrance in one of the turrets. The brick turret we have been looking at was where the masons entered the building, through a renais-sance portal added by Hendrick de Keyser and decorated with a relief illustrating a solemn builder with the tools of his trade. The masons built the tower themselves; the curious windows with small bricks laid at odd angles were done by

apprentices to test their skills.

The turret on the far left is particularly inter-esting to us, for it was here that the surgeons entered the Waag to go up to the anatomy theatre that they had added (the central turret with its large windows). The gate is inscribed with the words *Theatrum Anatomicum*, and, if we look closely, *Hippocrates*. Its nickname was *snyburgh* - the carving house. This was the door Rembrandt entered in 1632 when he came here to paint the *Anatomy Lesson of Dr Tulp*. Rembrandt was just twenty-six years old, and probably looked much as he does in the portrait on page 244, painted four years before.

Dr Tulp was thirty-nine when he performed the dissection on the body of a hanged criminal. Rembrandt painted Tulp cutting open the fore-arm, watched attentively by seven observers who are named on the sheet of paper held by one of them. Rembrandt had only recently arrived in Amsterdam from Leiden when he painted this major work. The surgeons must have been pleased, or they would not have given him another commission in 1656 to paint *The Anatomy*

Lesson of Dr Deyman, the sad remains of which we saw on Walk 1. The two paintings originally hung either side of the fireplace in the anatomy theatre, but were sold in the 19th century when the surgeons needed to raise cash to boost their pension fund. The *Anatomy Lesson of Dr Tulp* was bought by the King of the Netherlands, who gave it to the royal collection at the Mauritshuis in The Hague (it is still there), but the *Anatomy Lesson of Dr Deyman* was less fortunate. The painting had been damaged when fire swept through the Waag in 1723, and it spent some time in Cheltenham before being bought back by the city of Amsterdam for the Amsterdam Historical Museum in 1882.

The turret we see on the far right of Visscher's drawing once led to the meeting hall of the guild of St Luke. If we walk over there now, we will see a relief of St Luke above the entrance, along with a cow and a pen. These attributes of the Apostle who was mystically inspired to paint the portrait of the Virgin refer to the painters' guild, whose members met in one of the upper rooms. There are no records of Rembrandt belonging to this guild, though we know that the members banned him from working as an artist after he became bankrupt. He was saved from the prospect of total ruin by his companion Hendrickje and son Titus, who formed a company to sell his works.

A small market is held on the Nieuwmarkt, but it is nothing compared to the scene opposite, photographed in 1890 from the other side of the Waag. It shows the octagonal room at the top of the weigh house where Dr Tulp carried out his anatomy lessons, and a tall chimney in the distance belonging to the Boas factory on Nieuwe Uilenburgerstraat, a large diamond factory built shortly before this photograph was taken.

The woman we see in the foreground might have been heading to Jacob Hooy at Kloveniersburgwal 12, a chemist shop that has been curing Amsterdammers' aches and pains since 1743. Rare medicinal spices and herbs are stored in little wooden drawers and porcelain jars with neatly handwritten Latin labels. It is the sort of shop that might be expected to sell patent remedies for gout. Perhaps it does, but it also stocks

more everyday items such as washing powder and thirty-eight different varieties of Dutch liquorice.

IV. Kloveniersburgwal. Let us now go down this right side of Kloveniersburgwal. This was once the city moat, and if we look at the Anthonisz. map (page 117) we will see that there were convents on the western side of the water and meadows to the east. By Rembrandt's time, though, it had become a fashionable canal where several of his clients lived. In the 19th century, some of his greatest paintings hung in a building on the left side of the canal, No. 29. This splendid classical mansion known as the Trippenhuis was built from 1660 to 1664 by Justus Vingboons, one of the sons who lived in the house we saw earlier in the Sint Antoniesbreestraat.

It is in fact two houses disguised as a single mansion. Two brothers, Louis and Hendrick Trip, wanted a grand house, something in the style of the new town hall, so they pooled their resources and built two separate houses behind a single façade. The Trips were arms dealers, being the sons of Jacob Trip and Margaretha de Geer, whose portraits were painted by Rembrandt in 1661 (the elderly couple still hang next to one another in the National Gallery in London). Jacob's brother, Elias Trip, had founded the family business during the Eighty Years' War when he began importing weapons to supply the Dutch rebels. He went on to arm the Dutch East India company with muskets and cannons to protect their trading posts in the Far East. Jacob's marriage to Margaretha helped to form a business alliance with Louis de Geer, who controlled most of the Swedish copper and iron industry.

Jacob died soon after Rembrandt painted the portrait in London, and the brothers Louis and Hendrick inherited his vast empire which then included Swedish iron and copper mines, smelting ovens and cannon foundries. We might have expected them to have kept quiet about their trade, but they paid handsomely to have the house laden with military symbols, including two chimneys in the shape of 17th-century mortars, a classical frieze decorated with weapons of war, and a tympanum adorned with further armaments.

The family business slumped at the very time this house was being constructed; the Trip brothers lost their Swedish monopoly on gun-casting in 1662, which forced them to give up selling weapons. By the time the mortars had appeared on the roof of the house, the Trip fortunes were rapidly declining, and Hendrick died not long after the house was completed.

The Trippenhuis then passed through various owners until Louis Napoléon, looking for ways to recreate the allure of Paris in his damp northern kingdom, turned it into a national art gallery modelled on the Louvre. The walls dividing the brothers' two houses were knocked through, and the rooms filled with a collection of paintings and furniture. Van Gogh came here to look at Dutch paintings in 1877. Eight years later, he would have found it had moved to the new Rijksmuseum.

Before we move on, we might be amused to look behind us at the narrow house behind us, No. 26, called the Klein-Trippenhuis. The Small

Trippenhuis was apparently built in 1696 for one of the Trip family servants using stone left over from the construction of the large mansion. A broad house further down the canal, No. 47, was bought in 1669 by Dirck Tulp, one of Dr Tulp's sons. Young Tulp worked for the East India Company, and married Anna Burgh, who lived on the same canal at No. 23. He seems to have been fiercely ambitious, and bought himself an English baronetcy to advance his social position in Amsterdam. He had his portrait painted in 1653, but instead of Rembrandt he chose the elderly Paulus Potter to paint him riding a horse in a lush green landscape - a country gentleman rather than an official.

At the next bridge, we can see the building where Dirck Tulp pushed his pen, and the Trips came to sell arms. The East India House is down the narrow Oude Hoogstraat at No. 24, marked on the Florisz. map as the Oost Indisch Huys. The monumental entrance leads into a courtyard where merchants once gathered to discuss the latest news from the Far East. The building is now occupied by the university.

We now cross the bridge and turn right down the final stretch of Kloveniersburgwal. The sober Suassohuis at No. 75 was once the home of Augustus Pieter Lopez-Suasso, a 19th-century art collector from a rich Jewish family. He fell in love with his maid, Sophia de Bruijn, which chilled relations with his parents. The couple married secretly in England and later lived a withdrawn life in this house, where Pieter whiled away his days making drawings of the old stone tablets on Amsterdam houses. After he died in 1877, Sophia moved to another house on the Nieuwe Herengracht, where she amassed a vast collection of dubious antiques. She died in 1890, leaving a considerable sum to build a museum for her collection. It opened in 1895 and was briefly known as the Suasso Museum, though it was soon renamed the Stedelijk Museum, and, in the 1950's, purged of every last item from Sophia's bequest.

The Van Bambeeckhuis at No. 77 was once the home of Nicolaas van Bambeeck, a wealthy cloth merchant who commissioned Rembrandt to paint a double portrait of himself and his first wife, Agatha Bas, reproduced here. Rembrandt painted the couple in 1641 when they were living in a house in the Sint Antoniesbreestraat. The portrait of Van Bambeeck is now in the Musée des Beaux-Arts in Brussels, and the lovely study of his wife hangs in the Queen's collection in Buckingham Palace.

Van Bambeeck had this house built in 1650 by Philips Vingboons, who had been a neighbour when he lived in the Sint Antoniesbreestraat. It was one of Vingboons' earliest classical houses, featuring a pediment decorated with a star. The attic and cellars were filled with wool when Van Bambeeck lived here. The house was recently converted into sixteen luxury apartments.

Vingboons had already built the nearby Poppenhuis at No. 95 for Joan Poppen, the grandson of a wealthy German merchant. Poppen had inherited a vast sum at the age of seven, which provided a steady income for the rest of his life. He commissioned Vingboons to build this classical mansion with its six Corinthian pilasters, swags of fruit and classical pediment; he then proceeded to fill the cellar with good wine and

drink himself to death.

The building next door (No. 97) is now a youth hostel, but was originally a home for eight retired sea captains. Three doors down, at No. 103, we see a concave baroque wooden door carved in the 1720's. The house just before it (No. 101) was in Rembrandt's day the home of Anna Wijmer, the widow of Jean Six, the silk merchant. Their son Jan Six, a close friend of Rembrandt's, was thirteen when his mother bought this house in 1631. Ten years later, Rembrandt painted a portrait of the elderly Anna Wijmers (now in a private collection in Amsterdam).

If we look at the Florisz. detail on page 104, we will see a building called the Glas huys near the south end of the Oude Cingel (the old name for Kloveniersburgwal). This was a glassworks which stood (and apparently still partly survives) in the garden behind the three houses at Nos. 105 to 109. The factory was established here by Jan Jansz. Carel, one of the founders of the East India Company. Carel later sold the business to Jan Soop, who brought skilled glass makers here from Murano to produce drinking glasses,

mirrors and the colourful glass beads which Dutch traders took on their travels to barter for gold dust. We do not know if Rembrandt knew Jan Soop, but he certainly met his son Floris, who lived in the 17th-century house we see at No. 105. Rembrandt painted his portrait in 1654, when he was an old man of 50, dressed in a flamboyant standard-bearer's uniform. The portrait is now in New York's Metropolitan Museum of Art.

Continuing down Kloveniersburgwal, towards the bridge we crossed earlier on the walk, we soon reach the spot where Reinier Vinkeles stood in 1764 to draw the view of the Kloveniersdoelen opposite. The round tower, another survival from the original city walls, was the famous meeting place of the Doelisten, an early protest group. Led by a porcelain trader, Daniel Raap, the Doelisten agitated during the 1740's for power to be removed from the tightly knit oligarchy of the regents. Perhaps these stirring memories were behind Vinkeles' choice of a view, but he may also have had in mind the other role that the Kloveniersdoelen played in Amsterdam's history. To the left of the tower is the banqueting hall that

was once graced by *The Night Watch*, but the painting had been moved out by the time this drawing was made. When Koveniersdoelen was rebuilt in 1714, the *Night Watch*, after being trimmed - rather drastically - to fit, was rehung in the town hall on the Dam.

The painting has left a trace here however. Before we go straight ahead to reach to the Amstel, we should pause briefly to look across the water at the Doelen Hotel. The two statues just below the dome are copied, though not very accurately, from *The Night Watch*. The man on the left with the long boots is Lieutenant Willem van Ruytenburch. The other figure is Captain Frans Banning Cocq.

The Halvemaansbrug leads us across the Amstel. If we now turn left down Binnen-Amstel, we can stand on the spot (near No. 120) where the photograph opposite was taken one sunny day in 1891. The house with the neck gable, at No. 9, is still standing, as is the Zuiderkerk tower, partly hidden by trees, but who were these seven people who posed on the quayside? The two men on the left in their sailor caps look as if they might have just unloaded the wooden barrels from the boat, but were the others domestic servants, or perhaps the staff from a nearby shop? We will never know.

We now go right down the narrow Bakkersstraat to reach the Rembrandtsplein. Rembrandt would not recognise this square named in his honour, as it barely existed when he lived in Amsterdam. It was then just a patch of open ground behind the city gate. Nor, probably, would he recognise the iron statue unveiled in the middle of the square in 1852. It is meant to be Rembrandt, but it does not look at all like the shabby, morose, proud artist we know from the self-portraits. The figure in the middle of the bushes is too flamboyant, more like a 19th-century bohemian artist. Politics were to blame for this. The city needed something to match the magnificent Rubens statue erected by the burghers of Antwerp in 1840 and a down-at-heel, bankrupt Rembrandt was hardly the sort of person they had in mind.

Towards the end of the century, several fashionable cafés opened on the Rembrandtsplein, including the Mille Colonnes and the Café De Kroon. The first has gone, but the Café De Kroon has survived at No. 17. Designed by Gerrit van Arkel, this was one of the famous grand cafés of Amsterdam. It closed down in the 1960's, apparently for good, but the rooms on the first floor were recently restored to something approaching their original splendour. We can sit on plump sofas surrounded by glittering chandeliers and cabinets filled with exotic butterflies, or bask in the sunshine on the terrace watching the pigeons perched on Rembrandt's hat.

It is easy to miss the Café Schiller at No. 26. The covered terrace may look a bit dilapidated, but it is well worth pushing back the heavy curtain to glance inside. Once our eyes are accustomed to the gloom, we will discover this to be a nostalgic relic of the Art Deco age, for all the world like an old Roxy cinema that is about to be closed down. Not much has changed since the café opened in 1922; the ornate lamps still cast patches of yellow light on the marble walls, illuminating the portraits of Dutch cabaret stars of the 1930's painted by Frits Schiller. The lighting

creates a slightly theatrical air, but the only source of drama these days is when someone accidentally sits on the broken spring of an old sofa.

WALK 4

The Old Harbour

THE IJ *to* THE MARITIME MUSEUM

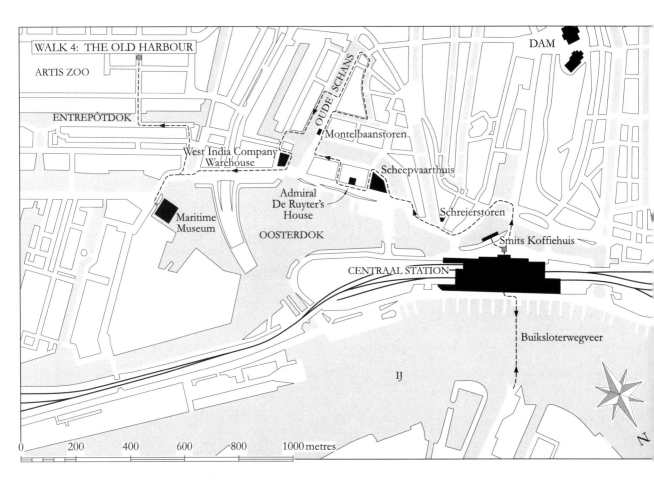

WALK 4: THE OLD HARBOUR

ARTIS ZOO

ENTREPÔTDOK

OUDE SCHANS

DAM

Montelbaanstoren

West India Company
Warehouse

Scheepvaarthuis

Admiral
De Ruyter's
House

Schreierstoren

Maritime
Museum

OOSTERDOK

Smits Koffiehuis

CENTRAAL STATION

Buiksloterwegveer

IJ

N

0   200   400   600   800   1000 metres

The Old Harbour

THE IJ *to* THE MARITIME MUSEUM

The old harbour is one of my favourite quarters, with its creaking Rhine barges, dark wood-panelled cafés, and nautical shops crammed with rigging and charts. In the course of this walk, we will cross a busy shipping lane, explore the maritime museum, and board an 18th-century ship. We should allow at least four hours and avoid Mondays in winter, when the maritime museum is closed. If we set off at 9 am, we should reach the museum soon after it opens at 10 am, leaving ample time to explore the collection before we begin to feel the need for lunch. The harbour area is not known for its restaurants, but we will find several cafés and restaurants in the fashionable Entrepôtdok warehouse district.

We begin back at Centraal Station, a blustery red brick building built on an artificial island in the 1880's. It was designed by Petrus Josephus Hubertus Cuypers, a Catholic who preferred the gothic style, though he put principles to one side in his public buildings, and adopted an eclectic blend of renaissance and gothic motifs. The station is laden with symbolic 19th-century sculpture proclaiming the virtues of industry and travel, including reliefs to the left of the main entrance representing the gods of steam and electricity, but perhaps the most curious feature is the dial on the left tower, which looks like a clock, but is in fact a wind vane.

We might stop for coffee at Smits Koffiehuis again (see page 30), or, for a change, in the café Eerste Klas in the station on platform 2b. This handsome wood-panelled café was formerly the first-class restaurant. It closed down many years ago, but has now been carefully restored to its original splendour. With its stained glass windows, dark brown woodwork and newspapers on wooden poles, it has all the allure of the old restaurant. The only difference now is that few of its customers hold first-class tickets.

I. The IJ. We are now going to do something that virtually no tourist ever considers, which is to walk through the station and out the back entrance, following the signs to Uitgang Noord. This brings us out on a busy road, which we cross to reach the IJ waterfront. This broad stretch of water is an inlet of the IJsselmeer, formerly the Zuider Zee. The name changed, as did the ecology of the region, when the Zuider Zee was enclosed by a dike, turning it from an inlet of the North Sea into a freshwater lake.

A sign indicates the Buiksloterwegveer, a free ferry that carries cyclists and pedestrians across the IJ every few minutes. The trip is short, but it allows us a glimpse of long Rhine barges, rusty Polish freighters and the occasional luxury cruise ship moored in the eastern docklands. When we arrive at the other side, the cyclists set off as if a starting pistol has been fired. After they have gone, we can walk to the end of the jetty, where we might find a sullen, lank heron perching on a wooden post. We are now near the spot where Willem van de Velde the Younger, perhaps sitting in a rowing boat, painted the exciting view opposite of the IJ in 1686. Most of the old town is now hidden by the station, but we can still see the spire of the Montelbaanstoren from where we are standing, just to the left of the station.

The main reason for coming here is to see that Amsterdam is still, as it was in Van de Velde's day, in the Golden Age, a busy port. Few tourists ever glimpse the harbour district, which is a pity. We do need not go any further, though another day, perhaps, we might rent a bicycle to explore the landscape to the north of the IJ (see page 278 for a suggested route). Today is a day for the harbour, so we should take the next ferry back to the station. As we near the pier, we see a curious black wooden building on the waterfront at

pier 7, just beyond Henk's Haring stand. This was built for a shipping company in 1919 in a style that hints at the indigenous architecture of the Dutch East Indies. To the right of the ferry, we will see Pier 10, a small restaurant located in a modern building at the end of the pier. We might return to eat dinner by candlelight here, watching ships sail past the curved glass window.

II. Prins Hendrikkade. We now go back through the station, braving the cacophony of Stationsplein, and cross the crowded bridge. But rather than following the flow down Damrak, we choose the quieter route that runs left along Prins Hendrikkade. This takes us over a bridge built to replace the crowded wooden structure named the Nieuwe brugh on Florisz.'s map (page 36). We then continue along Prins Hendrikkade past the blackened exterior of the St Nicolaaskerk, constructed during the 19th-century Catholic revival, and now, like so many Catholic churches in Amsterdam, suffering from a want of funds.

If we turn back to the Van de Velde, we will see a squat round tower to the right of the Oude Kerk

spire. This is the Schreierstoren, built in the middle ages as part of the city defences. On the Anthonisz. map opposite the tower is still a military installation, with cannons poking out and a privy stuck to the wall. More enormous cannons loom from the emplacement at the tip of the island - by the time Florisz. produced his map this area had been planted with trees and the tower had become a redundant relic, blocking the new bridge across the Geldersekade (called the Keulsche Kay on the map).

Tourist guidebooks tell us that the Schreierstoren, or weeping tower, was where wives and sweethearts would congregate as their men sailed off to the Far East. It is easy to believe this romantic tale, for many sailors died on the long sea voyages. A ship that set off from the Schreierstoren with a crew of two hundred might return, if it ever did, with some fifty fewer men on board.

But is the story of the weeping tower genuine? We can see an ancient cracked stone tablet inscribed *Schrayer houck* embedded in the brick wall, to the right of the entrance. It shows a woman standing on the ramparts as a ship sails off into a choppy sea. The message seems clear enough, but if we look more closely we can see that the woman is not actually weeping, but holding her hand up to her face. Could it be that she is concealing a smile? A local historian has cynically suggested as much, arguing that the woman is in fact looking forward to taking a lover.

This interpretation might not gain much support from the Greenwich Village Historical Society, whose members presented a bronze memorial in 1927 to celebrate the role played by the Schreierstoren in the history of New York. 'From this ancient Tower of Tears erected 1482 AD, Henry Hudson set sail April 4th 1609 on the vessel *Half Moon* on that voyage of discovery destined to bring him to the harbour of New York and the Hudson River,' it says. The plaque omits to point out that the English explorer had been sent by the Dutch East India Company to find a northwest passage to India, which he failed to do, having wasted his effort sailing up the river that would later be named after him. Robert Juet of Limehouse, an officer on the Half Moon,

recorded the first European sighting of Manhattan in his diary: 'We saw a very good piece of ground: and hard by it there was a Cliffe... It is on that side of the River that is called Mannahatta. There we saw no people to trouble us.'

Another commemorative stone is inscribed with the rousing motto *Navigare necesse est.* This one was put up by the Dutch in 1945, perhaps stirred into action by the New Yorkers. It commemorates the 350th anniversary of the first voyage to the East Indies, which meant far more to the Dutch than Hudson's chance encounter with Manhattan. Cornelis Houtman's fleet set off from the harbour east of here in 1595 and though they didn't bring back much booty, they paved the way for the following expedition, in 1599, which yielded huge profits. And profit, like navigation, necesse est.

The New Yorkers were back here again in 1959. This time, the New York Port Authority presented a plaque to commemorate the 350th anniversary of Hudson's voyage to America. One Dutch historian, fearing perhaps the collapse of the little tower under the weight of so many

memorial plaques, has argued that no more should be added. But the 400th anniversary of Hudson's voyage is due in 2009, and I suspect that someone in New York may have some more bronze up their sleeve.

The tower was later occupied by the harbour masters. It was they who commissioned the painting by Van de Velde on page 135, though it is difficult to imagine where such a long painting could have been hung in such a round tower. It now lives in the Amsterdam Historical Museum while the tower is occupied by L. J. Harri, a nautical shop which stocks practical sailing guides to Dutch canals, shiny brass instruments, and detailed navigation charts that could have saved Henry Hudson a wasted journey.

If we now walk a short way down the Geldersekade (but not too far or we will find ourselves back in the red light district), we can stand on the spot where the photograph opposite was taken in 1895. The building we see with the sign Ship Chandlers Warehouse (No. 8) was a chandler's run by J. & J. Vinke, who supplied coffee, peas, beans, salt ham, tar and pitch. The interior, now

used as a private restaurant, is still furnished with the old wooden drawers where ship's supplies were stored.

Back on Prins Hendrikkade, we turn right to reach a bridge called the Kraansluis. The crane can be seen on Anthonisz.'s map, but not the island opposite us. It was a harbour then. The quay ran to the right of the bridge, along the Oude Waal, which was originally an area of shipyards and warehouses known as the Lastage. By the time Florisz. drew his map, the shipyards had gone and the Lastage had become a residential quarter.

The strange building standing at the tip of the island is the Scheepvaarthuis, built in 1912 to provide offices for six shipping companies that ran services to far-flung places such as Java and Japan. It is a wonderful dark brick edifice laden with rippling ironwork, carved sea monsters and the faces of stern Dutch mariners. Designed by Johan van der Mey, Michel de Klerk and Pieter Kramer, it launched the Amsterdam School style, which briefly flourished in the Netherlands during the First World War and into the early 1920's. It is easily recognised from the flamboyant brick-work, curvaceous lines and romantic sea imagery. For a time, the city council adopted this as the official style, commissioning architects to design bridges, electricity substations and even the town hall extension on Oudezijds Voorburgwal, but it was an expensive style and was finally killed off by the Depression.

The Scheepvaarthuis is suffused with the romance of the sea. Just look at the entrance, which is guarded by four sea gods representing the oceans served by the shipping companies. Or walk down the side to examine the stone beams decorated with the busts of famous mariners and map-makers. There are twenty-eight in all, including Houtman, Barentz, Mercator and Blaeu, but no Henry Hudson, perhaps because he was English, or more likely because he failed his mission.

On closer study, we discover a wealth of tiny details, such as mermaids, galleons and the shoals of fish opposite. Even the railings are carefully shaped to suggest the rolling seas. This exuberant maritime imagery is no longer quite so apt, as the building is now occupied by the Amsterdam public transport authority, whose only link with the sea is the passenger ferry we took earlier.

The bridge to the right of the Scheepvaarthuis is one of my favourite spots in Amsterdam. I like the smell of woodsmoke, the creak of bicycles toiling across the arched bridge, and the houses nearby smothered in wisteria. Occasionally, a lazy Amsterdam cat will stretch itself out on a car roof, a saw will screech in a nearby workshop or a sluggish heron land on the deck of a houseboat; but nothing else ever disturbs the peace.

Looking from the bridge, our main landmark is the jaunty spire of the Montelbaanstoren. Following an attack from Gelderland in 1512, this tower was built to protect the Lastage ship-yards. As with the other towers we have seen, its military role was shortlived. It eventually fell into ruin, until the city council came to the rescue in 1606 by commissioning Hendrick de Keyser to add a spire in his breezy mannerist style.

We now turn down the Binnen Bantammer-straat, a lane to the left of the bridge. The residents here have nurtured potted plants and

climbing creepers to create a wild rustic abandon. We soon leave this bucolic corner behind and turn right onto the busy Prins Hendrikkade, where we have come to look at Admiral Michiel de Ruyter's House at No. 131. De Ruyter bought this house in 1661, soon after dealing a crushing blow to the Swedish navy in the Battle of the Sont. The house originally stood on the harbour front, which we see crowded with ships on the detail from the Florisz. map on page 145; the only vessels left now are cluttered houseboats, a floating restaurant and a hotel boat.

The next lane, Schippersstraat, leads us back to the quiet Binnenkant, where artists and writers settled in the 1950's and 1960's. The tall neck gable house just to our right, at No. 32, was once the home of the architect Aldo van Eyck. Members of the Cobra group gathered here in 1948 to discuss the future of art in the aftermath of the Second World War. One year later, Aldo van Eyck organised the first Cobra exhibition in the Stedelijk Museum. The vibrant abstract style was initially unpopular (we might remember that Karel Appel's mural in the town hall had to

be painted over), but the group gradually won over admirers; there is now even a Cobra Museum in the respectable suburb of Amstelveen, of all places.

We now turn left along Binnenkant to reach a sleepy stretch of Oude Schans. It appears on the Florisz. map as the Montelbaens Burchwal, a crowded canal where boats unloaded timber. If we turn right over the bridge and walk down the Oude Schans a short distance, we can stand near the spot where Jan de Beijer made this drawing at about four o'clock on a summer day in 1760. For once we cannot stand on the exact spot, as this was in the middle of a wooden bridge which appears on the Florisz. detail on page 145 (above the letter E), but is no longer standing. If we find a vantage point opposite No. 18 (a house we will look at later), we can see that the Montelbaanstoren has hardly changed. Even the mermaid wind-vane is still there on the top, and the bell-gable house on the left (No. 6) has kept its curious pair of painted women's heads. On the other side of the canal are some very strange chimneys, and lumberjacks poling tree-trunk

rafts. The drum on stilts was used to lift goods onto the barges. The building behind, half hidden by trees in De Beijer's view, was the West India Company warehouse.

More about that later, but first let us look at Jan Swammerdam's House at No. 18. The famous Dutch natural scientist was born here in 1637 in a house that appears on the Florisz. map (just to the south of the wooden drawbridge, where a timber barge is moored). His father Jan Jacobsz. ran a chemist shop on the ground floor and dabbled in science in his spare time, amassing a cabinet of curiosities that included such oddities as a unicorn, three Hottentot catapults, a mermaid's hand and a mechanical mouse.

The son followed in his father's footsteps, but concentrated on more serious natural history specimens. Eventually what this modest house contained was one of the greatest scientific collections in 17th-century Europe; visitors on the Grand Tour would sometimes come here to admire the rarities. On a visit here in 1668, Cosimo de Medici was so impressed that he offered Swammerdam a position in Florence and 12,000 guilders for the collection. Swammerdam turned down the offer, even though such a sum would have bought him a house almost as grand as Rembrandt's (who we remember splashed out 13,000 guilders in 1639).

Swammerdam lived here for most of his life, working on detailed descriptions of animals (insects were his speciality) and building up a vast collection of specimens, including the ear-drum of a walrus, a silkworm's testicles and a horse's nostrils. He developed his own method for preserving specimens with wax (still in use today), and discovered the existence of red blood corpuscles. His father, though, was unimpressed, urging him to become a doctor, rather than waste his time in 'a pursuit in which there is no profit'. Nothing daunted, the young Swammerdam plodded on with his investigations until his death in 1680, after which the collection was sold off. Nobody thought anything more about Swammerdam for another fifty-seven years, until his extraordinary drawings and descriptions of animals were published by Herman Boerhaave of Leiden University. The plaque we see on the wall of the house was added in 1880, declaring that: 'His research into nature remains an example for all time.'

We continue down Oude Schans, crossing another bridge and then turning right down Rechtboomsloot, a dark, mysterious canal lined with crumbling warehouses, some of them visible on the Florisz. map here. The warehouse at No. 42 is decorated with a curious carved stone named De Lastage and dated 1971. It shows a view of the nearby Waag boarded up with wooden timbers, a reminder of the destruction caused when the metro was built through this quarter in the 1970's.

Now we turn left along Kromboomsloot, a quiet, forgotten canal where cats slumber on sunlit windowsills and the rusted relics of abandoned bicycles remain padlocked to bridge railings for years, until a man from the council arrives to remove them with a sturdy metal cutter. A handsome old warehouse called Schottenburg (at Nos. 18-20) is not quite old enough to appear on Florisz. This rugged yellow brick building dates from 1636, according to the year

stone set in the wall. It is now a beer warehouse stocking dozens of potent brews from Belgium and Germany.

The classical building at No. 22 is an old Armenian Church, built in 1714 for Armenian merchants who settled in Amsterdam to trade in exotic products such as silk, gems and goat's wool. The first Armenian Bible was published in Amsterdam in 1666 and a sculptor versed in the Armenian script was found in 1749 to carve the text above the entrance, which includes the declaration: 'Johannes, a priest from Amasia, rebuilt the gate at his own expense and added the marble lamb.' A small group of local Armenians still worships here.

If we stand next to No. 49, just beyond the next bridge, we can see the bend in the canal sketched by Gerrit Lamberts in 1817 (opposite). Lamberts once again shows us a deserted street, with just one shadowy character crossing the bridge. Another stork-like chimney cowl sits proudly in the top right-hand corner. A few of the buildings in the drawing can still be seen, such as the Zuiderkerk spire, with its gilded cock still in place, and the attractive house on the corner of Keersloot, though most of the houses drawn by Lamberts were torn down when the metro was built.

At the end of the canal, we turn left along Snoekjesgracht, where Aldo van Eyck and Theo Bosch built the modern apartment block on the corner as part of the reconstruction of the neighbourhood. A brick building on the opposite quay (Nos. 32-52) was once the coach house of the De Pinto house. We now turn left down Oude Schans, where the quay opposite tends to be deserted during the day, but more lively in the evening when crowds come to hear improvised jazz in the Bimhuis (No. 73); then right across the modern bridge, and left down the other side of the canal. George Breitner, the plein air impressionist we met in Walk 1, rented a studio at No. 5. Willem Witsen (who drew the canal view on page 14) took it over in 1887, painting several views of Oude Schans, if not in the open air, at least from his window, including a view of the Montelbaanstoren we may have seen in the Amsterdam Historical Museum.

147

Continuing down the canal, we come to an inlet, where we turn right and cross an iron drawbridge. We then go left along 's-Gravenhekje to find the Dutch West India Company warehouse, the top still decorated with the row of stone balls we saw above the foliage in Jan de Beijer's view. Looking up at the solemn brick façade, we can read the completion date of 1642 (which makes it too late to appear on the Florisz. map) and the initials GWK inscribed on an ornate sandstone cartouche in the pediment. This sturdy building with its seven wooden hoist beams was built by the Dutch West India Company, which was founded in 1621 to profit from the Atlantic trade. The warehouse was once crammed with furs bought from the Indians, which the Dutch sold to Russia - surely a case of coals to Newcastle - and sugar from the Carribean slave plantations.

The company also ran the trading post on Manhattan, which had been bought from the Manhattoes tribe in 1626 for the famously low sum of 60 guilders. By the time the company built this warehouse, the Dutch settlement of New Amsterdam, at the southern tip of Manhattan, had barely 400 inhabitants. In the same year as the building was completed, a drunken Indian shot dead a Dutch farmer on Staten Island. The Dutch governor Willem Kieft ordered a punitive expedition the following spring in which more than 100 Indians were murdered at Pavonia by Dutch mercenaries. A Dutch settler, who watched the massacre from the ramparts of the fort on Manhattan, wrote: 'I saw nothing but firing and heard the shrieks of savages murdered in their sleep.'

The Pavonia massacre sparked off a war between the Dutch and the Indians, in which the settlement on Manhattan was almost destroyed. The Dutch governor wrote a desperate letter in the autumn begging for help to be sent: 'Almost every place is abandoned. We, wretched people, must skulk, with wives and little ones that still survive, in poverty together, in and around the Fort at the Manahatas where we are not safe even for an hour, whilst the Indians daily threaten to overwhelm us. Very little can be planted this autumn and much less in spring; so that it will come to pass that all of us who will yet save our lives, must of necessity perish next year of hunger and sorrow, with our wives and children.'

The company claimed that it could not afford to support the settlement on Manhattan, as a rebellion in Brazil had brought them close to bankruptcy, but as it happened the fort was finally relieved, just in time, when a ship arrived carrying soldiers fleeing from Brazil. The company's fortunes continued to decline, though, and in 1654 the governors were forced to vacate the headquarters on Herenmarkt (described on page 172) and move to this warehouse. The company finally collapsed in 1674.

We now turn right along Prins Hendrikkade, where we find an East India Company warehouse dating from about 1600 at No. 176. A gate to the right of this rugged brick building still bears the initials VOC and A, referring to the Amsterdam branch of the Verenigde Oost-Indische Compagnie. The East India Company had a shipyard on this waterfront in the 17th century, clearly visible on the detail from Florisz.'s map overleaf (to the right of the long warehouse).

The map shows ships in various stages of construction - the vessel next to the warehouse has its keel and stern fitted, and carpenters are now working on the hull; another to the right looks almost ready to sail, and a third ship, left of the warehouses, has just been launched, throwing up a cloud of spray as it hits the water.

The shipyards have gone, but this quarter retains a nautical atmosphere. If we continue along the former quay, we pass the Zeevaartschool, a nautical training school designed in 1878 by Willem Springer. Nearby, at Kadijksplein 18, the Zeemanshuis was built in the 1850's as a home for poor seamen. It was founded by an Amsterdam banker who had read a Dickens story about a sailors' home in New York.

III. The Maritime Museum. The most impressive nautical relic in this quarter is the Nederlands Scheepvaart Museum (Dutch Maritime Museum), which stands opposite us on an artificial island. We can put away our map now, for there is no mistaking this building, which stands in splendid isolation on the edge of the harbour, surrounded

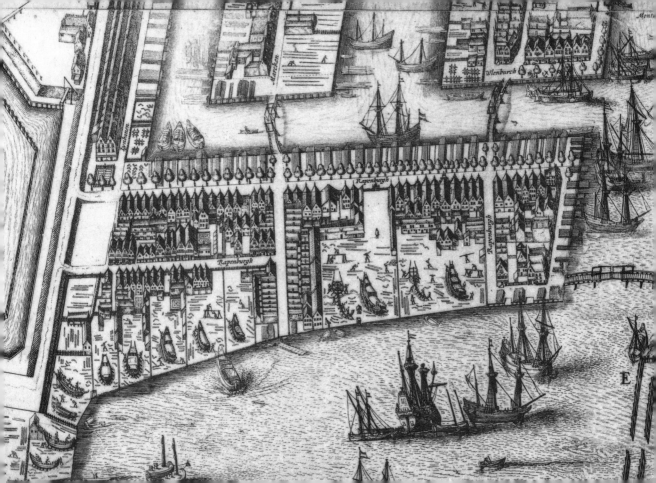

by various historic Dutch craft including a three-masted sailing ship that looks as if it might have been built in the shipyards on Florisz.'s map. The ship was in fact constructed a few years ago by a team of volunteers, as a faithful replica of an East India Company vessel that sank off the coast of England in 1749. More about that later, but first we have the museum to visit.

This stern classical building was designed by Daniel Stalpaert in 1656 as an arsenal for the Amsterdam Admiralty. This was where ships were fitted with rigging and sails, and equipped with weapons and food for the long sea voyages to the East Indies. We can still see the brass pumps in the courtyard used to supply the ships with drinking water, and several shipwrecked cannon dredged from the sea bed.

We have thirty crowded rooms to visit, so we will need at least an hour, and possibly much longer, depending how interested we are in model ships, figureheads, maps, globes, charts and paintings of sea battles. For those with a love of sea lore, a visit here could take up the rest of the day, for the museum also has a nautical

bookshop, a shop in the basement selling ship models and several historic vessels moored outside.

The first few rooms immerse us in the early days of seafaring, with models of mediaeval craft, gleaming brass astrolabes and detailed world atlases. We can pore over various maps of Amsterdam in room 1, comparing the Anthonisz. map of 1544 with Florisz.'s map of 1647 (the later version with the new town hall prematurely included). In the next room, we find a copy of Blaeu's map of the world printed on twenty-one sheets. It was drawn in 1648, by which time most of the planet has been correctly mapped, apart from the coast of Nova Hollandia, as Australia was called in those days.

We will find a portrait of Michiel de Ruyter in the same room, painted by Ferdinand Bol in 1667, six years after the admiral had bought the house we passed earlier. Bol shows De Ruyter soon after he had defeated the English fleet in the Four Day Battle of 1666. He is leaning on a balcony with his elbow resting on a celestial globe, looking very pleased with himself. 'The day after the victory I found him sweeping his own cabin and feeding his chickens,' a French writer wrote after this battle.

Room 5 contains an 18th-century *trekschuit* painted bottle green and gold. Almost every traveller in Holland had horror stories about these inland barges used on the Dutch canal network from the 17th to the 19th century. The services were reliable but tediously long. A traveller going from Rotterdam to Amsterdam had to spend eleven hours in a cramped cabin filled with pipe smoke, watching the dull flat fields glide past. Boswell sank into one of his deep melancholies during such a trip in 1763. 'I travelled between Leyden and Utrecht nine hours in a sluggish trek schuit without any companion, so that I brooded over my own dismal imaginations,' he wrote to a friend.

For a Dutch seaman, nine hours in a trekschuit was nothing. They were used to spending nine months on board the East India ships. The food they ate was hardly inspiring, as we can see from the menu displayed in room 10. They had grits with prunes cooked in butter for breakfast, yellow peas or beans with salted meat or stockfish for lunch, and the day's leftovers at 6 pm. The food was washed down with gin and beer at breakfast, wine for lunch and another tot of gin at night.

We might ourselves be feeling the need of a tot of gin by this time, but we still have one more floor to visit, where we can look at nostalgic photographs of transatlantic liners, poke around a reconstructed radio room and experience a simulated submarine attack on an Atlantic convoy. After that, one last thing remains to be done. In room 24, we will find a periscope. If we look through it, we will perhaps see people dressed in old costumes on the decks of the *Amsterdam.* It is time to go on board.

A team of volunteers toiled for several years to create a replica of the *Amsterdam,* which sank off the coast of Hastings on its maiden voyage (and whose remains were recently dug up on Hastings beach). The decks are nicely cluttered with ropes and barrels, and the cabins have been furnished in 18th-century style. We can stoop down to peer inside the captain's cabin, or clamber down the steep steps to poke around the vast storage space. During the summer, actors dressed as seamen sing old sea shanties or act out episodes from life on board the ship. The best moment to catch is the firing of the cannon, which takes place below decks amid much shouting of orders and Dutch naval banter.

We can then climb up onto the breezy poop deck to look out over the harbour. The port area has changed, of course, since the Amsterdam set sail in 1749, but we can still see Admiral De Ruyter's house, the warehouses of the West India Company and the Schreierstoren. If we stand here while the actors are singing lusty sea songs, or cooking a meal, we might almost begin to believe that we are about to set sail for Java.

After visiting the museum, we can go on to explore the harbour area to the east, or take bus 22 from outside the museum back to Centraal Station. If we are in the mood for exploring, we should take the pedestrian underpass to reach the other side of Prins Hendrikkade, then go through the impressive classical gate leading to the Entrepôtdok. We come upon a long row of massive brick warehouses named in alphabetical order

after various Dutch towns. The warehouses have now been converted into apartments, cafés, restaurants and offices.

We then go right across the Nijlpaardenbrug, whose name, if we are wondering, means Nile Horse - that is Hippoptamus - Bridge. The reason for the name is found not so far away, for we are close to Artis, Amsterdam's 19th-century zoo. We can probably leave that for another day, for our aim now is to find a café, my favourite here-abouts being De Plantage at Plantage Middenlaan 37, a brown café decorated with old Colonial photographs, vague maps of imaginary islands and old lamps salvaged from an Art Deco cinema. We might try a glass of Wieckse Witte here, a delicious tangy Dutch wheat beer brewed in Maastricht. We can then catch a tram back to the centre, or walk along the Plantage Midden-laan through the former Jewish district. But that is another story.

WALK 5

Singel

THE HAARLEMMERSLUIS *to* THE FLOWER MARKET

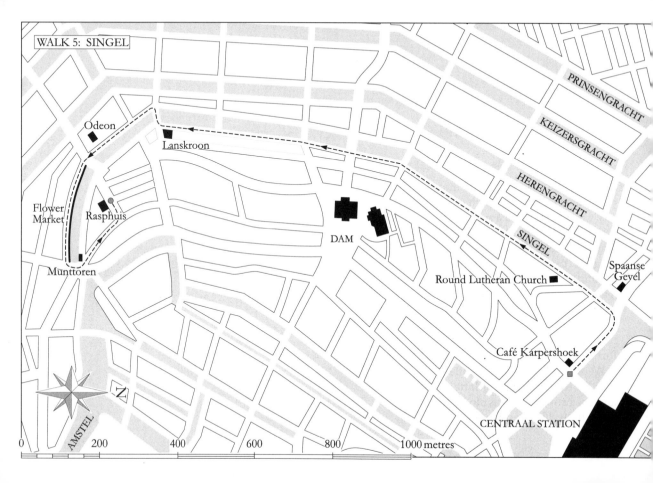

WALK 5: SINGEL

Odeon

Lanskroon

Flower
Market

Rasphuis

Munttoren

DAM

Round Lutheran Church

Café Karpershoek

Spaanse
Gevel

PRINSENGRACHT

KEIZERSGRACHT

HERENGRACHT

SINGEL

CENTRAAL STATION

AMSTEL

N

0   200   400   600   800   1000 metres

Singel

THE HAARLEMMERSLUIS*to* THE FLOWER MARKET

When Anthonisz. drew his map in 1544 (page 33), Singel formed a stretch of the moat, with the city wall along the east side and watery meadows lying to the west. When the city pushed westwards in the early 17th century, this became an elegant canal where people such as Frans Banning Cocq and Rembrandt's son Titus lived. This is a short walk we can do whenever we have an hour to spare, in the course of which we will discover a barge for stray cats, a floating flower market and a house that celebrates its former owner's enormous nose.

We might begin with a coffee in the nostalgic café De Karpershoek at Martelaarsgracht 2. This ancient brown café has stood on the waterfront since 1629. The wooden interior looks as if it has not changed much since then, apart from the addition of a large clock kept a few minutes fast so that commuters do not miss the last train home. On leaving the café, we turn left along the old harbour front, marked on the Florisz. map as the Harinckpackery (herring packing works), but now the Prins Hendrikkade. The only herring we will come upon now are the delicious *maatjes* sold at Stubbe's fish stall on the bridge that crosses Singel. These small cured herring are served with a dash of raw onion, and eaten on the spot - whole, if possible. We then say *dag*, and are on our way.

I. The Haarlemmersluis. The herring stand is near a lock, the Haarlemmersluis, where seagulls

swoop around looking for scraps. A lock-keeper cycles here every evening between 7 pm and 8 pm to crank the sluice shut, then returns again in the morning to open the gates, purging the canals of the day's rubbish. This ritual, or something like it, must have been familiar to the great landscapist Hobbema saw when he painted his only true townscape, now in the National Gallery. When he was 30 he was given the post of wine gauger to the city and came to live round the corner from here - and never painted again.

Before we start walking, we can look at one of the oldest houses in the city has stood here since 1610 (and so appears on Florisz.). The red-brick house at No. 2 is called De Spaanse Gevel (The Spanish House) after Spanish inscriptions were found on the beams. The original owner, a man called Cruywagen, was a ships' chandler. The carved stone above the warehouse door is a play on his name - Mr Wheelbarrow, as it were. The musty shop is still a chandler's, crammed with rigging, ropes and flags. A life assurance company commissioned the corner building, dated 1843, next to the lock at Haarlemmerstraat 2. The directors indulged a romantic whim by adding the blue guardian angel of insurance we see on the roof, perched on top of a globe.

We set off now down the other side of Singel, keeping to the side with the odd numbers to admire the tall houses opposite, such as Vriesland at No. 24, whose flamboyant baroque balustrade is decorated with a splendid carving of a ship battling against a stormy sea. Another house called Zeevrugt (literally 'harvest of the sea') at No. 36 has a sailing ship above the door and a rococo balustrade decorated with a reclining figure of Mercury, looking unusually relaxed for the god of trade.

We now come upon the Round Lutheran Church, whose dome can be seen quite clearly in the photograph on page 30-31. This unusual church was built in the 1670's by Adriaen Dortsman for the Lutheran church, but Lutherans are thin on the ground now, and the church, renamed the Koepelzaal, is used only for the occasional conference or classical concert. Directly opposite the church, a barge called the Poezenboot has been for many years a refuge for stray cats.

Another nautical detail can be spotted further down this side of the canal (at Nos. 23-25). An unusually broad house has a bell-gable bearing the motto *Vita Hominum Similis Naviganti* ('the life of a man is like a voyage'). A house opposite, at No. 56, has a Roman emperor on the gable top, but its almost pair, No. 60, more curiously, has a splendid 18th-century baroque crest decorated at the top left corner with two cherubs. One boy, presumably representing Cupid, sits on a helmet holding a cluster of arrows. The other is dressing up in his helmet; perhaps he is Mars, the god of war.

If we stand on the bridge called the Lijnbaansbrug, looking south, we will see one of the most curious houses on Singel. We have to look closely at No. 116 to discover the reason for it being called the Huis met de Neuzen (House of the Noses). The story goes that in the 1750's, when this house was being built, some friends of the owner offered to pay for the decoration, but only if they were allowed to include portraits of the owner and his two sons. They may have regretted the decision on seeing the gable.

159

A short stroll further down the canal brings us opposite the handsome double step gable called De Dolphijn at Nos. 140-142. This blushing red brick house was built in about 1600 by Hendrick de Keyser, who leafed through his books of Italian renaissance designs for the fanciful motifs such as the scrolls and obelisks we see on the front. This was the home of Captain Frans Banning Cocq, the man leading the city guard in Rembrandt's *Night Watch* (detail here). Cocq was once described as the stupidest man in Amsterdam, though clearly he was also one of the richest.

Let us now look at the narrow red house at No. 166, which is hardly wider than the front door. If we stand here long enough, we will probably see a tourist boat chugging along the canal, while the guide describes this building, in four languages, as the smallest house in Amsterdam. It is an amusing idea, but quite false, for the building is much wider at the back.

II. The Torensluis. From the next bridge, Torensluis, looking south again, we will be able to see several interesting buildings. The tall 18th-century house at No. 186, which must have been built by a merchant, has the familiar wooden hoist beam for lifting goods into the attic and a bust of Mercury on the roof. The next house, No. 188, is decorated with a carved stone from 1737 naming it as De Roo Oly Molen (The Red Oil Mill). Two doors further, the house at No. 192 once belonged to a wine merchant who put up a stone tablet decorated with a bunch of grapes. And finally, in this neighbourhood, an ancient, weathered carved stone from 1663, attached to No. 194 but moved here from elsewhere, shows various cobbler's tools. It once identified the guild house of the clog makers.

Carrying on down Singel, still on the same side, we pass the attractive Faculty of Literature, built in the 1980's by Theo Bosch. We should pause briefly opposite the warehouse called Theeboom, No. 210, to look down the lane called Driekoningenstraat. This lets us glimpse the Bartolotti House, designed by Hendrick de Keyser, and the Westerkerk tower, built by his son Pieter. We will look more closely at the Bartolotti House on our next walk, and visit the Westerkerk, perhaps even climbing the tower, on Walk 8.

We now have to cross Raadhuisstraat, watching out for trams, and then proceed down Singel, keeping to the side with the odd numbers so that we can appreciate the gable top of No. 288, which ruffles its plumage like an exotic bird. This flamboyant rococo house was built in the 1750's using costly grey sandstone shipped from Germany. The owner was a merchant, though I suspect he might have been trying to disguise the fact here. We can hardly spot the hoist beam, which is carved with a dolphin's head. The loft doors are likewise concealed by a flourish of rococo detail.

Another 18th-century merchant built the house at No. 326, but he had no qualms about his trade. The two figures on either side of the attic door are Mercury and Neptune. The neighbouring house, No. 324, has a splendid swan carved on a stone. If we now stand on the next bridge, we will see a white house opposite, at No. 358, identified by a carved stone as In de

Vergulde Haringbuys (In the Gilded Herring Boat). This was briefly the home of Rembrandt's son Titus and his wife, but the gilt has worn since their time.

The sinuous railings pictured here can be spotted at Nos. 351 to 353, two houses which retain their 17th-century wooden fronts. On the opposite side, we see a Vogel Struis (ostrich) on No. 370. The quay we are on is marked as the Appelmarkt on Florisz.'s map, though nothing now remains of the apple trade apart from a curious stone on the house at No. 367, carved with Adam and Eve under the apple tree.

On the opposite side of Singel, No. 390 is a sumptuous 18th-century baroque house with two reclining figures on the cornice representing Apollo and Minerva. We can see a carved medallion above the door supported by two cherubs, though we probably cannot make out the word *Bouwkunst* (architecture). We should now stop briefly in front of No. 400, not to admire the architecture, but because Otto Frank worked here for the Opekta jam company. A photograph in the Anne Frank Museum shows Anne standing on this doorstep, waiting for her father.

Now let us turn our attention to Lanskroon, at No. 385, one of the best cake shops in town. Local office workers steal out in mid-afternoon to tuck into a moist slice of bilberry tart or a rich piece of Sachertorte before returning to their computer screens. The shop is cramped and the queue can be long, but it worth putting up with any amount of discomfort to sample one of Lanskroon's cakes.

Beyond the next lane is the best map shop in town at No. 393. The people who run Pied-à-Terre stock a vast range of maps and guidebooks for adventurous travellers. We will find walking guides to Wales, cycling maps of the Netherlands and guidebooks to every country visited by Dutch globetrotters. The noticeboard in the entrance hall is crammed with requests for travelling companions to remote places. A few years ago, everyone seemed to be heading for China, but South Africa and Russia are now the places being explored.

For now we might now cross over to the other side of Singel to look at the modern jewellery in the window of Jorge Cohen at No. 414. This Argentinian craftsman produces jazzy red and black jewellery inspired by the interiors of the Tuschinski cinema, sometimes incorporating fragments of old bracelets and necklaces found in the flea markets of Paris.

We continue across Beulingsloot, a narrow canal that laps the walls of the houses, like a small corner of Venice. An Italian restaurant called Casa di David stands on the corner as if to complete the scene. We soon come to a tall brick church called De Krijtberg at No. 446, another empty relic of the Catholic revival. The Old Lutheran Church opposite, built in 1633, is now used by the university for graduation ceremonies. The university has also taken possession of the Bushuis at No. 423, a mannerist building of 1606 where the guild of crossbowmen once stored their equipment. The new university library at No. 425 stands on the site of the meeting hall of this guild, whose members pose in the painting by Cornelis Anthonisz. in the Amsterdam Historical Museum (see page 74). We can also see their successors in a group portrait by

Bartholomeus van der Helst in the Rijksmuseum, part of which is shown opposite. The Van der Helst work is particularly interesting because it shows the crossbowmen celebrating the Peace of Münster in the banqueting hall that stood here. The windows are open, allowing us to glimpse two buildings on the opposite side of Singel.

One of them was a brewery called The Lamb, which had a lamb on the roof. The brewery has gone, and the site, at No. 460, is now occupied by the Odeon, a dark red neck gable house built by Philips Vingboons in 1662. We might recognise the typical Vingboons touches such as the festoons, oval windows, and neck gable. The floorboards now shudder each night to the noise of a disco and the bar, open from 10 pm, occupies the grand front room of the house.

III. The flower market. The flower market takes up the last stretch of Singel. Floating glasshouses are filled with rampant house plants, garden gnomes, daffodil bulbs, bags of peat, flower pots and pails of freshly-cut flowers. The shops sell big bunches of yellow tulips in the spring, gaudy sunflowers in midsummer, and chrysanthemums to brighten up damp autumn afternoons. A jaunty tower called the Munttoren stands at the end of the canal, its tinny carillon playing a folk tune every hour. The ornate spire was built by Hendrick de Keyser on the brick stump of a mediaeval tower. The building attached to the tower was once a guard house; it is decorated with a carved stone depicting the Amsterdam legend - two fishermen in a boat with a very miserable dog.

There is one last sight to look at in this neighbourhood, which we find by walking down the busy Kalverstraat shopping street and turning left into Heiligeweg. An extraordinary renaissance gateway at No. 19 once led to the Rasphuis. The gate was designed by Hendrick de Keyser in 1603 in a sober Doric style, with the Maid of Amsterdam seated on top, wielding a whip to control two chained prisoners. A Latin motto declares *Castigatio*, which hardly needs translation. The panel below is carved with a rumination by Seneca: 'It is virtuous to tame that which everyone fears.'

What lay behind was once a house of correction. It was built in 1596 on the site of an old convent to provide a model prison based on the 16th-century writings of Dirck Coornhert. At a time when branding and torture were common, Coornhert argued that imprisonment was a more humane punishment. The city eventually took up his ideas after a boy of sixteen was hanged for theft. Travellers visiting Amsterdam in the 17th century would be brought here to watch the inmates shaving hard Brazilian wood - we see the tree trunks in the relief - for use in the dyeing trade. John Evelyn noted his impressions in 1641. 'We were carried to see the Rasp-house, where the lusty Knaves are compelld to labour; and it is a very hard labour.'

Evelyn failed to mention one feature of the Rasphuis that astonished another English traveller, Thomas Bowrey, in 1698. Prisoners who refused to work were 'put into a Cellar into which the water runs, and there is a Pump. If they will Pump Hard, they will keep the water Low; if not, it rises and Drownds them.' Simon Schama writes about the drowing cellar in *The Embarrasment of Riches*, but concludes that the story is a myth. Michael Pye was so taken with the idea that he wrote a historical novel called *The Drowning Room*.

Our walk is over, and all that remains is to mention a few good restaurants in the neighbourhood. An elegant little Italian restaurant called Tartufo at Singel 449 serves delicious pasta dishes such as tagliatelle with fresh salmon and chives in a cream sauce. Dishes can be ordered in small or large portions, depending on how hungry we are after our walk. If we are very hungry, we might head back to the Munt to eat in Indonesia at Singel 550, a large, bustling Indonesian restaurant where we can order an enormous rijsttafel.

Herengracht

THE WEST INDIA HOUSE *to* THE WILLET-HOLTHUYSEN MUSEUM

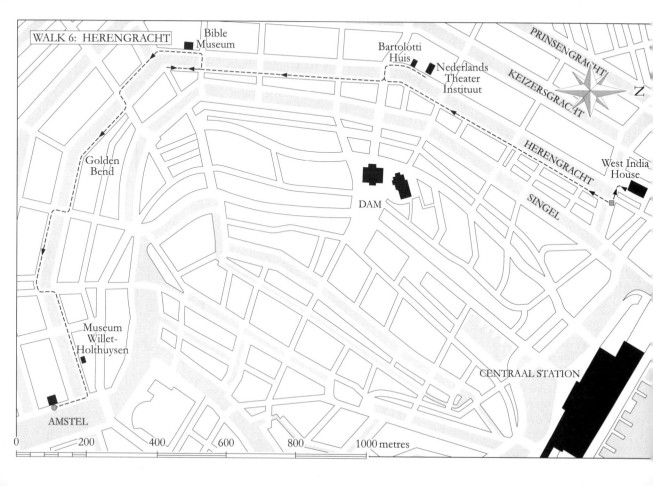

WALK 6: HERENGRACHT

Bible Museum

Bartolotti Huis

Nederlands Theater Instituut

PRINSENGRACHT

KEIZERSGRACHT

Z

Golden Bend

HERENGRACHT

West India House

DAM

SINGEL

Museum Willet-Holthuysen

CENTRAAL STATION

AMSTEL

0   200   400   600   800   1000 metres

Herengracht

THE WEST INDIA HOUSE *to* THE WILLET-HOLTHUYSEN MUSEUM

It is time now to stroll down the Herengracht. This is a walk for a summer day, as it is mostly out of doors, apart from the three canal houses we visit along the way. Two of the houses are closed on a Monday, and the first one we visit does not open until 11 am, so we are best leaving this walk until the afternoon. In the course of our stroll, which will take us about two hours, we will see some of the most splendid houses in Amsterdam and gaze on cherished views painted by 17th-century artists.

For over two centuries, a home on the Herengracht was the ultimate proof of success in Dutch society. It meant that its owner was a rich banker, a successful merchant, or perhaps a slave trader. He probably owned a large collection of porcelain, a country house on the Vecht, perhaps even a Rembrandt. Any house on the Herengracht above the 200's was a mark of distinction, though the 400's and 500's were particularly coveted, and the ultimate achievement in the Dutch Golden Age was to live on 'the bend in the Herengracht'.

If we look at a map, we will see that the Herengracht actually has four bends, but everyone knew that *the* bend was the one at Nieuwe Spiegelstraat. The richest families in Amsterdam employed the best architects of the day to build neo-classical palaces on this stretch of Herengracht. The painting by Berckheyde on page 191 shows the bend soon after the original houses had been built. The scene looks strangely bare compared with the views we have seen of the old town. There are no carpenters working in the street, no barges unloading barrels onto the quayside - and no trees! The trees would come later, but the carpenters and brewers would be kept away by the strict planning regulations which banished noisy and noxious trades from the upper end of the Herengracht.

I. The old end. There is an older part of Herengracht, which is quieter and more modest. That is where we begin this walk, at the spot where Brouwersgracht joins Herengracht. A convenient bench placed at the end of the canal will let us enjoy the view down the gracht. Or, if it is open, we can go into the Belhamel at Brouwersgracht 60, an intimate restaurant where we might, if we are lucky, get a window table looking down Herengracht. The staff are friendly and the menu is inspired. For some, indeed, it is the perfect Amsterdam restaurant.

If we study the detail opposite from Florisz.'s map, we can see that this corner of the city has hardly changed since 1625. We are looking at a district laid out under the Plan of the Three Canals drawn up in 1609. Hendrick Staets, the city carpenter, is credited with creating the basic outline, which gave Amsterdam its unique canal network. The Dutch Republic was in an euphoric mood when the Plan was drafted; the long war with Spain had just ended with the signing of a truce (though it lasted only twelve years), and the population of Amsterdam was rising fast, swollen by Protestant refugees from Antwerp and Sephardic Jews driven out of Spain. Once the new canals were dug, wealthy Amsterdam merchants were able to sell their homes in the crowded old quarters to the east and move into the new district. Some of the more wealthy Flemish families settled there, too, though the Jews preferred to be on the east side of town near the synagogues.

The 1609 Plan was so ambitious that it took the best part of a century to complete, as we saw in the picture on page 77. The digging of the canals was begun when Rembrandt was just three years old and it was barely half completed when he died. Houses and bridges were being built in this district while Manhattan was being settled,

Descartes was flirting with his Dutch maid, and Tasman was mapping the coast of Australia. The canal ring was built in two separate stages, beginning with the northern section, from Brouwersgracht to Leidsegracht, and moving on, in 1665, to the southern section, from Leidsegracht to the Amstel. When Florisz. produced his 1625 map, only the northern section had been built. We can see from the detail on page 181 that the Herengracht ended abruptly at the Beulingsloot (the Heeredwars Burchwal on the map). The Leidsegracht was a moat, and everything beyond was farmland.

This walk gives us a vivid impression of the evolution in architectural styles during Amsterdam's Golden Age. We are now at the old end of the canal, where the houses on the left side were built facing the city wall in the 1590's and early 1600's. Some have been modified, of course, but many still retain features that go back to those early years of the Dutch Republic. As we move down the canal, beyond the bridge with the five arches we see in the distance, the character of the buildings changes. As the merchants

became richer and more sophisticated, they began to choose courtly French architecture instead of the the cheerful Dutch Renaissance style developed by Hendrick de Keyser. Some of the most splendid houses were built during the second phase, after 1665, using the accumulated wealth of half a century of Dutch trade.

The older part of Herengracht, where we begin, is still mainly residential, but as we progress towards the newer end, we will find that most of the houses have been turned into banks, lawyers' offices and design studios. By the time we reach the grand palaces built after 1665, there are few signs of domestic life; the former dining rooms are now crammed with computers and fax machines, while the stuccoed hallways have been turned into reception areas.

All that comes later, after our stop for coffee and cake. We begin at the Herenmarkt, a forgotten little square to our right. Staets intended this to be a market - and so it was, briefly. We can see it marked on the Florisz. map as the Varcken-markt, the pig market. Later in the 17th century the square gained a louche reputation which led to it being known locally as the Hoerenmarkt (whores' market). The Herenmarkt (which means gentleman's market) is now empty of both pigs and prostitutes; nor is there even the usual jaunty fish stall selling pickled herring (the nearest one is at the end of Singel).

II. The West India House. Only the most inquisitive tourist ever stops to examine the brick West India House on the north side of the square, marked West-Indisch Huys on the Florisz. map. At the time of the map, the building was occupied by the Dutch West India Company, which had moved here in 1623. The map shows the building with three wings, but it gained a fourth in the early 19th century. By that time, there was no longer any Dutch West India Company, nor was there much work in Amsterdam, and this splendid building had become the headquarters of the poor relief board.

Things were very different when Florisz. drew his map. The West India House was bustling with activity, as the directors pored over maps of America in search of new trading opportunities.

The first Dutch settlers left for North America in the same year that the company moved here. Three years later, in 1626, Peter Minuit bought Manhattan island from the local Manhattoes tribe in exchange for some cloth and trinkets. When the news of the deal reached Amsterdam, Peter Schagen wrote a letter to the States General in The Hague. 'Our people have purchased the island Manhattes from the Indians for the value of 60 guilders,' he informed them, little realising that they had struck the greatest property deal ever.

The directors were more impressed by the exploits of Piet Heyn, the Dutch captain who attacked a Spanish fleet carrying silver in 1628. The treasure was brought back to Amsterdam and stored in this building. Two years later, Michiel Pauw (whose house we will visit very shortly) bought some land at Hobocan Hacking on the banks of the North River opposite New Amsterdam, where he created the colony of Pavonia. The deed signed by Pauw is the oldest document held by the New York City archives. Yet the link with Manhattan was brief. The company was badly run, leading to the loss of its trading settlements in Brazil and New Amsterdam. The finances became so shaky that the directors had to abandon their headquarters here in 1654 and move into a company warehouse in the port area (we passed it on Walk 4).

If we go through the entrance at No. 93, we can see from the mail boxes that the West India House is now occupied by organisations ranging from the John Adams Institute to The Flying Hippo. A cigarette company, proud of its brand name, gave the bronze statue in the courtyard depicting Pieter Stuyvesant, the governor of New Amsterdam from 1647 to 1664. Stuyvesant had lost a leg trying unsuccessfully to capture the island of St Martin from the Spanish, and was known to the Indians as 'the big Sachima with the wooden leg'.

If we now turn round, we can see a stone tablet put up to commemorate the foundation of New Amsterdam in 1626. The sculptor has carved a view of the early settlement at the tip of Manhattan island, including a windmill and gallows. This town had grown considerably by the time

the Costello Plan, on which the map opposite is based, was drawn up in 1660. The plan shows the Dutch settlement four years before the English took over New Amsterdam, renaming it New York. We can see that the Dutch were already busy building canals, laying out streets on a grid pattern and constructing gable houses with formal Dutch gardens. They might well have gone on to plant elm trees, if they had not lost it all to the English in 1664. The formal baroque gardens now lie buried beneath the skyscrapers on Wall Street and Broadway. Nothing now remains from thirty-eight years of Dutch settlement except for the occasional Dutch place name.

On leaving the courtyard, we go back to Brouwersgracht, and cross the canal not by the iron bridge straight ahead, but over the narrow iron footbridge to the left, known as the Melk-meisjesbrugetje (Milkmaid's Bridge). It was built in 1882 to replace the old wooden bridge on the Florisz. map and takes us down the old side of Herengracht, where the first houses were built in the last decade of the 16th century. The Heren-gracht in those days was just a narrow strip of water running inside the 1585 city wall. The modest gable houses built on the left side had a view of the city wall for almost thirty years; had the Spanish ever laid siege to Amsterdam, the early residents of Herengracht would have been the first to know about it.

The outlook changed after the city expanded westwards in the 1610's. The old town wall was demolished and the Herengracht was widened considerably. The houses on the opposite side were often grander, as we can see from Nos. 12 and 14. The plots were bigger too, so that by contrast with the crowded conditions on the old side of the canal, the new houses were able to have large and elaborate gardens. How much the Dutch enjoyed their gardening we can guess from Florisz.'s bird's eye view of pleached trees and parterres. Later on this walk we will be able to visit one of these gardens.

For now, though, we have to be content with the façades. Some have playful details, such as the fish at the top of No. 21, which is a pun on the original owner's name of Visser (a *vis* being a fish in Dutch). We also find warehouses at this end of the canal, such as the two at Nos. 37 and 39 built in the mid-18th century. A few steps further, we pass two smaller warehouses, Fortune and Noah's Ark, at Nos. 43 and 45. These are the oldest buildings on Herengracht, built in about 1590 when the area was still on the trading outskirts of Amsterdam.

After crossing the Blauwburgwal, we come to De Tijd at No. 105. This modern building, the headquarters of a Dutch magazine publisher, is undistinguished apart from a large iron clock on the wall and a curious stone tablet, which shows a 17th-century paper mill where the workers are busily making paper while a man lies fast asleep in the attic. This stone originally decorated a building on Damrak.

III. The first bend. We come upon another pair of warehouses at Nos. 155 and 157. These date from the 18th century, as we can tell from the gable tops decorated in flamboyant French style. The next bridge takes us over the lovely Leliegracht, after which the buildings on the right side become more stately. We have reached the first bend in the Herengracht. Though not *the* bend, this spot drew the artist Jan van der Heyden, inventor of the fire hose, here on a breezy summer day in the 17th century. When we get to the next bridge, we will be able to stand on the spot where Van der Heyden painted the view opposite (now in the Louvre). A barge is being unloaded onto the quay as three swans glide past. We see five houses, the last two almost hidden by the elm trees. Not much has changed in this corner of the city; though the first house on the left (No. 174) has lost its ornamental step gable, the splendid house next door (Nos. 170 to 172) is still standing, as is its neighbour (No. 168).

The next two houses, hidden behind the trees, have changed considerably since this painting was done. No. 164, which was rebuilt in 1743 in Louis XIV style, is named Messina. A pious 18th-century owner decorated No. 166 with the inscription *Soli Deo Gloria* - glory to God alone. This was not a sentiment shared by the neighbouring Pauwhuis (No. 168), where Michiel Pauw trumpeted his own glory in the pediment, so living up to his name, which in Dutch means

peacock. Two lions of St Mark originally flanked the Pauw family coat of arms to remind everyone that Pauw belonged to the Order of St Mark; Pauw, we remember, also attempted immortality by naming the colony he founded in America after himself, Pavonia. His house, built in 1638, was Philip Vingboons' first commission. It represented a new style of architecture, in which grey Bentheim sandstone replaced red brick, and a classical neck gable was considered more fitting than the jaunty Dutch step gables we see next door (Nos. 170-2).

The coat of arms was still there when Van der Heyden painted the scene, but it has now gone. A widow called Maria Luyken bought the Pauw house in 1730 and made various changes to the decoration. No doubt the owner of *Soli Deo Gloria* would have been pleased with her efforts, for she hacked off Pauw's heraldry and substituted a pair of hands holding a Bible. The two thistles on the roof (the Pauw family symbol) were removed, and replaced by the classical vases we now see. The pediments above the windows also vanished.

The widow attacked the interior with equal zeal. Jan van Logteren was employed to create a lavish stucco staircase, and two rooms were painted by the landscape artists Jacob de Wit and Isaac de Moucheron. As we might have expected, the widow chose Biblical themes to decorate her walls, including the story of Jephthah, the Israelite judge who made a pact with God on the eve of battle, promising to sacrifice the first creature he saw if he was victorious in battle. Of course, the first person he met after winning was his own daughter.

The widow bequeathed her house to the Reformed Church, but it is now occupied by the Nederlands Theater Instituut (Dutch Theatre Institute). Maria Luyken would surely not have approved of her house being used for the display of miniature theatres, circus posters and other frivolities. The building was closed for restoration when I last passed, so it is difficult to know exactly what it will look like when it reopens, though we can be fairly confident that the delightful miniature theatre of Baron van Slingelandt will still be on display. Whatever the changes, it is worth going inside simply to see the purple and gilt wood-panelling, stucco ceilings and neo-classical paintings. There are few enough opportunities to enter a Herengracht house, and this is one of the best.

The house next door (Nos. 170-172) was built by Guillielmo Bartolotti. Bartolotti was not his real name, but plain Willem van den Heuvel. He adopted the more flamboyant Italian name after making his fortune as a brewer and banker. The Bartolottihuis is just as grandiose as its name would suggest. It was built in 1617 by Hendrick de Keyser. The façade, which curves slightly, is a wonderful bustling blend of red brick, white sandstone, stone vases, curled volutes and cartouches. We can still read the two plaques Bartolotti had inscribed with his Latin mottos. 'By ingenuity and hard work,' one says; 'By religion and virtue,' the other. After the house was rebuilt in 1971, a third plaque was inserted at the top of the gable to celebrate the renovation.

If we were trying to follow the Florisz. map, we would be confused by the next stretch of canal. Instead of an elegant arched bridge we discover the busy Raadhuisstraat, built in 1895 to link Dam with the western suburbs. A row of historic houses was demolished to allow the road to be built. George Breitner made a painting of the scene in the winter of 1895 (reproduced on page 202). A workman is breaking the frozen earth with a pick, while two figures struggle through the sludge. A row of houses on the east side of Keizersgracht was also demolished, allowing Breitner to paint the houses on the west side (Nos. 200 to 212). Some of the interiors were saved; they could be seen in the Stedelijk Museum at the beginning of this century, but they vanished after the last war.

We are looking here at the first significant breach in the canal ring since it was laid out in the 17th century. The buildings on either side of Raadhuisstraat were constructed soon after Breitner painted the scene. Before we cross the road, we can admire an early work by Berlage at Herengracht 184, hewn from rugged red sandstone in 1897. Across the street, we find a curious shopping arcade built on the spot where the workman with the pick stood in Breitner's painting. The arcade was designed by a prolific architect, A. L. van Gendt, and his two sons in a strange neo-gothic style, featuring carved beasts such as leopards, crocodiles and griffins.

We cross back to the side with the odd numbers, for this allows us to look across at an usual pair of houses at Nos. 218 and 220 known as 'the father and son'. The two houses, one slightly taller than the other, were built in about 1620 in Dutch renaissance style. Further down the canal, we see a splendid pair of baroque crests on Nos. 250 and 252. The latter house, which dates from about 1730, has a carved stone under the balustrade giving its name as Meelbal, the flour bag. Further along this stretch, De Witte Leli goes one step further, sporting a vase of white lilies with the name carved on the stone underneath to look like billowing blue cloth. The house next to the White Lily was once the home of Alexander Voûte, the 19th-century coffee dealer said to be the model for Max Havelaar in Multatuli's novel.

We now come to the splendid baroque Van Brienen House at No. 284, an 18th-century sandstone house with enormous sash windows. The building is now occupied by the Hendrick de Keyser Foundation, an organisation established in 1918 to protect historical Dutch houses. It now owns about seventy houses in Amsterdam, including this magnificent building. The foundation unfortunately failed to save the seven houses that once stood directly opposite their own office, which were torn down in 1920 and replaced by the ugly office block outside which we are now standing (Nos. 293-305).

Let us move smartly on and now look briefly at No. 319. If we are doing this walk in the afternoon, we should find the gate of this traditional gin tasting house open. De Admiraal occupies a quaint neo-gothic building with a turret and a stone tablet giving the completion date of 1899. We might come back later to sample one of the gins poured here, which come from the Ooievaar distillery in the Jordaan. We can sip an oude jenever sitting in a bench fashioned from an old gin keg, or, if we have a wedding to celebrate, a romantic Bruidstranen ('bride's tears') in one of the candlelit alcoves hung with tapestries. De Admiraal is open from noon on weekdays and from 5 pm on Saturdays, but is closed on Sundays.

We now continue south to look at the row of three houses on the opposite side, No. 338 to No. 342. The first of these was built in 1730 and is called Het Roode Kruis from the red cross that once decorated the coat of arms at the top. The third house is a splendid baroque building constructed about ten years earlier, but the house in the middle (actually called 't Roode Kruis), though it looks quite in keeping with the others, was in fact built in 1874 by an architect who obviously wanted to preserve the architectural harmony of the canals.

In fact the canals became a hodge-podge of styles quite early on. On Florisz.'s map of this section all the houses have step gables, and in fact we can see the last step gable house on Herengracht a little further along, on our side of the canal at No. 361. By the 1650's, when this house was built, the more fashionable Herengracht residents had adopted the Vingboons style. No. 361 is called Huis Sonneberg, the House of the Sun Mountain. We see a tiny brass plaque near

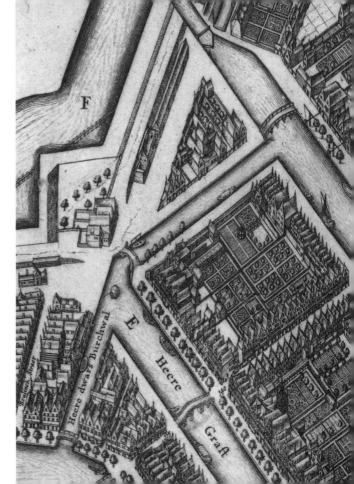

the door with three Amsterdam crosses, which identifies the house as one that has been restored by Stadsherstel, an organisation founded in the 1950's to renovate historic Amsterdam buildings.

IV. The second bend. We are now approaching another bend. Though still not *the* bend, this is a most attractive spot all the same. Someone in the city administration must agree, for there are rows of benches here - a rare treat in Amsterdam. If we are fortunate, we will find an unoccupied bench right on the bend where we can sit down to admire the view.

The two identical neck gables to the left of the bridge opposite are known as 'the twin sisters' (Nos. 396 and 398), not to be confused with the two more modest houses behind our bench which are called 'the twin brothers' (Nos. 409 and 411). Another set of twins stand to the right of the bridge (Nos. 390 and 392). If we can see through the foliage, we should be able to spot a man and woman at the top of each gable holding a length of rope between them.

When Florisz. drew his 1625 map, the canal in front of us did not exist. Nor did the houses to the left of the bridge. The Herengracht came to an abrupt end directly opposite our bench. The painting opposite by Jan Wijnants (in The Cleveland Museum of Art) shows the stretch of the gracht opposite us as it must have looked around 1660 from a spot just north of the old ramparts, which we saw on the detail from the Florisz. map. The painting shows two arched bridges (at Huidenstraat and Wolvenstraat) and an empty site with timber stacked against the fence. A merchant called Hendrick Cromhout had bought two separate plots of ground on either side of the timber yard in 1614, and wanted to buy the ground in between, but the yard belonged to a stubborn wood merchant called Cornelis Jansz. Kerfbijl who refused to sell. We can just make out the empty plot on the Florisz. map, above the H of Heere Graft, and with a timber-laden barge alongside. Cromhout died before he had built anything, but his son Jacob commissioned Vingboons to build three houses - two large houses to the right of the timber yard (Nos. 364 and 366) and a smaller house to the left (No. 370). Kerfbijl

did finally sell his timber yard to the Cromhout son in 1660 - soon after this painting was done - and Vingboons added another small house (No. 368) to complete the row. The two large and two small houses are affectionately known as the father, mother and twins.

Vingboons was at the height of his popularity at the time - we can count no less than six of his houses from where we are sitting - but the Cromhout Houses were his greatest achievement. Almost a quarter of a century had passed since he had designed the Pauw House at Herengracht 168, and his neck-gable style has become increasingly refined. The façades are decorated with swags of fruit, stone carved like drapery and bulls' eye windows.

Jacob Cromhout himself lived in the large house to the right of the timber yard (No. 366). A carved stone above the door shows a piece of bent wood, alluding to the literal meaning of Cromhout. The house was owned in the 18th century by Elizabeth Cromhout, who in 1717 employed Jacob de Wit (whose work we saw inside Herengracht 168) to decorate the ceiling in the main room with classical scenes. We can visit the house, now occupied by the Bible Museum, by going back to the bridge and crossing the canal. The De Wit ceiling is in a room at the back.

When we leave the museum, we turn right past No. 368, where the wood was stacked in the painting. We soon come to the flamboyant mansion at Nos. 380-2, built in 1889 for Jacob Nienhuijs, whose money came from tobacco plantations. He commissioned A. Salm to construct a replica of the William K. Vanderbilt Mansion on New York's Fifth Avenue, which was itself modelled on a Loire castle. The Vanderbilt mansion has gone, but New Yorkers have this house as a reminder of what they have lost.

We are back with Vingboons for the Huis van Gerards at No. 386, though it does not look at all like his style. A mere three years after the Cromhout houses, Vingboons seems here to have abandoned the neck gable style in favour of a classical mansion decorated with pilasters and a pediment. This house was built for Carel Gerards, whose daughter Cornelia married the wool merchant Nicolaas van Bambeeck (pictured with his first wife Agatha Bas on pages 124 and 125). In fact Vingboons had built a similar mansion for Van Bambeeck fifteen years earlier at Kloveniersburgwal 77, so this extra grandeur seems to have been his standard solution to the double-width house.

The neck gable next door (No. 388) may look like a regular Vingboons, but it is not. It was built in the Vingboons style for Johannes Elison, the son of a Norwich preacher. Rembrandt painted a pair of portraits of the elderly preacher and his wife Maria Bockenolle in 1634. The portraits once hung in this house, but are now in the Boston Museum of Fine Arts.

We now cross the Leidsegracht, pausing to admire the twin houses at Nos. 396-8, built soon after this stretch of canal was dug in 1665. If we stand near the water and look back the way we have just come, we will see some of the houses painted in the bright and breezy view of 1783 by Isaak Ouwater overleaf. The twin neck gables on the left are still standing. So, too, is the house on the opposite corner, and the twins to the right.

We can also spot the Cromhout Houses in the distance, now four in number. The other buildings are not so easily recognised; the white house with a large barrel outside was sacrificed, along with its neighbour on the left (and their fantastic Y-shaped chimneys), to build the mock Vanderbilt Mansion we saw earlier.

We find one more Vingboons house at No. 412, but again we are unlikely to recognise the master's hand. It is another double house (these were becoming more common in the 1660's), built for a French Catholic merchant called Guillaume Belim la Garde. Two doors down, we see a house that looks more like an early Vingboons, though it is not. Once again, the pious sentiment *Soli Deo Gloria* crops up on the gable.

An entirely different style of building appears once we are on the far side of the Leidsestraat. The houses are no longer built of red brick, but of grey sandstone. The change of building materials reflect a change in the Dutch temperament in the 1660's, from the blustery optimism of the new Dutch Republic to the cynical grey face of the mature state. In this stretch of Herengracht,

we will miss the step gables, the warehouses, the little shops, the endless quirky details, but most of all we will miss the cafés. The hiss of an espresso machine is a sound rarely heard on this part of Herengracht, so we may consider turning right down Leidsestraat to visit one of the cafés on Keizersgracht such as Metz at No. 455 or Walem at No. 449.

V. The Golden Bend. Fortified and back on Herengracht, we should walk down the side with odd numbered houses to appreciate the best houses on the Golden Bend. The house we see opposite at No. 436 looked considerably better when it was originally built in 1672. In 1895, the double flight of steps was removed, leaving the front door up in the air. If it had not been so badly mistreated, it would now look rather like the De Graeff House at No. 446, built in the same year for Andries de Graeff, who served three times as burgomaster. De Graeff's brother Cornelis lived at Herengracht 216 and his sister was a short stroll away at Nos. 254-256. Andries built this sober baroque house in 1672,

the 'disaster year' when the Dutch Republic was attacked on all sides by English, French and German armies. De Graeff had his own disaster year in 1674, when he had to flee the city to escape the tax authorities.

Notice how flat the rooflines have become, compared with the old part of Herengracht. Even Vingboons was forced to conform to the stark horizontal style when he designed the Deutz House at Herengracht 450 in 1670-72, omitting the pilasters, swags and pediments that made the Cromhout Houses so attractive; but he made up for it with very delicate rustication. This house was built for Joseph Deutz, who made his money importing Swedish tar for the Amsterdam shipyards. It is now owned by a bank, whose employees, when they look up from their computer screens, can look across the water at one of the handsomest houses on the whole Herengracht.

This exquisite house (at No. 475) was designed by Daniel Marot, a French architect who worked mainly in The Hague, where he designed elegant town houses in Louis XIV style. The house we see here was built in about 1730 when the sober style of the 1670's had become a thing of the past. Look at the flamboyant entrance, and the figures on the balustrade. There is even a globe on the roof, though we may not see it unless we step back, carefully, to the edge of the quay.

We have a good impression of the 18th-century interior of this house from the painting opposite by Adriaan de Lelie, now in the Rijksmuseum. It shows the merchant Jan Gildemeester's private art gallery on a Sunday afternoon in 1794 or 1795. The sunlight is filtering through the front window as Gildemeester shows his friends around his collection of 17th-century Dutch paintings. The dark green walls were covered with Dutch masters, including, in the corner above the man in the red coat, Rembrandt's *Portrait of a Preacher* of 1637 (now in the Duke of Sutherland's collection in Scotland). The officer in Revolutionary uniform we see standing in the doorway suggest that De Lelie painted this scene soon after the French invasion of 1795. The art lovers are unconcerned, brandishing a fine array of eyepieces, kneeling on the floor, leaning on chairs and even running up ladders to get a closer view of the paintings.

An essay by De Bruyn Kops of the Rijksmuseum has identified most of the characters in the painting. De Lelie himself is the one kneeling to the right; and behind him, talking to the man in uniform, is none other than our old friend Pierre Fouquet, who had supplied many of the paintings in the room.

Now at last we come to the Golden Bend, where rich families built splendid town houses in the 1670's. And is this *the* bend? we may ask, for it is a rather disappointing spot. The city fathers have not even considered it worth putting up a bench. Many of the houses were built here in the 1670's, which was, as we have seen, a sober period in Dutch architecture. The soberest architect of them all was Adriaan Dortsman, who built the Greek classical house opposite us in about 1670 (No. 462). The statues above the entrance represent Faith and Love. Two others on the balustrade depict Welfare and Trade. None of those virtues mattered as much as peace, which was soon to be shattered two years later

in the disaster year.

The house on the corner of Nieuwe Spiegel-straat (No. 466) looks as if it has hardly changed since the 17th century. Yet this building was entirely demolished in 1894; a few architectural relics were put into storage and later incorporated into the new building. The pediment decorated with an eagle is a 17th-century relic; the baroque gable on the corner dates from the 18th century.

If we walk on now to the Vijzelstraat, we can stand on the spot in the middle of the bridge where Gerrit Berckheyde painted the very sober picture opposite (in the Rijksmuseum). Berck-heyde was a Haarlem artist who specialised in views of Dutch cities. He painted the Grote Markt in Haarlem several times (there is a version in the National Gallery in London), as well as various views of the Golden Bend in Amsterdam in the 1670's and 1680's. This particular version was painted in 1685, before the elm trees had been planted or Van der Heyden's street lamps had been installed. We will recognise some of the buildings such as the sombre Dortsman house, with the two statues on the balustrade marking it out from its neighbours (on the left side, just beyond the patch of sunlight), and the house on the corner of Nieuwe Spiegelstraat, before it was knocked down and then rebuilt.

We should also recognise the splendid house on the left with a carriage parked outside (No. 476). This building, which dates from the 1670's, is still standing, though it has been altered. The pediment has gone - it was removed in the 1740's when the house was owned by the cloth merchant David de Neufville. An admirer of Marot, De Neufville had already paid the French architect to redecorate his country house in Louis XIV style. He then asked Marot to modify this house by removing the pediment and installing a flamboyant balustrade decorated with the family coat of arms and surmounted by an eagle and vases. A later owner removed the double staircase, but the admirable Hendrick de Keyser Foundation, which now owns the building, has put everything back to Marot's design.

The ten-floor ABN Bank building which we see to the left of the bridge (at Herengracht 482) was built in 1926 by Karel de Bazel. This was

another project that required, like Raadhuis-straat, the demolition of eight historic houses. The building stands on a rugged granite base, with statues representing Europe and Asia next to the main entrance on Vijzelstraat.

If we stay on the middle of the bridge, but cross to the other side, we can see the sombre former residence of the mayor of Amsterdam at No. 500. A handsome building opposite is named De Vergulde Turkse Keyser (The Gilded Emperor of Turkey), at No. 527. The house was built in about 1668 in the sober neo-classical style of Vingboons, but the name is something of a mystery. The pediment is decorated with a figure, but it is an eagle, not an emperor, gilded or otherwise. Nor does the house appear ever to have been the home of a Turkish emperor, though it has seen some distinguished guests, including Tsar Peter the Great, who stayed here in 1717 as the guest of the Russian merchant Dimitri Solowjow. Almost a century later, the building was acquired by King Louis Napoléon, but he was such an epitome of bourgeois life that he could hardly be the gilded emperor.

We now walk down the side with even numbers. The Tsar may have been amused by the row of four houses almost opposite his residence (Nos. 504-10). Dating from the late 17th century, the houses have curious carved figures in the neck piece. The first has climbing dogs, though what it is on top of No. 506 is unclear. The next house features splendid Tritons blowing horns and the last (No. 510) has sea gods riding on the backs of dolphins.

Further down we can look across to the beautiful mansion at No. 539, recently restored by a bank. The architect charged with restoration studied an 18th-century Grachtenboek (Canal Book) in which the house was illustrated, to return the building to its original state. The statues supporting the balcony are a delightful touch, though they failed to capture Albert Camus's attention in 1954 when he walked along this canal looking for inspiration. His eye fell instead upon the 17th-century building opposite (No. 514), which has two Moors' heads, a man and a woman, above the door. Camus remembered the house when he wrote his novel *The Fall* some years later. 'Charming house, isn't it?' the narrator says. 'The two heads you see up there are the heads of Negro slaves. It was a shop sign. The house belonged to a slave trader. Oh, they weren't squeamish in those days.' Perhaps not, but Camus got it wrong: the house never belonged to a slave trader.

The other side now opens up into Thorbeckeplein, a little square where we find a statue of the Dutch prime minister Johan Thorbecke. Unveiled in 1872, it shows the statesman standing up to address parliament, with his hand resting on a pile of documents. Thorbecke is not an obvious politician to honour in Amsterdam, as it was his government that pressed ahead with the construction of Centraal Station, despite strong opposition from the city council. Perhaps he is admired for his role in drafting the 1848 constitution, which created the tolerant climate Amsterdammers now enjoy. Thorbecke is facing away from a cluster of sex clubs which are, I suppose, the consequence of his liberalism.

We cross over, but continue down the canal, now on the odd numbered side, where we soon come to a row of four houses (Nos. 571 to 581) where a rare meeting of minds occurred in 1664. Four owners of adjoining plots agreed to build houses 'of the same height and under one cornice,' though the contract went on to say that 'each of the owners shall be free to decorate the house with such ornament as shall please him.' A rich biscuit manufacturer called Pieter van Schoorel took full advantage of the exemption clause to decorate his house (No. 579) with a statue of the Archangel Michael, with a fine head of gilded locks, slaying a dragon. The elephant's head we see below was the biscuit manufacturer's trade mark. Unlike the two Moors' heads Camus noted, this really was a shop sign.

We now cross the lively Utrechtsestraat, a bustling street with clanking yellow trams, flower shops that spill out onto the street, and an excellent cooks' equipment shop. More to the point, it has several good restaurants such as the convivial Sluizer at Nos. 41-45. The menu ranges from plain, substantial Dutch food to grilled fish, Belgian fish stews (*waterzooi*) and crab casseroles.

That is for later. We still have a short stretch of Herengracht to walk down, keeping to the side with the odd numbers. We do not often get to see inside the houses on this stretch of Herengracht (most are banks or offices), but the Willet-Holthuysen Museum (No. 605) is open to us. Built in 1687, and fresh from a recent restoration, this house is a handsome example of Louis XIV style, complete with a double staircase. Not that we get to use the staircase - we humble folk have to enter by the tradesmen's entrance below the steps, though we should not complain too loudly, for it gives us a chance to glance inside the 18th-century Dutch kitchen with its polished copper pots and gleaming Delft tiles painted with caged parrots.

The last occupants of the house were Abraham Willet and Sandrina Louise Holthuysen. The wife bequeathed the house to the city when she died in 1895, but insisted on it being kept as a museum. Some councillors wanted nothing to do with the house (they were already struggling to cope with the awkward terms of Sophia-Augusta's bequest, which eventually became the Stedelijk

Museum), but they finally, grudgingly, accepted the gift. The museum opened in 1896, and Baedeker considered the porcelain and glass collection good enough to merit a star in his guide. Even so, few people ever came here, leaving the first curator with ample time on his hands to write a scandalous novel about the couple's unhappy love life, and the widow's lonely last years as she died of cancer in this house full of cats.

The museum now gets a few more visitors, but we might still find ourselves wandering alone across the creaking floors, listening to the timid chimes of a clock. The most impressive interior is the Blue Room at the front, where the walls are covered with vivid blue Utrecht velvet. The painted ceiling depicting *Dawn chasing away Night* is by Jacob de Wit, though he did not paint it for this house. He did it for a house at Herengracht 250, next door to one we saw called The Flour Bag.

The garden at the back is the only one we can visit along Herengracht. It has been replanted in 18th-century style with low box hedges and gravel - just the sort of style that irritated David Hume on his visit to the Netherlands in 1748. He considered such gardens to be 'scrawled and flourished in patterns like the embroidery of an old maid's work bag.'

One of the oldest houses on this stretch stands further along this side at No. 619. This classical building has little decoration apart from a puzzling gilded motto above the door that reads: SALUS HUIC DOMUI. The motto means 'Health to this House', but it is also a chronogram that reveals the date of the building (1666) to anyone with a head for adding up Roman numerals.

The architect was Adriaan Dortsman, and the commissioner Jan Six. Six came from a family of wealthy French Huguenot refugees who owned dye works and silk mills. He became burgomaster of Amsterdam and married Margaretha Tulp, the daughter of Dr Tulp, in 1656. Six befriended Rembrandt and commissioned him to paint his portrait some twelve years before this house was built. He even lent Rembrandt money when the artist's lavish lifestyle began to catch up with him, but then appears to have let his friend down rather badly by selling Rembrandt's promissory note to someone else, who then demanded payment. By the time Six and his wife moved into this house, the friendship was over and Rembrandt had been forced to decamp to a modest house on Rozengracht. The portrait of Six was hanging in this house when Baedeker wrote his 1905 guidebook. It is now in a private collection near here. Guidebook writers are not allowed to reveal the whereabouts, but perhaps the tourist office can help those who would like to see this extraordinary painting.

We are now nearing the end of our walk. Herengracht ends with an elegant arched bridge over the river Amstel. The long building we see on the opposite side of the river is the Amstelhof, which was built in the 1680's as a home for elderly women and still serves the same purpose today. Turning right along the Amstel, we find another Dortsman house at Amstel 216, dated 1671 in solid Roman numerals. If we look up at the top, we might just be able to make out the coats of arms of Van Beuningen and Jacoba Bartolotti van den Heuvel. Van Beuningen was

195

a successful burgomaster and ambassador, who moved into this house in 1686 with his young bride. He was a grey-haired old man of sixty-four-while his wife was a spirited forty-six-year-old. Not surprisingly, the marriage ended in disaster. Van Beuningen lost his property and went mad.

A local legend has it that he painted mystical Hebrew symbols on the front of the house with his own blood. We can clearly read his name on a stone to the left of the door. Perhaps the story is true after all.

WALK 7

Keizersgracht

BROUWERSGRACHT *to* THE MUSEUM VAN LOON

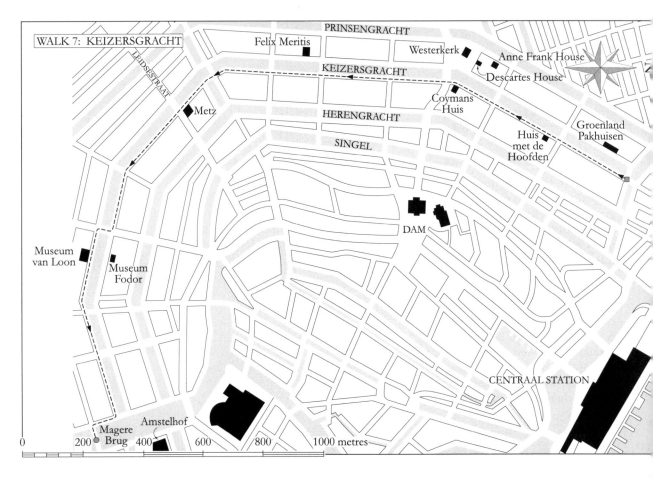

WALK 7: KEIZERSGRACHT

PRINSENGRACHT

Felix Meritis

Westerkerk

Anne Frank House

Descartes House

KEIZERSGRACHT

Metz

HERENGRACHT

Coymans Huis

SINGEL

Huis met de Hoofden

Groenland Pakhuisen

DAM

Museum van Loon

Museum Fodor

CENTRAAL STATION

LEIDSESTRAAT

Magere Brug

Amstelhof

0   200   400   600   800   1000 metres

Keizersgracht

BROUWERSGRACHT *to* THE MUSEUM VAN LOON

This walk takes us down Keizersgracht, the second of the great canals. The early stretch is as grand as Herengracht, but it becomes less interesting after we have crossed Leidsestraat, as many Herengracht owners built coach houses on this stretch of Keizersgracht. The best day to do this walk is on a Monday, when we can visit the café on the sixth floor of the Metz department store, the Museum van Loon and perhaps even catch the plant market on the Amstelveld. Timing is important. If we set off at about 10 am, we should get to Metz for coffee soon after 11 am, before it gets too busy. Resuming the walk at 11.30 am, we should reach the end of Keizersgracht, where it joins the Amstel, in good time for lunch.

I. The old end. We begin the walk at the old end of Keizersgracht, where it joins Bouwersgracht, keeping to the side with the odd numbers. This is the stretch of canal John Evelyn strolled down in 1641, noting in his diary: 'nothing more surpriz'd me than that stately, and indeede incomparable quarter of the Towne, calld the Keisers-Graft, or Emperors Streete, which appeares to be a Citty in a Wood, through the goodly ranges of the stately and umbragious Lime-trees, exactly planted before each-mans doore.'

Evelyn would presumably have passed a row of five brick warehouses on the opposite side of the canal, three of which are still standing at Nos. 40-44. The Groenland Pakhuizen were built in 1621 by the Greenland Company for storing whale oil. Further down the canal, the house at No. 64, built in Louis XIV style in 1738, owes its current splendour to restoration by the Stadsherstel organisation in 1973. The flamboyant top with two reclining children had to be rebuilt from scratch, using an 18th-century drawing.

We then cross Herenstraat, an attractive shopping street which we might explore briefly, looking at the shop selling tin toys and Chinese lanterns at No. 38, noting a useful cobbler at No. 33, and admiring the artistic arrangements of potted plants at No. 2.

Back on the Keizersgracht, the splendid House with the Heads, on our side at No. 123, was built in 1622 for the merchant Nicolaas Sohier. It was designed by Hendrick de Keyser just before he died in 1621; he was working at the same time on the nearby Bartolotti house on Herengracht, and the style is similar, though the six heads on the ground floor add a bizarre touch. According to an amusing, but unlikely local legend, the heads represent six burglars beheaded by a maid who caught them breaking into the house. In fact they are Greek deities: Apollo, on the far left,

wearing a laurel wreath; Ceres, next to him, with ripe ears of corn in her hair; Mars, wearing a helmet; Pallas Athene, also helmeted; a tipsy Bacchus with bunches of grapes, and Diana, identified by a half moon in her hair.

When Evelyn passed this way, the House of the Heads was owned by Louis de Geer, who had bought the building in 1634. De Geer was the son of a Protestant iron merchant from Liège forced to flee to Holland to escape the Spanish terror. The son settled in Amsterdam, where he carried on his father's trade, and married one of the daughters of Jacob Trip. Louis de Geer developed close ties with Gustavus Augustus of Sweden, arranging loans for the king and even lending ships to Sweden during the war against Denmark.

High on the front of the house, the stone tablet in Czech recalls John Amos Comenius, the exiled Moravian educationalist. He moved here as a guest of Laurens de Geer in 1656, soon after writing the world's first picture book for children. Comenius lived here until his death in 1670, and was buried in a chapel in Naarden, east of Amsterdam. The House with the Heads is now

200

occupied by the city department for the protection of historic monuments.

Just before we cross the Leliegracht, we pass a house at No. 149 with a statue of the King of Sweden on the wall. A splendid office stands on the other side, just beyond the bridge, at Nos. 174-176. It was built in 1905 by Gerrit van Arkel for a Dutch life insurance company whose initials EHLB still decorate the top, even though the building is now occupied by Greenpeace. The large tile picture at the top of the tower shows the guardian angel of life insurance protecting a mother and child, which might just as well serve as an advertisement for the present tenants.

II. The first bend. A short stroll further brings us to the first bend in the Keizersgracht. The classical Coymans House, on the bend at No. 177, was designed by Jacob van Campen in 1625 for the rich Antwerp merchants Balthasar and Joan Coymans. The house was completed just in time to appear on the Florisz. map - the long roof can be seen facing the Kerckhof in the detail here. The house was built just one year after the House

with the Heads, but the style is quite different; Van Campen has dispensed with pinnacles, vases, heads, masks, gables and other mannerist fancies, introducing Amsterdam to the more measured Italian classical style.

We now cross Raadhuisstraat and continue down the side with the odd numbers. The row of houses opposite appear in this painting by George Breitner of *The widening of the Raadhuisstraat in winter*. It must have been chilly painting, so it has been assumed that Breitner photographed the scene and returned to his studio to work on the canvas - a working habit that paradoxically helped give his paintings their sense of immediacy. The row of houses we see in the painting run from Westermarkt 1 (the corner building on the right) to Keizersgracht 212. The arched cornice of No. 212 is still there, as is the neck gable of No. 210 and the bell gable on No. 208. The corner house at Westermarkt 1 still has an old sign advertising the EHLB insurance company we passed earlier.

The house at No. 210, partly hidden by a tree in Breitner's painting, was bought in 1619 by Dr Tulp, the surgeon in Rembrandt's *Anatomy Lesson of Dr Tulp* (now in the Mauritshuis in The Hague). Dr Tulp was a strict Calvinist, who opposed all forms of idle amusement. On being appointed burgomaster of Amsterdam in 1654, he introduced a regulation to limit the amount that could be spent on a wedding feast, as well as the time at which the guests had to leave. His daughter Margaretha had the bad luck to marry Jan Six that same year.

Perhaps Dr Tulp mellowed in old age; he certainly did not protest at the lavish feast laid on in 1672 to celebrate his 50th year on the city council. The guests sat down to a twelve course meal, drank enormous quantities of wine and praised the elderly surgeon, who was then 79, in a series of Latin poems. Everyone finally rolled home at the unholy hour of eleven in the evening.

The house next door (No. 208) was bought by Dr Tulp for his son-in-law Arnout Tholincx, who had his portrait painted by Rembrandt in 1656 - two years before the artist was declared bankrupt and forced to move to a modest house not far from here. A few doors down, No. 216 was the

home of a 17th-century preacher who did not have to look far to find a wife. He married the daughter of Balthasar Coymans, who lived hardly a dozen houses down the canal. The wedding took place some years after Dr Tulp's regulation, so we can assume that the guests were safely in bed at an early hour.

A handsome house on our side, at No. 209, has an 18th-century figure of Hope perched on the balustrade. Hope is represented by a woman holding an anchor amid a stormy sea, though we risk falling into the canal if we try to admire her from this side of the canal. This house was once owned by Gerrit Reynst, a wealthy merchant who moved here in 1634. He owned a remarkable collection of curiosities which he had bought from Andrea Vendramin of Venice, including paintings, fossils, coins and Egyptian relics. Visiting the house in 1662, Melchior Fokkens was full of praise: 'A house with an interior worthy of a royal palace, displaying all the decorative variety of India and Ancient Rome. All these rarities are worth at least three tons of gold, if not more.'

The house next door to Hope (No. 211) was

called Charity, but sadly I cannot find any evidence showing that No. 213 was ever called Faith. A few doors down, at No. 215, a more prosaic owner identified his modest home with a relief showing a small white cabbage. Another interesting stone tablet showing a copper mill is at No. 225. This detail was added in the 18th century by Rudolphus Knuijse, who owned a copper mill in the countryside, and put his initials (RK) and those of his wife (EW) above the door.

Just after crossing Hartenstraat (another good shopping street), we will see a splendid pair of identical twins, Nos. 244 and 246, built in 1730 and crowned with a lavish baroque confection. Yet amid the swirling stonework, allowance always had to be made for attic doors and hoist beams.

We turn right across the next bridge, and head down Berenstraat, straight ahead, to look at the building named Amsterdams Welvaren at No. 7. The front is decorated with a sailing ship and the initials J. W. They stand for John Warder, a British Quaker who refused to accept the insurance money due to him after the sinking of a Dutch ship called *Amsterdams Welvaren* in the Fourth Anglo-Dutch war. His descendants had no scruples about claiming the money, and using some of it to build this mock gothic nursery school in 1864.

Back on Keizersgracht, we now turn right down the side with the even numbers, past a house called Inde Stat van Bordee at No. 320, with a 17th-century carved stone showing a detailed view of Bordeaux. Further along, the handsome neoclassical building at No. 324 has the words *Felix Meritis* (happy through merit) at the top. This building was constructed in 1788 by a scientific society whose motto this was. The members were strict Calvinists who sought this happiness through the pursuit of literature, physics, music, drawing and, of course, trade. The five panels on the front of the building illustrate the disciplines, while a beehive in the pediment symbolises the busy diligence of the members. Distinguished visitors such as Tsar Alexander and Napoleon were invited here by the members. They would have been shown the museum and perhaps led onto the rooftop observatory to gaze at the stars.

In the 19th-century, famous musicians such as Brahms and Grieg performed in the concert hall, where the members also conducted gravity experiments using a hole in the ceiling. All in all, this society was a model of enlightened beliefs, though its view of women remained somewhat old-fashioned. At the opening of the building, a local professor declared that women ought not to concern themselves with science; they should be more interested in the smiles of their babies or the merry bustle of children running around the house. Happiness through motherhood, one might say. The society finally wound up its affairs in 1889, and the building went through various owners until the Dutch Communist party took it over in 1946. The building became famous in the 1960's for radical plays staged by Ramses Shaffy. It is still the base for various experimental theatre and dance companies.

Just beyond here, we should pause to look across the canal at the Sohierhuis at No. 319, a white neck gable house with cheery red shutters built by Philips Vingboons in 1639. Walking on, we pass a curious classical gateway at No. 384, which is all that remains of the old municipal theatre. Built by Jacob van Campen in the style of Palladio's Teatro Olimpico in Vincenza, the theatre was destroyed in a fire in 1779. The Theatre Museum at Herengracht 186 has a model showing the building before it burnt down.

On reaching Runstraat (whose delightful shops are described on page 235), we cross over the bridge and continue down the side with the odd numbers. The splendid 17th-century gateway we see at Nos. 365-7 was originally the entrance of the Oudezijds Herenlogement on Grimburg-wal, built by Philips Vingboons in 1647 as a residence for distinguished guests. We can see this gate in its original location on the print on page 89, just to the right of the bridge; it was moved here after the Herenlogement was demolished in the 19th century.

Continuing down this side, we pass a handsome neck gable house at No. 387 built in 1667, perhaps by Justus Vingboons, brother of Philips. The gate to the left of the house still has the gilded star that gives the house its name, De Vergulde Ster. We then come upon another

French city depicted on a carved stone, at No. 401. This house, named Marseille, shows the French port of Marseilles in astonishing detail. If we look closely, we can see the Vieux Port and the Fort St Jean at the southern tip of the town.

The magnificent baroque house opposite us, at No. 446, was built in about 1720 by a banker. The façade is encrusted with motifs borrowed from the Louis XIV style, including cherubs, shells, hunting horns and vases. In the 19th century, it was owned by another banker, Adriaan van der Hoop, who filled the mansion with a remarkable collection of Dutch paintings, including Rembrandt's *Jewish Bride*.

III. Leidsegracht. If we walk on, we come to one of the most alluring corners of Amsterdam, where Keizersgracht joins Leidsegracht. This is as far as Evelyn would have walked, as the city wall lay beyond here until the second phase of the Plan of the Three Canals was begun. The city stonemason's yard, where Quellien carved the sculpture that decorates the town hall, ran along the inside of Leidsegracht. An interesting carved stone identifies a house on the opposite side of Leidsegracht, at No. 23, as De Maenne Schijn - Moonshine.

Now for coffee. We face a difficult choice here, for there are three good cafés in the neighbourhood. The first to consider is Land van Walem at Keizersgracht 449, one of the first cafés in Amsterdam to abandon brown decor. Walem looks like a De Stijl interior of the 1930's, and the large front window is, in fact, a genuine De Stijl relic, designed by Gerrit Rietveld in 1933. The furniture is now rather dented, and most of the fashionable set have migrated elsewhere, yet Walem remains a friendly café offering excellent crusty *broodjes*, frothy cappuccinos and delicious chocolate cake. There is even a small garden at the back where we can sit on summer days.

If Walem is too busy, we might try Morlang next door, at No. 451. This café, which occupies the ground floor and basement of an 18th-century canal house, tends to be a bit less crowded, particularly in the basement. The interior is vaguely baroque, with a painted canvas hung from the ceiling and big mirrors everywhere.

The final café to consider is found on the sixth floor of Metz & Co, a department store at Keizersgracht 455. This splendid corner building laden with massive caryatids was designed in 1891 by Jan van Looy. A century ago, we would have found the offices of the New York Insurance Company located here, but the clerks moved out in 1908, and the building was taken over by Metz, leaving just the letters NY carved on the stonework as evidence of its former occupants. Metz was founded in 1740 by a draper from the northern French city of Metz. The company won exclusive rights to distribute Liberty fabrics in the Netherlands in 1902, and in the 1930's promoted modern European designer furniture such as Rietveld's zig-zag chairs and Sonia Delaunay's carpets. We can now shop here for Liberty prints, handbags, kitchen utensils or even a reproduction Rietveld.

This was once the tallest building in Amsterdam, bringing a hint of the early American skyscraper style to the old canals. It is still the tallest building in this district, and the view from the café is worth the climb. A few years ago, we would have found ourselves in a bare postmodern café designed by Cees Dam, but that style suddenly went out of fashion as Amsterdammers began to look for something more like an English club. Not daring to seem old-fashioned, Metz ripped out the post-modern furnishings and turned the café into a Dutch approximation of an English country house. We thus now sip our coffee amid wood-panelled walls, still-life paintings and lamps with fake leopard-skin shades. We can even enjoy a full English afternoon tea at Metz, at least until that, too, becomes unfashionable.

The views are fascinating. Looking in one direction, we can see the familiar spires of the Zuiderkerk and the Montelbaanstoren, while in the other direction the Rijksmuseum and American Hotel are visible. We also discover unexpected details such as secret roof terraces and odd bits of back garden we never knew existed. Before we leave Metz, there is one floor left to explore. A spiral staircase leads from the café into a circular glass penthouse, added to the building in 1933 by Gerrit Rietveld. The architect intended it to be an experiment in architectural innovation; even now, more than 60 years later, it is a sensational structure that almost floats above the city.

After we leave the shop, we should cross the bridge at Leidsestraat, pausing to admire the wrought iron railings photographed here, designed by P. L. Kramer in the Amsterdam School Style. We should also take note of the quaint corner house at No. 508, built in 1881 in a florid French renaissance style. The house was completed exactly 300 years after the birth of the Dutch poet Pieter Hooft, inspiring the owner to add the poet's bust above the door. Hooft lived in Muiden Castle on the River Vecht, where he invited the distinguished Dutch writers and intellectuals of his day - the jurist Hugo Grotius, Joost van den Vondel, the poet of endless odes, and Maria Tesselschade, whose grave we failed to find in the Oude Kerk.

This is perhaps a good moment to buy some postcards. If we walk down the even side of Keizersgracht, we will find the best postcard shop in town at No. 510. Art Unlimited has a card

for every occasion, neatly arranged in rows of boxes classified by artist or category, so that we can hunt out Van Gogh and Van der Heyden, or sift through headings such as 'Cemeteries,' 'Belgium,' 'Giraffes' and 'Fat People'. A few years ago, ballet dancer's legs were in fashion. Then came eccentric Italian cooking utensils, Amsterdam bicycles, teddy bears, and now Dutch colonial scenes. Whatever next? Thin Belgians, perhaps?

The next stretch of Keizersgracht is slightly disappointing, especially the side with the odd numbers, for this is the section parallel to the Golden Bend on the Herengracht which was bought up to build coach houses for the grander addresses. The building at No. 481 was originally a coach house, as was No. 485. Other buildings, such as Nos. 487 and 493, were warehouses, while the massive building we see at Nos. 497-9 was put up in 1683 by Joseph Deutz, the rich tar importer we met on our walk down Herengracht, and who evidently needed both stables and a warehouse.

Once we have crossed Nieuwe Spiegelstraat,

things begin to pick up. We should now walk down the side with the odd numbers, for that affords us the best view of the handsome double house at No. 596, built in about 1740, and the equally grand house at No. 604, which was constructed, according to the inscription at the top, *Int derde Vredejaar*. The 'Third Year of Peace' was 1670, three years after the Treaty of Breda was signed, ending one of the wars between the Dutch and English, and leading to the exchange of the islands of Manhattan and Surinam.

The two houses on the left, Nos. 606 and 608, are splendid baroque buildings with flamboyant neck gables. The house at No. 610 was originally built in the same style, but a later owner, falling victim to the flat cornice fad of the 1790's, had the top removed. But whatever aristocratic disguise was adopted, these remained merchant houses with goods hauled up with the hoist beams, through the attic doors to be stowed away in the top two floors.

An odd house at Nos. 569-71 was built in 1923 in Venetian Gothic style. On the opposite side, the row of seven houses at Nos. 634 to 646 were once identical septuplets, but various owners have modified their properties over the years, removing a stair here or a gable there, so that only Nos. 636 and 638 are now the same.

We now have to cross the busy Vijzelstraat, beyond which lies the Fodor Museum at No. 609. This former warehouse was bequeathed to the city by the coal merchant C. J. Fodor, who owned a vast collection of paintings and prints, including etchings and drawings by Rembrandt. Fodor gave them to the city on condition that they converted this former warehouse into an art gallery, and displayed the works there. The museum opened three years after Fodor's death, in 1863, and in the days of the old Baedeker guidebooks it did indeed contain an impressive collection of 161 paintings and 300 drawings. But the city council moved the collection after the last war, and the building was converted into a modern art gallery.

IV. The Van Loon Museum. Fodor lived in the adjoining house, No. 611, where he enjoyed a splendid view of the two Dortsman mansions

opposite, at Nos. 672 and 674. The house on the left, No. 672, is now the Van Loon Museum. It was built, along with its neighbour, for two brothers in 1672. One had a well-paid job in the Dutch East India Company and the other was a merchant with a seat on the board of the Amsterdam Exchange Bank. They also bought four adjoining lots on the Kerkstraat to enable them to build coach houses at the rear of their houses. The brothers employed Adriaen Dortsman to build two identical palaces in the sober style of the 1670's. Dortsman, as usual, dispensed with picturesque details such as neck gables and garlands, producing a cool classicism.

This museum offers us a rare opportunity to see behind the façade of a stately canal house and savour the slight air of dilapidated grandeur. The chairs are too frail to use, and the rococo mouldings are crumbling, but the house is suffused with history. One of the earliest owners was Ferdinand Bol, one of Rembrandt's pupils, who lived here until 1680. Subsequent inhabitants have left their mark on the interior - the intertwined initials of Abraham van Hagen and

Catharina Trip are worked into the staircase balustrade, and the monogram of Hendrick Sander can be seen in the master bedroom. The house was acquired in 1884 by the Van Loon family, and it still remains in their hands. The rooms are filled with their family mementoes, including a fascinating collection of fifty portraits of distinguished ancestors, beginning with oil paintings of 17th-century Dutch rebels and ending with sepia photographs of aristocratic Van Loons of the 1920's. We can also wander in the garden pictured here, with its carefully clipped box hedges and coach house in the style of a Greek temple. The painting by Cornelis Troost from the Rijksmuseum, opposite, shows us how a similar garden would have looked in the 18th century.

If we are here on a Monday, we should be able to catch the plant market on the Amstelveld before the growers pack up. The market is on the Prinsengracht, which we reach by continuing along Keizersgracht to the next canal, Reguliersgracht, then turning right. The plant market is held next to a curious wooden church called the Amstelkerk, which was originally envisaged under the 1609 Plan as a large brick church, but the site proved marshy and a temporary wooden building was erected while drainage experts worked out what to do. They never did find a solution, and the plan was eventually abandoned, leaving the square, with its sagging brick paving, looking somewhat desolate for six days of the week. It bursts into colour on Mondays, however, when local plant growers lay out ferns, geraniums and begonias on the square. The church itself is rarely open, but we can pause for a coffee or lunch in the attractive café Kort, located inside an annexe. Open from 11 am, it has a seductive terrace shaded by elm trees.

We might want, for the sake of completeness, to wander along the last stretch of Keizersgracht. If we go back down Reguliersgracht and turn right along the odd numbered side, we come to a shop called Ditjes and Datjes, at Keizersgracht 709, where we can find every possible culinary item, including Danish cress scissors. A short stroll brings us to the Amstel, close to the wooden Magere Brug at the end of Kerkstraat. If we wait here long enough, we can watch the bridge being

raised to allow a barge to pass through. It happens every 30 minutes or so. All that remains after that is to look for somewhere to eat - perhaps in one of the restaurants on Utrechtsestraat.

Prinsengracht and the Jordaan

THE ANNE FRANK HOUSE *to* RUNSTRAAT

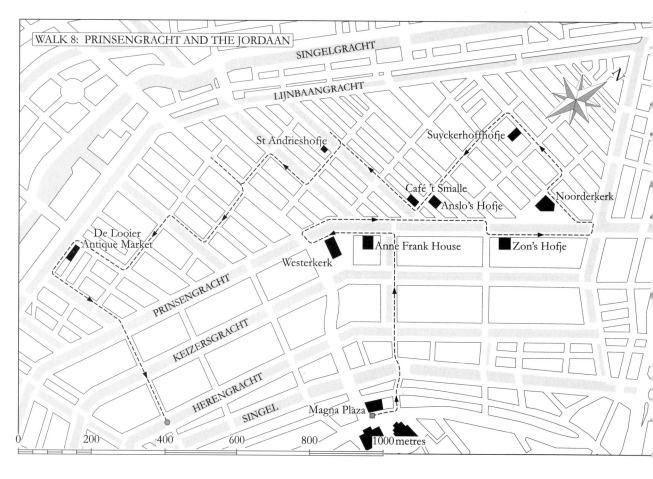

WALK 8: PRINSENGRACHT AND THE JORDAAN

SINGELGRACHT

LIJNBAANGRACHT

St Andrieshofje

Suyckerhoffhofje

Café 't Smalle

Anslo's Hofje

Noorderkerk

De Looier
Antique Market

Westerkerk

Anne Frank House

Zon's Hofje

PRINSENGRACHT

KEIZERSGRACHT

HERENGRACHT

SINGEL

Magna Plaza

0   200   400   600   800   1000 metres

Prinsengracht and the Jordaan

THE ANNE FRANK HOUSE *to* RUNSTRAAT

This is one of the most enjoyable walks in Amsterdam, particularly in the summer months when most of the cafés put out a few metal tables on the narrow pavements, and we can sit in a patch of sunlight watching cyclists rattle along the streets. The walk is best done on a Monday morning, when we can rummage in the flea market on the Noordermarkt before it packs up at about 1 pm, and perhaps even catch the plant market on the Amstelveld (which goes on until 6 pm). If we don't have a Monday to spare, we might set aside a Saturday morning when a bird market takes place on the Noordermarkt, or time our walk to begin on a Tuesday morning so that we can catch the carillon concert in the Westerkerk tower (performed from noon to 1 pm).

The one day to avoid is Friday, when the indoor antique market on Elandsgracht is closed. The walk can be done in a couple of hours, but if we wander into second-hand bookshops or linger on a café terrace we are more likely to spend a whole day here.

We begin once again on the Dam, stopping for a coffee in the Bijenkorf, or, for a change, Ovidius in the Magna Plaza shopping centre, where a sign above the door announces *Veni, Vidi, Verbazi*. The spacious interior has the nostalgic mood of a traditional brown café, with wooden furnishings and a large reading table piled with copies of the *Volkskrant* and *Vogue*. After finding something suitable to read, we can sit down and order the best *caffè latte* in Amsterdam.

On leaving Magna Plaza by the main entrance, we turn left down Nieuwezijds Voorburgwal, then left again down Molsteeg, a narrow lane with tiny shops selling jewellery and antiques. Once we have crossed Spuistraat, we continue down Torensteeg, named after the *toren*, or tower, which once stood at the end of the lane. The tower has gone, though, leaving an unusually wide bridge where, a few years ago, a rugged bronze statue of Multatuli, the 19th-century writer, was unveiled. In the summer, when the café Villa Zeezicht puts out tables on the bridge, it is difficult to resist stopping here for a coffee. Perhaps not now, though. Our route continues down Oude Leliestraat, which has a useful dry cleaners called Sneeuwwit at No. 11. Should we fail to get this little joke, a statue of Snow White stands in the window to make the point clear.

We then walk down the lovely Leliegracht, where shops sell wooden toys, bicycle parts and old TV's. Once across Keizersgracht, we come to a little enclave of specialised booksellers, dealing in art books (No. 36), architecture (No. 42) and architecture and gardens at Architectura &

Natura (No. 44), where the piles of unsorted books seem to grow higher every day. It is almost like wandering in an overgrown garden, where we might, if we dig deep in the undergrowth, find an interesting old volume on Dutch landscape theories, or even a book that will tell us something about the fanciful Art Nouveau insurance office on the other side of the canal (described on page 201).

We also pass Christophe at No. 46, which is, most people agree, one of the best restaurants in Amsterdam. The interior is designed in a sober modern style which has no truck with traditional Dutch decor. The specialities on offer include lobster, Texel lamb and pigeon. A few doors down, Herb Lewitz's orderly Book Traffic at No. 50 sells second-hand English novels, film guides and travel books, along with the odd abandoned copy of Hugo's *Dutch in Three Months* - abandoned no doubt because almost everyone in Amsterdam speaks flawless English.

I. Prinsengracht. At the end of Leliegracht we turn left along Prinsengracht, keeping to the side with the odd numbers. This canal, the outer-most of the three great canals, was built in the 17th century for craftsmen and shopkeepers. We still find massive brick warehouses and corner shops with 18th-century windows, yet perhaps the greatest appeal of Prinsengracht is its slightly bohemian charm, with clematis growing up walls and roses planted in old tin drums. The atmosphere is enhanced by the houseboats gently rocking in the wake of the tour boats. Each boat has been lovingly painted and decked with geraniums; it seems hardly believable that they once, twenty years ago or so, sailed down the Rhine carrying sand or coal to Germany.

The Prinsengracht is about two miles long, so we may not have time to look at each one of the 1,000 or so houses along its length, but we must at least visit the Anne Frank House at No. 263. There is likely to be a large crowd of tourists gathered outside, as this narrow 17th-century canal house, where Anne Frank wrote her diary during the Nazi occupation of the Netherlands, is now the most visited house on the canals. In the summer, the queue often stretches around the block, in which case we should perhaps come back another time. If we read the diary, we learn that the house was desperately crowded when there were only eight people hiding here. More than half a million visitors now tramp through every year.

Once inside, we can climb the creaking wooden stairs, peer at the hinged bookcase that hid the entrance to the annexe, and squeeze into the tiny back bedroom where Anne wrote. As we shuffle through her parents' bedroom, we can see pencil marks on the wall marking the height of Anne and her sister Margot. In Anne's tiny bedroom, the damp brown walls are still plastered with Anne's collection of photographs of Deanna Durbin, Greta Garbo and the British princesses, alongside a touching English illustration entitled *The Lark's Song*.

Otto Frank and his family had left Frankfurt in 1933, soon after Hitler came to power. Even in those early days, he sensed the horrors that were to come. The family moved to Amsterdam, renting an apartment at Merwedeplein 37. Otto Frank set up in business selling Opekta jam at Singel

400 (which is where he took this photograph of Anne), while Anne settled into a local Montessori school. After the Germans invaded the Netherlands in 1940, Otto acquired this house on the Prinsengracht. Two years later, when Hitler's Final Solution was being ruthlessly enforced, he began to convert the annexe at the back into a hiding place. Soon after Anne's thirteenth birthday, the family went into hiding here, along with four other Jews.

Otto had given Anne a diary as her thirteenth birthday present, and she used it to record the family's twenty-five months in hiding. It is full of teenage thoughts, complaints about the food and accounts of family rows. Yet there are also lyrical descriptions of the Westerkerk bells, and the chestnut tree in the garden. 'From my favourite spot on the floor I look up at the blue sky and the bare chestnut tree, on whose branches little raindrops glisten like silver, and at the seagulls and other birds as they glide on the wind,' she wrote on 25 February 1944.

Anne was just fifteen when the police burst into the annexe after being tipped off by an informer.

The eight people hiding there were deported to the concentration camps. Anne and her sister ended up in Bergen-Belsen, where they both died of typhus in 1945; of the eight, Otto Frank was the only survivor. After the war, he was given Anne's diary by a Dutch woman who had salvaged the scattered pages from the floor soon after the family had been arrested. Anne had called it *Het Achterhuis* (The Annexe), which was the title of the original Dutch edition. In one of the entries, she dreamed of becoming a famous writer one day. The diary has now sold more than 13 million copies in 50 languages, and so, in a way, her ambition has been achieved.

On leaving the Anne Frank House, we turn left and left again onto the Westermarkt. The house where Descartes spent the summer of 1634 is at No. 6. He stayed here with a French school-teacher, Thomas Jacobsz. Sergeant, and wrote an enthusiastic letter to a friend in praise of Amsterdam: 'Where else in the world are all life's commodities and every conceivable curiosity to be found as easily as here? Where else in the world can one find such absolute freedom?'

Descartes took advantage of this freedom to have a brief affair with the schoolteacher's Dutch maid, Helena Jans. A daughter was born called Francintje, who later died of scarlet fever at the age of five. Descartes, normally quite irascible, was deeply affected by the death. 'It was the worst thing that ever happened to me,' he confessed.

Descartes' house faces the Westerkerk, whose bells consoled Anne Frank while she hid in the attic nearby. The church seems strangely empty after the crush in the Anne Frank House. On some days, we may find ourselves wandering alone in this vast white church, which was begun in 1620 by Hendrick de Keyser and completed, after he died the following year, by his son Pieter. The nave, with its lingering gothic affectations, is clearly the work of Hendrick, but the wonderful tower, which we glimpse from odd angles as we walk through the Jordaan, was surely Pieter's design. Hendrick could never have produced such an orderly classical composition, without at least adding a few gothic pinnacles or perhaps a roaring lion's head. The church was built in

221

record time, so that it appears to have been finished by the time of the 1625 map, right up to the cockerel perched on top of the imperial crown (see page 201).

The latter harks back to the middle ages, when Maximilian of Austria granted the city the right to use the Hapsburg imperial crown. He did so in 1489, and though the Hapsburg link was broken during the Dutch Revolt, the city still chose to add the crown to this Protestant church. Rembrandt, who lived nearby after his bankruptcy, seems to have been quite fond of the tower, for he sketched it several times. It can be climbed, at least in the summer, for a view of the Jordaan.

Rembrandt's companion, Hendrickje Stoffels, was buried here in 1663, and Titus, his only surviving son, in 1668. A little over a year later, Rembrandt himself was laid to rest in an unmarked grave in the church. A stone memorial is now attached to one of the pillars on the north wall. It was put up in 1906, 300 years after Rembrandt's birth, in a belated attempt to honour the city's greatest painter. The oval memorial

carved with cherubs and sea creatures which might seem pure invention, but it is actually copied from a carved memorial stone just visible at the back of *The Night Watch*. Of Titus and Hendrickje, no trace remains in the church, not even a plaque.

When we leave the church, we turn left, coming to a square with a flower stand and a fish stall. The tiny statue of Anne Frank on the left is easy to miss, standing next to the church, often with a bunch of flowers left by a tourist. Not far away, a monument formed out of three pink triangles stands on the edge of the Keizersgracht, commemorating homosexual victims of the Nazis.

We now cross the bridge over Prinsengracht and turn right down the canal, where a delicious smell of roasted coffee has been wafting out of Keizer, at No. 180, since it opened in 1817. The porcelain shop at No. 172 sells Delftware from De Porceleyne Fles factory in Delft, which is one of the few places where plates and tiles are still painted by hand. A large Delftware vase is possibly too fragile for us to carry home, though a little tile decorated with a tulip or a cherub ought to survive the journey.

We continue down Prinsengracht to Leliegracht, where we should pause on the bridge to admire a flamboyant rococo confection adorning the house at No. 126. The top was carved in the mid-18th century by a sculptor clearly besotted by the courtly French style of Louis XIV, thought its original progenitors would have been surprised to see it used on a narrow merchant's house in the Protestant north.

De Prins at No. 124 is another tempting place to stop for a coffee. The interior of this 18th-century house is decorated in brown café style with wooden tables and old photographs. If we are up early on a Sunday, we can breakfast here royally on toast, eggs, ham, cheese, pumpernickel bread and a spicy Dutch gingerbread called *ontbijtkoek*.

De Prins is not the only tempting café in the neighbourhood. There is another on the next canal we cross. If we stand on the bridge called Pansemertbrug, we will see it on the far side of Egelantiergracht, at No. 12. It is called 't Smalle

and is, as the name says, rather small - even by Dutch standards. It occupies an 18th-century house smothered in ivy, where a famous ginmaker, Pieter Hoppe, once ran a distillery and tasting house. The interior has been tastefully restored with old wooden fittings and stained glass windows that evoke the taverns of Jan Steen. The main problem with 't Smalle is that is almost always crowded, even when the customers spill out in the summer onto the wooden landing stage beside the canal.

We continue down Prinsengracht to No. 235, pausing here to look at the pediment, which is carved with a scene now familiar to us, depicting two men in a boat accompanied by a seasick dog. This illustration of the foundation of Amsterdam is all that remains of a 17th-century poor house that once stood at No. 237. The 19th-century building that now occupies the site was originally a fire station.

We turn right across the next bridge, the Prinsensluis, and left down the other side of Prinsengracht. The original owner of No. 175 was a bit out of touch with fashions, building this step gable in 1661 when his more stylish neigh-bours were investing in classical neck gables, such as the lovely example at No. 36, on the opposite side, built eleven years earlier. The owner of No. 175 decorated his house with a puzzling row of carved stones which depict an old sheep, a spotted ox and a young lamb. After pondering what this could possibly mean, we can then turn our mind to the carved stone on No. 36, which illustrates De Veersack ('the bag of feathers').

The house at Nos. 159-171 may not look much, but it conceals a secret almshouse called Zon's Hofje. Push open the door and go to the end of the passage to find a leafy garden filled with birdsong. A curious carved stone attached to the wall on the left shows various domestic animals preparing to board Noah's Ark. This came from a Mennonite church which once stood here. The clock on the wall cannot be trusted, nor can another we pass in a few minutes on the roof of the almshouse at Nos. 89-113. This is Van Brienen's Hofje, built in 1790 in a sober classical style. It is not open to the public.

The only reliable clock hereabouts is on the Noorderkerk, opposite us, which is where we are heading now. On the way, we pass a house at No. 7 called De Posthoorn, the post horn, which once concealed a 17th-century church where Augustinian monks from Flanders worshipped. When the ban on Catholic worship was lifted, the congregation employed Pieter Cuypers to build a magnificent neo-gothic church on the nearby Harlemmerstraat. It is still there, though it is now an art gallery.

The café 't Smackzeyl at Brouwersgracht 101, on the corner of Prinsengracht, is located in a cheerful rosy-faced canal house dating from the 17th century. The café is named after the carved stone above the door depicting a sail, and it indeed feels quite like a ship inside, with its creaking wooden floorboards, and cramped little spaces barely large enough for a table and a hatstand. This is the perfect café to sip a Dutch beer, ideally sitting at a window table, where we can watch the seagulls swoop around boat's rigging as Vivaldi gently plays in the background.

Across the canal, at Prinsengracht 2-4, the café

Papeneiland occupies the ground floor of a corner house dating from 1641. The interior is furnished like an old Dutch painting, with gleaming Delft tiles and antique brass lamps. The view from the front window was a favourite of George Breitner's.

II. The northern Jordaan. We are about to explore a district set aside in the Plan of the Three Canals for carpenters, masons, artists and other tradesmen. The Jordaan is not an area we visit for its architecture (most of the houses are plain 19th-century buildings), or for its canals (most of which have been filled in), but to hunt out whimsical carved stones on house façades, secret almshouses hidden down narrow alleys and little shops selling all kinds of curios.

The city could not afford to dig grand canals in the Jordaan, so the surveyors simply followed the lines of old drainage ditches, which run at odd angles off the main canals. This area was only partly settled when Florisz. was at work in 1625, as we see from the many empty sites on the map. By the end of the 17th century, most of the

gaps had been filled, and many of the new houses were occupied by Huguenots driven out of France when Louis XIV revoked the Edict of Nantes. Some local historians even argue that the name Jordaan is a corruption of the French *jardin*, a theory backed up by canal names such as Rozengracht (Rose Canal), Leliegracht (Lily Canal) and Lauriergracht (Laurel Canal). But if we look at the Florisz. details, it is immediately noticeable how few gardens there are in the Jordaan compared with the Herengracht or the other grand addresses of Golden Age Amsterdam. Here the houses are small and crammed close together; the few empty spaces are mostly yards.

The Jordaan has a logic of its own which even Amsterdammers sometimes find mysterious. 'Amsterdam sees the Jordaan as one big revolt,' it says on a plaque in Anslo's Hofje, quoting the writer Bordewijk. 'The Amsterdammer doesn't understand the Jordaaner, whose town has its own map, a town within a town.' To those who don't speak Dutch, the problem is made that much worse by narrow streets bearing baffling names, such as Eerste Rozendwarsstraat - literally the first street across Rozengracht. To add to our confusion, seven of the Jordaan's eleven canals were filled in during the 19th century, so that Rozengracht now has neither rozen nor any gracht.

Not that this matters. The appeal of the Jordaan lies in the quirky little boutiques that last a season or two, the tiny art galleries created in empty shop windows, and the corner cafés that seem barely to have changed since Rembrandt lived here. We are quite likely to lose our direction in the confusing warren of narrow streets but, even if we get woefully lost, we are sure to find something of interest along the way. It might be an inspiring art gallery or a café where the locals burst into song at the slightest excuse. Anything is possible.

We begin on the Noordermarkt, which we reach by turning left down the even side of Prinsengracht. This cobbled square is empty for most of the week, but becomes transformed on Monday mornings when a flea market is held here, and again on Saturdays as bird dealers turn up to sell canaries and chickens in the shadow of the church. The site of the market was once a walled cemetery, as we saw on the Florisz. detail, where a burial can be seen taking place in the graveyard.

After the cemetery was closed down, the site was used for a market. The print overleaf by Hermanus Schouten shows the market in the 18th century, when it was obviously a good place to hunt for baroque cabinets, carpets, clothes and whatever is stacked in the basket next to the church. The market now has stalls piled with second-hand clothes that were fashionable, if they ever were, twenty or more years ago. Young Amsterdammers like to rummage around in search of something wild or weird to wear at Roxy or Mazzo, or wherever is currently fashionable on Saturday nights.

The Noorderkerk was begun by Hendrick de Keyser in the same year as the Westerkerk, which suggests that when De Keyser died the following year, it may have been from overwork. Here he finally abandoned his beloved gothic and designed a church in the form of a Greek cross. This arrangement appealed to the Protestants

Angeliers Graft

Noorder
Kerck

Kerckhof

Prince Graft

Linde Graft

Goutbloem Graft

Palm Graft

146

145

Brouwers

Sluys

Brouwers Graft

as it allowed the preacher to stand in the centre surrounded on all sides by his flock. But Dutch pragmatism got the better of the design, and little houses were added between the arms of the church almost as soon as it was completed. A quick glance at the detail opposite shows that they were already there when Florisz. drew his map in 1625.

A memorial on the church wall relates the beginning of the dock workers' strike on this spot. 'At six o'clock on the evening of Monday 24th February 1941, members of the outlawed Dutch Communist Party addressed 250 fellow citizens. They called for a strike in protest at the deportation of 400 Jewish Amsterdammers by the German occupying forces. The next morning the February strike broke out.' It was quickly crushed.

An intriguing shop behind the church (at Noorderkerkstraat 18) has sold antique spectacles and plastic sunglasses for as long as I can remember. It used to keep an impressive stock of artificial eyes, but these had disappeared the last time I looked in the window. The owner seems to have become slightly irritated with inquisitive callers who ring his bell at all hours, for he recently put up a notice that says: 'We are normally open from 11 to 6. Do not ring the bell before 11. We will not open up, but you will disturb us.' He also runs the shop across the street, which is crammed with old mangles, beer glasses and antiquated dentist's chairs that nobody, not even someone in need of spectacles, could possibly want to own.

We turn right down Noorderkerkstraat to reach Lindengracht. The gracht has disappeared, and the lindens were probably never a feature, but this is still an attractive street, enlivened by several quirky façade stones added in recent years. If we turn right, we will find one called Het War-Gaarn (the tangled yarn) at No. 53, showing two apes and a dog fighting over a tangled reel of yarn. My favourite, though, is 't Hcargnednil at Nos. 55-57, which turns out to be the street name in reverse. The date (1972) is written upside down, but what does the tree with the fish in its branches mean?

While pondering this riddle, we should now

walk in the opposite direction down Linden-gracht to look at the Suyckerhoff-Hofje at Nos. 149-163. This alms house is named after a Jan Suyckerhoff, who built nineteen small houses in 1670 for Protestant widows of good morals and 'a peaceful disposition'. If we push open the door and go down the narrow passage, we can glance in the courtyard, which is planted with roses, foxgloves and lavender.

On leaving the hofje, we turn left, then left again down Tweede Lindendwarsstraat. The playground on the right stands on the site of a Carthusian Monastery. After crossing Wester-straat, we continue down Eerste Anjeliers-dwarsstraat, past a flower shop that does occasionally sell anjeliers (carnations). Landré's music shop, at No. 36, stocks a good selection of second-hand scores, and Het Poppenhoekje at No. 2 sells antique porcelain dolls from the days when blinking glass eyes were considered the last word in sophistication. Once we reach Egelantiers-straat, we should turn left to glance at Anslo's Hofje, Nos. 36-50, an alms house founded in 1615 by the cloth merchant Claes Claesz. Anslo.

It is not normally open, though we might be able to glimpse the courtyard through an open door. The house to the left, at No. 52, belonged in the early 17th century to a teacher, who presumably thought up the witty name De Schrij-vende Hand (The Writing Hand).

We now continue down Eerste Egelantiers-dwarsstraat, past a house with tile pictures in the doorway (No. 60), to emerge on Egelantiers-gracht, which is still a gracht - and a very attractive one at that. We have already considered the nearby café 't Smalle (at No. 12) as a possible place to linger, though our walk takes us in the opposite direction. Turning right, we pass a splendid set of three Louis XIV neck gabled houses at Nos. 66-70, and a house on the opposite side, at No. 63, decorated with a stone showing a red hooded falcon.

If we stand near No. 482 and look back towards the bridge, we can see almost the same view as was sketched by Gerrit Lamberts in this drawing. He stood here on a bitter winter day, the canals frozen, the streets piled up with snow. Three children are shown skating on the ice while a

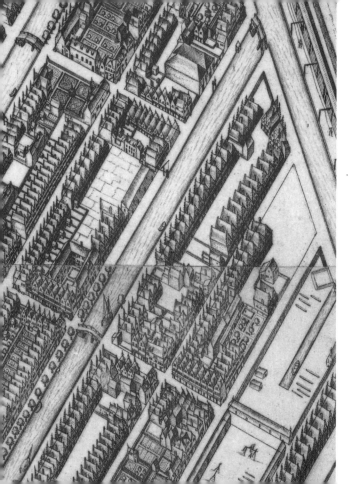

woman sweeps the pavement outside No. 143. The main difference now is that we can only see the crown on top of the Westerkerk tower, as the long building opposite has had an extra floor added.

This building is the Sint Andrieshof, an alms house built by a cattle farmer in 1615, and so clearly visible on the detail from Florisz.'s map. If we cross the bridge, we can go inside (it is numbered 105-141). A long tiled corridor leads into a quiet garden planted with lavender, giant daisies and rhododendrons. The decoration is simple, with just a stone water pump and a 17th-century stone bearing the figure of Christ and the words *Vrede sy met u* (peace be with you). The inscription is perhaps a polite way of asking visitors to keep the noise down.

On leaving the hofje, we turn right along the canal, then right again down Eerste Leliedwarsstraat. We might be tempted to stop when we reach the corner café De Reiger at Nieuwe Leliestraat 34. This handsome brown café is a favourite haunt of the artists and students who make up much of the Jordaan's population. The walls are hung with sentimental 19th-century watercolours with titles such as *Betwixt the Hills* and *A Peaceful Backwater*, which is one reason I like De Reiger. The other reason is for the view of the Westerkerk, though that requires us to sit at one particular table in the front of the café. If it is already taken, we will have to settle for a glimpse of *Betwixt the Hills*.

From De Reiger, we continue down Eerste Leliedwarsstraat to Bloemgracht, a handsome canal sometimes described as 'the Herengracht of the Jordaan', though that did not stop the cartographer Blaeu from setting up a large printing works on this canal in 1637. If we turn right along the canal, then left across the first bridge, we can look at Nos. 65a-71, an old wood dealer's store, where, if all goes according to plan, the 17th-century mansion of Joan Huydecoper will one day be rebuilt (we may remember that it was destroyed when a British bomber crashed on Singel in 1943). Some of the masonry was salvaged and the current intention is to reconstruct the house to accommodate a private library of esoteric knowledge known as the Bibliotheca

Philosophica Hermetica.

Further down this side is an intriguing row of three houses at Nos. 87-91 known locally as De Drie Hendricken; they date from 1642 and are identified by carved stone tablets showing a city dweller, a country man and a seaman. All three were restored by the Hendrick de Keyser Foundation, which perhaps explains why they are known as 'The Three Hendricks'.

We continue down this canal as far as the Tweede Bloemdwarsstraat, which, if our Dutch is making any progress, we should recognise as the second street to cross Bloemgracht. Turning left down this street, we come to the busy Rozengracht, which was a canal when Rembrandt moved here in 1658 with his mistress Hendrickje, Titus and the few remaining possessions that had not been seized by the bailiffs. It is no longer a canal, but a busy tram route connecting the centre with the western suburbs. If we turn right, we will see a splendid 17th-century gable house at No. 106 which has survived intact from Rembrandt's day. Hidden in its quiet courtyard is the Bols Taverne, a restaurant named after

Pieter Bulsies, or Pieter Bols as he preferred to be called, who founded a genever distillery near here in 1649. The building contains an excellent fish restaurant furnished in old Dutch style with antique cabinets and breezy 19th-century marine paintings.

Not far beyond here, we reach the site of the house where Rembrandt lived during the last eleven years of his life (at No. 184). The house itself has gone, and all that remains is a plaque on the wall above an antiquarian bookshop called, with due regard for history, Rembrandt. The Doolhof pleasure gardens which stood opposite Rembrandt's house have also gone, their place taken by a grim 19th-century almshouse, the Rozenhofje.

II. The southern Jordaan. We now go back down Rozengracht, turning right down Eerste Rozendwarsstraat. This leads to Lauriergracht, one of the four canals that survived the 19th-century urge to fill in the city's waterways. This canal has literary associations for anyone who has read Multatuli's great 19th-century Dutch novel *Max Havelaar.* 'I am a coffee dealer and I live at 37 Lauriergracht,' announces the wonderfully-named Batavus Droogstoppel in the opening sentence of the novel, repeating the statement on numerous other occasions, until the address is firmly embedded in the reader's mind. Many 19th-century travellers came here in the hope of finding the famous address, but all they discovered was an empty site. A modern building now stands at No. 37, but it has nothing to do with *Max Havelaar.* We can look at it if we are curious, but it would perhaps be better to seek out the house at Herengracht 276, which was apparently the home of the real life Amsterdam coffee dealer on whom Batavus Droogstoppel was based.

We now turn right down Lauriergracht, and cross over the next bridge, then continue down Hazenstraat, past The English Bookshop at Lauriergracht 71, where we will certainly find a copy of *The Diary of Anne Frank* and perhaps even an English translation of *Max Havelaar.* Hazenstraat is a wonderful street for browsing in little shops that sell jewellery, hats and second-hand clothes. The restaurant Het Stuivertje at No. 58 is a friendly bistro named after the Dutch five-cent coin. Decorated in old Dutch style, it is a popular place for a simple steak or a dish of the day.

At the end of Hazenstraat, we turn right along Elandsgracht, which is a gracht no more. A shop called Baobab, at No. 128, is filled with exotic treasures brought back from the owner's travels in the Far East. On the opposite side, the Antiekmarkt De Looier at No. 109 is a vast antique market where dealers sell old books, street organs, nautical equipment, Art Deco lamps and anything else that comes their way, even if it is a rusty scythe without a handle. It's open every day except Friday from 11 am to 5 pm.

We continue to the end of Elandsgracht and turn left along Lijnbaansgracht, where the 17th-century rope works once ran along the edge of the city walls. If we turn left down Looiersgracht, we will find another indoor market, not so well organised, at No. 38 (open the same hours as De Looier). We now continue to the end of Looiersgracht and turn right along Prinsengracht, where we find an old door between Nos. 338 and 340. This once led to the Doolhof, a 17th-century pleasure garden run by a man from Frankfurt. Behind this door, visitors would have found an exotic garden containing a maze, elaborate fountains and a collection of mechanical figures, including the splendid figures of David, Goliath and a landsman, all carved by Albert Vinckenbrinck now in the Amsterdam Historical Museum.

We have now seen something of the Jordaan, though we could easily spend another day wandering around streets we have not yet visited. For the moment, though, we have probably done enough, and all that remains is to find a final café. Let us try down Runstraat, the street that runs straight ahead. This is one of my favourite streets in Amsterdam; most of the good things in life can be found here. It is hard to resist the delicious smell of baking bread that wafts out of the Paul Annee bakery, at No. 25, or the eclectic collection of beers sold at No. 23. The Kookboekhandel at No. 26, run by a genial gourmet known locally as the pudding professor, is well stocked with second-hand cookbooks, and the Witte Tandenwinkel at No. 5 has an inspiring range of toothbrushes displayed on a miniature revolving ferris wheel. As I said, all the good things in life are found here, including several appealing restaurants - Tout Court at No. 13, Sauvage at No. 17d and the Indonesian restaurant Cilubang at No. 10. We will also find a friendly brown café called De Doffer at No. 12, decorated with antique clocks and nostalgic Heineken posters. The dark wooden interior is lit by flickering candles until well after midnight.

WALK 9

The Museum District

THE RIJKSMUSEUM *to* THE VONDELPARK

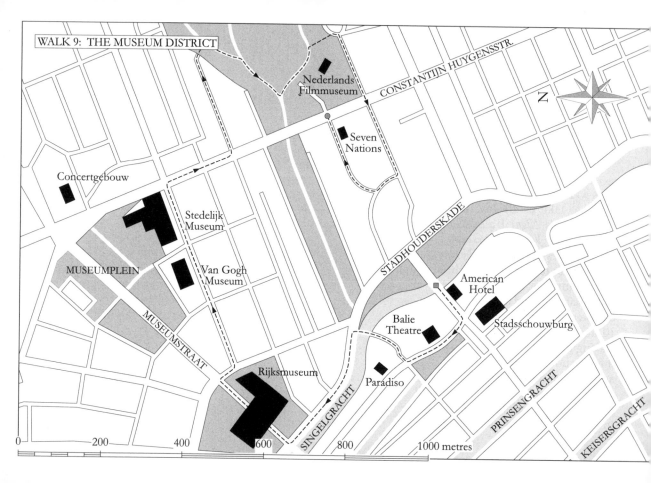

WALK 9: THE MUSEUM DISTRICT

Nederlands
Filmmuseum

CONSTANTIJN HUYGENSSTR.

Z

Seven
Nations

Concertgebouw

Stedelijk
Museum

STADHOUDERSKADE

MUSEUMPLEIN

Van Gogh
Museum

American
Hotel

Balie
Theatre

Stadsschouwburg

MUSEUMSTRAAT

Rijksmuseum

Paradiso

SINGELGRACHT

PRINSENGRACHT

KEISERSGRACHT

0   200   400   600   800   1000 metres

The Museum District

THE RIJKSMUSEUM *to* THE VONDELPARK

This walk does not cover much ground, but it is likely to take us all day. We are about to see Rembrandt's *Night Watch*, Vermeer's *Milkmaid*, Van Gogh's *Vase of Irises* and countless other masterpieces of Dutch art. Nor is that all. We will also encounter historic Dutch furniture, mediaeval sculpture, Japanese porcelain, French Impressionism and contemporary video art. If we can be at the Rijksmuseum soon after it opens at 10 am, we can stop for lunch at about 1 pm, leaving the Van Gogh and Stedelijk museums for the afternoon. This walk is ideal for a rainy day, as it takes in the three main museums, which are so close to one another that we may not even need to carry an umbrella. And if the skies begin to clear, as they so often seem to be doing in

Ruysdael's paintings, we can end up by taking a brief stroll through the affluent 19th-century streets around the museums.

The Leidseplein, where we begin, is constantly busy; even at four in the morning in the dead of winter, someone will be about, cycling home from a party, or staggering towards the taxi rank. Once the site of a city gate, this square began to change in the 18th century when the new city theatre was built here. The American Hotel, designed in 1902 by Willem Kromhout in an eclectic mixture of Venetian Gothic and Art Nouveau, added an exotic, though not particularly American allure. If anything, the City cinema designed by Jan Wils in 1935 looks more American, with its Modernist glass tower shining like a beacon in the night. Now there are restaurants bars, night clubs and any number of cafés, though none quite so grand as the Café American at Leidseplein 28, whose soft golden lamps glow invitingly behind the trees. The American brought a new grandeur to Amsterdam café life, with its vaulted ceilings and languid murals. The decor is still spectacular, though the service can be brusque, and the hotel has never received a good press since it banned hippies in the 1960's, leading the satirical writer Gerrit Komrij to describe the waiters as 'unemployed knife throwers'. The American still claims to be the haunt of writers and artists, though most of them decamped years ago to nearby brown cafés such as Reijnders at Leidseplein 6 or Eijlders at Korte Leidsedwarsstraat 47. Even so, the American is undeniably a grand setting, so perhaps we can ignore its shortcomings, order a coffee from a knife-thrower, and settle down to read this brief history of the Rijksmuseum.

I. The Rijksmuseum. One of the world's great museums, the Rijksmuseum was built in the 19th century to display the national art collection of the Netherlands, which at the time was crammed into the Trippenhuis on Kloveniersburgwal. The collection had been established in the early 19th century by the French King of the Netherlands, Louis Napoléon, who wanted to create something to rival the collection his brother had amassed in the Louvre. Louis initially filled the royal palace on the Dam with paintings that came his way, but the collection soon outgrew the palace and had to be moved to the Trippenhuis.

That, too, soon became too small to contain the Dutch treasures. Pieter Cuypers was given the job of designing a new museum on land beyond the old city walls. The government wanted a 17th-century renaissance building harking back to the Golden Age. Cuypers was a Catholic, and so neo-gothic was his preferred style, though the original design he submitted, which won the open competition, was a pure renaissance building. When work began on the museum, however, much of the renaissance detail was quietly dropped, and neo-gothic elements began to creep in. The central gable was originally designed to look like a renaissance canal house, but it ended up with a tall window plainly intended to evoke a gothic church. The Dutch king was so upset at the result that he refused ever to set foot in the building, calling it 'that monastery'. We are unlikely to be quite so fussy. Indeed, if the Rijksmuseum had a more monastic atmosphere, it might be easier to appreciate the art. As it is, the building is crowded, noisy and confusing.

We may find ourselves quickly overwhelmed by the collection. There are 250 rooms to visit and an impossible number of pictures to admire. The book *All the Paintings in the Rijksmuseum* is a weighty volume - and that is just the paintings. There are dozens of rooms filled with porcelain, sculpture, costumes and historical relics. The one consolation is that it was much worse in the early days, before Dr Schmidt-Degener became director in 1922, and purged much of the dross, sparing only the greatest paintings. Hundreds of lesser works were packed away in dark basement rooms or lent out to provincial museums.

Over the years, the museum has tried various ploys to make its collection more accessible. If we were here a few years ago, we might have seen visitors poring over folders describing various routes through the museum, based on themes such as townscapes or technical tours de force. These did not quite succeed in their aim. All too often, visitors would end up hopelessly lost in a remote room, looking for a porcelain macaw or an elusive view of Haarlem. The leaflets were eventually withdrawn, and the museum then turned its mind to the maps and direction signs. A Dutch design firm was contacted to produce new signs and a three-dimensional map. The signs are still there, with details taken from Dutch paintings to symbolise the services - a door in a De Hoogh painting indicates the exit, a motley group of peasants guides us to the information desk, and an angel signifies the museum lift. The new maps proved too confusing, though, and visitors now steer themselves around using an old-style floor plan.

Two plans, in fact. One covers the main collection, and the other shows the layout of the new South Wing. We should pick up a free copy of each, as otherwise we are all too likely to get hopelessly lost, especially if we are trying to track down the less visited departments such as Dutch history or Delftware, though I should add that it sometimes only by getting lost that we discover some hidden treasure, such as the marvellous Art Nouveau room (No. 34) hidden away in the basement. So much for the preliminaries. It is time to go.

On leaving the café, we turn left, pausing briefly to admire the Stadsschouwburg, a flamboyant theatre built in 1894 by Jan Springer. This was the scene in 1968 of the 'tomato protest', when a disgruntled audience hurled tomatoes at the actors during a performance of Shakespeare's *Tempest*. Dutch theatre has never been the same since. We turn right, crossing the street to Klein Gartmanplantsoen, and continuing past the Alfa cinema and the Balie theatre, which has an attractive modern café looking out on the square. We soon come upon a new square, Max Euweplein, which older Amsterdammers remember as a prison. A grand mock classical portal leads into a square where we might stop to watch a giant games of chess being played. The portal is inscribed with the words: *Homo sapiens non urinet in ventum*, a wise man does not piss in the wind.

A wise man also does not go in the front entrance of the Rijksmuseum. He goes round the back, and uses the quiet south entrance on Hobbemastraat. This is done by turning left on Stadshouderskade and following the 17th-century moat, past a row of 19th-century villas buried in ivy on the opposite bank.

The Rijksmuseum is the building on our right. We may think we have been here before, for it looks strangely like Centraal Station. The Rijksmuseum has the same long brick front with twin towers and a central gable, though it lacks a wind vane. The similarity is due to the fact that Cuypers designed both buildings. He built the Rijksmuseum first, sneaking in the tall church window in the central section, above the tunnel that takes bicycles and pedestrians under the museum. If the light is right, we might be able to see the gilded details and fanciful ironwork on the roof - perhaps even the bell-ringers below the clock faces and the cute little heads peering out of dormer windows. These represent the four winds, which makes one wonder if perhaps there *is* a wind vane somewhere on the building.

It is time to go in, using the rear entrance where we can slip in without much ado. We reach it by walking through the tunnel under the museum, passing perhaps a lone saxophone player, or the human statue who stands perfectly still on a plinth until someone drops a guilder in his hat, whereupon he performs a brief dance before resuming his rigid pose. Once inside the museum, we should consult the map to find out the best route to the front hall. The stained glass windows in this echoing hall are all that survive of Cuypers' bold design for a gothic hall where visitors could meditate on great art. Oddly enough, it now feels more like a railway station, with milling crowds, souvenir shops and even a meeting point.

Room 201 is off this hall. This is where the mediaeval collection begins. It fills just four rooms, since most Dutch mediaeval art was destroyed in the Reformation. Even the surviving works are often damaged, like *The Seven Works of Charity* by the Master of Alkmaar,

painted on seven small wooden panels in 1504, where the monks' faces have been slashed by a knife, though the figure of Christ in each scene has been spared. The painting has also been ravaged by damp, but it still gives a fascinating insight into life in a mediaeval Dutch town.

We find other early Dutch paintings by the Master of the Spes Nostra and Geertgen tot Sint Jans, but we are soon through with the middle ages and into the renaissance, where we can see the influence of Leonardo in Jan van Scorel's *Mary Magdalene.* One of the most bizarre artists of the day was Maerten van Heemskercke, whose *Erythraean Sibyl* of 1564 shows the prophetess sitting on a hill above a distant city that, apart from the mountains beyond, closely resembles Delft.

We soon leave behind the renaissance and enter the 17th-century rooms. The Rembrandt paintings are in rooms 214 and 215 - or at least some of them. Others are in the Gallery of Honour, and *The Night Watch* has a room to itself. The Rijksmuseum now has seventeen Rembrandts, having recently lent *The Anatomy Lesson of Dr Deyman*, partly destroyed by fire, to

243

the Amsterdam Historical Museum. No other museum in the world has so many of his works, and some have fewer than they once believed, thanks to the formidable research work of the Rembrandt Research Project. The Gemälde-galerie in Berlin was devastated a few years ago on being told that their *Man in a Golden Helmet* was a mere 'school of' Rembrandt. The two self-portraits reproduced here, however, are both genuine. The one on the left, in room 214, dates from the beginning of Rembrandt's career, when he was a cocky young artist in Leiden. His face is half hidden by a tangled mop of hair that would certainly have had him ejected from the American Hotel. Despite the tousled look, Rembrandt was already doing well for himself, with his own studio in Leiden where he taught two pupils. Contantijn Huygens visited him there the following year and praised his work, though he hinted that a tour of Italy might help to polish his style. Rembrandt ignored the avuncular advice and moved instead to Amsterdam.

The other portrait, in which Rembrandt is dressed as the Apostle Paul, turns up in room 229.

It shows him at the age of 55, with his crumpled face and sad, hurt eyes. Rembrandt had suffered many woes in the years between these two paintings, having been widowed, declared bankrupt, sued by a former nurse, forbidden to sell his paintings, and forced to sell his house.

This was 1661, and was not the end of his troubles. Nor was it the end of the transfiguring energy he gave to his art. He painted *The Jewish Bride* in 1667, when he was 61. Hendrickje had died four years before, leaving Rembrandt alone except for his sickly son Titus, but still able to produce this deeply moving painting of two people in love.

We are likely to find a familiar painting by Pieter Saenredam of *The Old Town Hall at Amsterdam* in this section (it was in room 214 the last time I saw it). This was the painting Saenredam did after the town hall had been demolished (it is reproduced on page 57). Notice how fastidiously he recorded the mouldering stonework and rotting wooden window frames. The closer we look, the more we discover, such as the inscription on the bookshop canopies, which

records: 'Pieter Saenredam drew this from life with all its colours in the year 1641 and painted it in the year 1657.' In the course of those sixteen years, the old town hall had burnt to the ground, and the new town hall had risen in its place. If we look at the pavement under the arcade, we can read another inscription which looks as if it has been chiselled into the stone. 'This is the old town hall of Amsterdam, which burnt down in the year 1652 on the 7th July and in three hours was destroyed,' it says.

Saenredam enjoyed hiding secret messages in his paintings, disguising them as scribblings on a church column or carvings on a stone. Another painting which is probably hanging in the same room shows the St Odulphus Church in Assendelft, where Saenredam has added his signature to look like a carved inscription on a pew. The tombstone in the foreground is inscribed with the name Johannes Saenredam, the artist's father.

We should find the paintings by Vermeer and De Hoogh in room 222. The museum owns four works by Johannes Vermeer, which may not seem many, but only thirty-six survive altogether - the four we see here, two more in The Hague and the others scattered around the world. Little is known about Vermeer's life, apart from the fact that he ran a tavern on the market square in Delft and sold paintings in an adjoining shop. He married a woman called Catharina and they had eleven children, some of whom may have posed for their father.

The French invasion in 1672 ruined Vermeer and he died at the age of forty-three. Other odd facts have emerged in recent years, such as a document showing that almost two-thirds of his paintings were owned by the Delft collector Pieter Claesz. van Ruijven. They were sold for virtually nothing. The painting of the girl with the pearl ear-ring (now in the Mauritshuis) fetched a mere two and a half guilders, and *The Art of Painting* was bought by a saddler for an apple and an egg.

The Kitchen Maid was painted in the late 1650's and shows a sturdy woman, possibly the family maid, pouring milk into a jug. If we can get close enough, we can examine the tiny details that

Vermeer does so convincingly, such as the broken window pane, the nail knocked in the wall and the pock-marked plasterwork.

The Little Street in Delft, reproduced here, was painted about the same time as *The Kitchen Maid*, and probably shows the view out of an upstairs window in Vermeer's house. The building on the left has been identified as an almshouse that once stood across the street, though the other building was probably invented by Vermeer. This is another painting we need to examine closely to appreciate the crumbling bricks and discoloured whitewash. It is a scene of utter domestic bliss, in which each figure occupies a safe sheltered enclosure. Yet Delft was far from being a haven of peace; a few years earlier, a massive explosion at a munitions store destroyed almost a quarter of the city and killed 200 people. The cracks we see on the building where the lace-maker is working might have been caused by the blast. A few streets to the north of here, the artist Carel Fabritius was killed in his studio. Most of his paintings were destroyed, apart from a tantalising handful of

exquisite works, such as a self-portrait in the Boymans-van Beuningen Museum in Rotterdam and *The Goldfinch* in the Mauritshuis in The Hague.

Vermeer's *Woman in Blue Reading a Letter* shows a heavily pregant woman - perhaps his wife Catharina. With her eleven children, she would have spent much of her life wearing the blue maternity gown we see here. Catharina - if it is her - is standing in front of a map of Holland and West Friesland by our old friend Balthasar Florisz., published in Amsterdam by Willem Jansz. Blaeu. The west coast is at the top of the map, with the Rhine delta above Catharina's head and the Haarlemmermeer, where Schiphol airport now stands, near the top right corner.

We find a painting by Jan van der Heyden in a side room (No. 219), but what a strange one it is. The label reads: *The Nieuwe Zijds Voorburgwal with the Old Haarlemmersluis (with topographical liberties)*. We should be able to spot one of the topographical liberties if we turn to Van der Heyden's painting on page 177. The Pauw House at Herengracht 168 appears in both paintings.

Can we ever trust Van der Heyden again?

While we are pondering this, most people around us are heading for *The Night Watch*, which hangs in its own special gallery, built in 1906. The painting is permanently guarded, having been attacked some years ago; there are also fire extinguishers close at hand, perhaps to avoid it suffering the fate of *The Anatomy Lesson of Dr Deyman's*. The painting shows a group of eighteen city guards armed with harquebuses and pikes. Each guard paid one hundred guilders to be included and some were apparently none too happy with the result, complaining that they were hidden in the shadows. Whether the story is true or not, at least two of the guards would certainly be horrified now to find they no longer appear in the painting at all. The canvas was originally larger, but it was cut down in 1715, when it was moved from the Doelen banqueting hall to the town hall on the Dam. Two of the guards who stood on the left side were lost, though we know what they look like from this copy of *The Nightwatch* made by Gerrit Lundens soon after the original; and we know their names

from the list of twenty members of the company written on an oval memorial plaque attached to the pillar above Lieutenant van Ruytenburch.

The painting was once much darker than we see it today, as the canvas had been blackened by smoke from the banqueting hall fireplace; hence its name. Now that it has been cleaned, we can see the scene is taking place in broad daylight, with sunlight glinting on the guards' helmets. Nobody, though, seriously suggests that it should be renamed 'The Day Watch'. The old name, unlike the grime, has stuck.

A side room contains Rembrandt's *Syndics of the Cloth Guild* (page 105), painted in the same year as the *Self-Portrait as the Apostle Paul* we have just seen. Though plagued by personal problems, Rembrandt rose above everything to produce this sober and balanced composition showing the five Staalmeesters gathered around a table in the Saaihal to assess the quality of cloth, as they did several times each week. The man standing up was Volckert Jansz., who owned a house on the Nieuwendijk containing a famous cabinet of curiosities. Sitting to his right, with a book of samples open on the table, is Willem van Doeyenburg, a wealthy cloth manufacturer. The old man on the far left is Jacob van Loon, who owned a large house on the Dam; the hatless man hovering in the background is the caretaker.

The signature at the top right was forged in the 18th century, though there is a genuine one, almost invisible, in the centre of the table cloth. An American writer recently claimed to find other secrets in the painting, such as the word SEX hidden in the paint. He also argued that the officials of the cloth guild were looking not at a book of cloth samples, but a volume of erotic prints. This sensational theory was quickly debunked by scholars who pointed out that the word 'sex' did not exist in 17th-century Dutch.

One of the side rooms in the gallery of honour contains four marine grisailles by the Van de Veldes. These spectacular action drawings of sea battles were often sketched in the thick of the fighting. In *The Battle of Terheide*, we can see Willem van de Velde the Elder sitting in a fishing boat, at the bottom of the canvas, sketching the sinking ships and drowning sailors. Another work shows Admiral Jan van Galen's ship *De Witte Olifant*, which we may remember seeing on his tomb in the Nieuwe Kerk.

We will find works by Frans Hals and other Dutch artists elsewhere, but perhaps we should move on, as there are still three floors of applied art in the west wing to visit. The earliest works are found in the rooms off the Night Watch Gallery, where we find sculpture by Adriaen van Wesel in rooms 241-2, renaissance furniture in room 250 and a remarkable classical room salvaged from a Dordrecht house in room 252. A side room (No. 258a) contains a splendid fireplace rescued from the Huydecoper mansion built by Philips Vingboons on Singel, the one that might one day be rebuilt on Bloemgracht.

One floor down, we wander through a maze of 18th-century rooms, observing the transition from the Louis XIV style popular during the reign of King William III, to the more frivolous Louis XV of the mid-century, and then the severer Louis XVI style that developed towards the end of the century. Some may find these rooms rather oppressive, but one little room (No. 164) containing dolls' houses is not to be missed. You can climb a special staircase to peer inside the miniature Dutch interiors furnished with tiny Delftware cups and patiently-crafted furniture.

We have still not looked at Dutch history, which occupies a series of isolated rooms on the ground floor. If we make it there, we should find a set of panels depicting the St Elizabeth's Day Flood, when the sea broke through the dikes to the south of Dordrecht, creating the Hollands Diep inlet. We may also be struck by a mysterious painting called *Fishing for Souls*, which deals with the religious quarrels of the 17th century. These led to the imprisonment of the famous lawyer Hugo Grotius, who finally escaped from Loevestein Castle in the bookchest we see here - unless it was in the bookchest that is in Delft. Each of them has its loyal supporters. We should also hunt for the painting of the Battle of the Haarlemmermeer, which showing a battle in which the Spanish fleet, then based in Amsterdam, defeated the Dutch rebels and captured Haarlem. The lake where the battle was fought is no more; it is now the site of Schiphol airport.

If we had more time, we could look at the mementos of Admiral de Ruyter, including a section from the stern of the English flagship *The Royal Charles*, carried off as a souvenir by the Dutch when they sailed up the Medway. The relics of the Dutch settlement at Nagasaki are also fascinating, though we may have to leave this for another visit, as we still have the South Wing to visit. This striking new addition highlights works that were formerly overlooked by most visitors. The 18th-century paintings are now crammed onto the walls in the style of the period, as we saw in *The Picture Gallery of Jan Gildemeester Jansz.* on page 189. Indeed, if we search this room, we should find Jansz.'s picture gallery, as also the Amsterdam town garden painted by Troost in about 1745 (page 213). The setting has never been identified, though we can safely assume from the grandeur of the buildings that it stood somewhere on Herengracht or Keizersgracht.

The Dutch Impressionists have been rescued from oblivion in the new wing, so that we can now appreciate Breitner, Mauve and Israels. One familiar picture we may be able to track down is Breitner's view of Damrak reproduced on page 47. This done, we can leave the museum without guilt, perhaps glancing briefly at the collection of costumes or the Japanese rooms. If we go out by the South Wing entrance, we will find ourselves in the garden, outside an extension added in 1900 known as the Fragments Building. The door we left by bore the initials P. P. P., revealing that it came from the Rotterdam Admiralty. The outside wall incorporates a classical arcade from Constantijn Huygens' house in The Hague.

Turning right, we go through a weathered gateway that once graced a building belonging to the Teutonic Knights in Utrecht. The formal garden beyond, designed by the versatile Cuypers, is filled with fragments salvaged from Dutch buildings torn down in the 19th century. Straight ahead of us, a solitary renaissance gateway known as the Bergpoort was built by Hendrick de Keyser in 1619 as one of the city gates of Deventer, though it is now simply a place to shelter from the rain. On the other side is the Herenpoort from Groningen, a vigorous Dutch renaissance gate built in 1621.

There are other curiosities to be found dotted around the garden, including the wrought iron gates from Over Amstel, a country house on the Amstel, and the Waterpoort from Gorinchem, a city gate decorated with a clock tower. Some of the relics can be identified, but the rusty iron signs on others are illegible. If we go back through the Teutonic Knights' gate, we come to an elegant rococo summer house covered with carved stones salvaged from old houses, including one with a peat porter and several showing ships.

On leaving the garden, we should turn left to admire the back of the Rijksmuseum, where the tile pictures were designed by Cuypers' craftsmen to illustrate the history of Dutch painting. If we are here in the late afternoon, and the sun is shining, we might be able to make out the intriguing relief on the Night Watch Extension, which shows Rembrandt in his studio working on *The Staalmeesters*. The panel on the left shows two of his pupils admiring the portrait of Elisabeth Bas, which hangs in the museum, though now with an attribution to Ferdinand Bol.

The roof of the extension is decorated with the figures of four craftsmen at work on the building - two masons building walls, a carpenter boring a hole in a beam and a blacksmith hammering an iron decoration. But the oddest details are the two figures peering around the corners of the two main towers, at the level of the gutters. The man on the left is Cuypers, holding a measuring tool; the other, on the right, is Victor de Stuers, a civil servant who wrote a pamphlet persuading the government to construct the Rijksmuseum in the first place.

We may find ourselves needing lunch by now. If so, there are several possibilities on the nearby P. C. Hooftstraat. We might manage to squeeze into Sama Sebo at No. 27, an exotic Indonesian restaurant where we can sample an inexpensive rijsttafel. Or there is L'Entrecôte at No. 70, where we are offered a simple choice of veal or steak, served in the French manner with salad and chips, and accompanied by a Côtes du Rhône or a white Burgundy. Once fortified by lunch, we can head for the Van Gogh Museum, just behind the Rijksmuseum at Paulus Potterstraat 7.

II. The Van Gogh Museum. This modern concrete building was designed by Gerrit Rietveld, the architect of the Metz penthouse, but was only completed after his death. It opened in 1973 to display the paintings and drawings that Vincent had left in his brother Theo's apartment in Paris, hoping that Theo might finally find a buyer. Theo, who died just six months after his brother, left the collection to his son Vincent, who gave them to the Dutch state. And so the paintings ended up here, in a beautiful light-filled museum on the edge of a park.

The paintings are displayed in chronological order, beginning on the ground floor with the early works painted in the Brabant village of Nuenen. This is where we find the bleak view of Nuenen church and the famous *Potato Eaters* of 1885. Then come the paintings Van Gogh produced in Paris, such as the lovely portrait of Augostina Segatori, a former artist's model who ran the café Du Tambourin, where the tables, as we can see, were made from drums. Van Gogh sometimes ate his meals here and may even have had a brief affair with Augostina.

We now climb to the first floor, where Van Gogh's style suddenly changes. Early in 1888 he left Paris, feeling, he told his sister, 'utterly wretched'. He went south to Arles in search of a better climate, but found snow on the ground. Within a few months, he was painting spring blossom and the creaky wooden bridge outside Arles, which happens to look just like the Magere Brug in Amsterdam. In the summer, Van Gogh went on a trip to the beach at Les Saintes-Maries, painting brightly-coloured boats drawn up on the sand; when autumn arrived, he headed east to paint the wheat being harvested on the plain of La Crau. By then he had found some rooms to rent in a building called the Yellow House, which was near the station, and furnished them after receiving a large sum from Theo. He celebrated by painting *The Yellow House* that September.

This was where where Gauguin came to stay in the late autumn. They did not get on as well as Van Gogh had hoped; just before Christmas a violent quarrel erupted after which came the famous episode in which Van Gogh mutilated his ear. The following spring, he was admitted to an asylum near St-Rémy, where he painted extraordinary views of the asylum garden and a reaper working in the walled field beyond, under a huge yellow sun.

The following January, Theo wrote to announce the birth of a son called Vincent. Van Gogh immediately painted the wonderful *Branches with Almond Blossom* we see here. He sent it to Theo to hang above the couple's bed, where, according to Theo, the young Vincent was fascinated by it. This was the Vincent who eventually inherited Van Gogh's paintings.

Van Gogh left the asylum in April 1889 and stayed briefly with Theo in Paris before going to Auvers to seek help from Dr Gachet. He painted several portraits of Gachet, but none of these are here. We only have the bleak *Wheatfield with Crows*, painted in July, just a few days before he shot himself.

If we climb to the top floor, we will probably find Van Gogh's collection of Japanese prints, or else a temporary exhibition with some connection to Van Gogh. We then go back to the ground floor, perhaps picking up some postcards in the museum shop, before heading on to the Stedelijk Museum next door.

III. The Stedelijk Museum. We might see other works by Van Gogh in the Stedelijk. Or we might not. This modern art museum has been in a state of flux since the end of the Second World War. It was then that Willem Sandberg, the director, disposed of much of the old collection and whitewashed the walls, ceilings and even the staircase railings with their carved thistles and goats' heads. All that remains of the old Stedelijk are the tiled pictures in the entrance hall.

Poor Sophia Augusta Lopez-Suasso would be devastated. We may remember meeting Sophia on Kloveniersburgwal. She was the maid who married the rich art collector Augustus Pieter Lopez-Suasso. She seems to have become slightly unbalanced after her husband died, moving to a house on the Nieuwe Herengracht and proceeding to cram it with an enormous collection of antiquities, the bulk of which was worthless junk. She bequeathed everything to the city on condition that it was displayed in a public museum to be called the Sophia-Augusta Foundation.

The city commissioned the city architect Adriaan Weissman to build the new museum in a picturesque Dutch renaissance style. Weissman did not see the job through, for he was dismissed from his post when an affair came to light. It was originally called the Suasso Museum when it opened in 1895, though it had become the Stedelijk Museum - Municipal Museum - by the time Baedeker's 1905 guide was published. It had a very eclectic collection in the beginning, including a portrait of Sophia, a bust of her husband, a medical museum, an old apothecary's shop and a room described by Baedeker as an 'Insane Room from the old Dolhuis, with old apparatus for demented patients'.

All this was thrown out in 1945, along with the old Amsterdam kitchen, the Chinese furniture, the collection of uniforms and several furnished rooms rescued from houses demolished during the widening of the Raadhuisstraat. Nothing remained except a few 19th-century Dutch Impressionist paintings. This purging of the past is a familiar Dutch obsession. It happened in the 16th century when the Calvinists cleared the churches of statues and painted the walls white. It occurred again, as we learnt over coffee this morning, when Schmidt-Degener purged the Rijksmuseum, and it happens, too, every Monday morning when Dutch housewives in the provinces make a big show of scrubbing out their houses. It is a somewhat manic urge, which leaves a lingering sense of loss, though in the case of the Stedelijk, it turned a dusty old museum into one of Europe's best modern art galleries.

Directions are difficult to give, as the collection is constantly changing. Rooms are sometimes closed and favourite paintings moved to storage. The best advice I can offer is to pick up a floor plan at the information desk and study the layout of the collection. We might choose to do so in the comfort of the museum café, where local artists gather to discuss art or fill in applications for subsidies. There are now so many artists at work in the Netherlands that the government has nowhere to store the paintings bought under subsidy schemes; a purge of these is almost inevitable but seems not yet to have happened.

We will probably find modern photography displayed in room 14, a video screen flickering in the small amphitheatre sunk below this room, and prints on the mezzanine floor. If we are lucky, we will glimpse the Busy Drone, a gaudy mechanical dance hall organ built in Antwerp in 1924 (in the concert hall, room 21A). Room 12 contains an exhibit that we might at first take to be the Insane Room from the old Dolhuis mentioned in Baedeker, but is in fact a work of Funk Art by Edward Kienholz called *The Beanery*. This bizarre object is modelled on a louche Los Angeles bar once frequented by artists. We can if we want to squeeze into this grimy dive crammed with salvaged relics of American consumerism covered in wax. A scratchy record is playing and dusty human dummies with clocks for faces prop up the bar.

We should look through the floor plan to see if the Cobra group are listed. They should be. Willem Sandberg was a great admirer of this group, which included the Danish painter Asgar Jorn, the Belgian Corneille, and the Amsterdammer Karel Appel. They first met in Paris in 1948, coining the name Cobra from the initial letters of Copenhagen, Brussels and Amsterdam. The artists shared a vague agenda based on old Nordic myths and an admiration for children's paintings. Willem Sandberg was so taken with the style that he commissioned Karel Appel to decorate the walls of the museum coffee shop - the Appelbar (numbered 15C on our plan).

The plan will also tell us if the Malevich collection is on display. This was given to the Stedelijk by Kasimir Malevich to provide a record of his development in the 1910's from Realism to Suprematism. We may also find works by Cézanne, Monet, Kandinsky, Matisse and Mondrian, but it all depends on the whim of the director. On my last visit, I was amazed to see William Holman Hunt's *The Awakening*, a sentimental Victorian work of 1853. Whatever we find on our visit, we can be certain that none of it will relate to poor Sophia Augusta.

IV. A walk around the Vondelpark. If we have an hour to fill before dinner, we might explore the 19th-century quarter around the museums, taking in the Vondelpark, a riding school and the curious villa Cuypers built for himself. We begin outside the Stedelijk Museum, turning left to reach Constantijn Huygensstraat, then right until we come to P. C. Hooftstraat, where we go left to reach the Vondelpark, a large park landscaped in romantic English style in 1865 by J. D. and L. P. Zocher. A century after its creation, the park lost its staid English atmosphere when it became a popular hippy camping ground. Those days are long over, but the park still attracts an eccentric population of fire-eaters, jugglers, buskers, poets and performance artists.

We head for the blue bridge straight ahead of us, watching out for bicycles, roller skaters and the occasional pupil from the circus school wobbling along on a unicycle. The bridge leads to the curious Ronde Blauwe Theehuis (Round Blue Tea House), a daring modern building of 1937 with flat round roofs that vaguely recall a flying saucer in a 1950's science fiction film. We might stop here for a coffee, but there is another, perhaps better, café not far from here. After we have passed the bandstand, we continue straight ahead, crossing an elegant wrought iron bridge, then turn right past a splendid statue of Vondel put here in 1867. The base was designed, like almost everything hereabouts, by Cuypers. The four angels at the corners represent the literary forms used by Vondel.

Continuing alongside the lake, we come to the Filmmuseum, a grand 19th-century building that began as a fashionable lakeside café. We can sit on the café terrace in the summer watching the ducks on the lake, or shelter from the rain in the spacious modern café inside. After coffee, we leave the park by the lane next to the museum, which brings us to the Vondelkerk, a fanciful 19th-century neo-gothic church bristling with gargoyles and wrought-iron vegetation. The church was built in 1880 by Cuypers in his favourite neo-gothic style. Until a few years ago, it was a dank, forgotten ruin, but it has now been turned into a business centre. What would Cuypers have thought of this? 'What does it matter?' he might have said. This is the inscription he put on his own house, which we find near here at Vondelstraat 77-79. Built in 1882, this rather gloomy mansion has features reminiscent of the Rijksmuseum, including a row of tiled pictures that hint at the architect's personal problems. The first depicts an architect, the second a craftsman, and the third a critic. 'Jan thought of it, Piet created it, Claes destroyed it,' the gothic text laments. 'Art is long, life is short,' another inscription sighs, and it ends with an exasperated snort: *Och, wat maeckt et:* What does it matter?

It is easy to miss the doorway of the Manège further along the street at No. 140. But if it is open, and there are no signs saying *verboden toegang*, we should take a look inside. A narrow passage leads to an impressive neoclassical riding school, designed in 1881 by Adolf van Gendt. If we hit the right day, we might even catch a glimpse of riders trotting around the ring.

Back down the Vondelstraat, we pass a house with wistful flowers etched into the plaster at No. 51 and a splendid mansion with mock battlements at No. 49. After crossing the perilous Eerste Constantijn Huygensstraat, we turn right, then left into Roemer Visscherstraat. We have come here to admire the Zeven Landen at Nos.

20-30A. This eccentric row of seven houses is best seen from the other side of the street, for only then can we appreciate the whimsy of Tjeerd Kuipers when he built them in 1894 using the traditional building styles of seven different countries. The English house at No. 30A has a half-timbered attic and mock battlements; the Dutch house at No. 30, like many houses in this quarter, has a renaissance gable; No. 28, the Russian house, has been given a splendid blue onion dome; No. 26 is Italian with renaissance details. No. 24, the Spanish house (photographed overleaf), is the most striking with its Moorish door and red and white bands of stone, while the French house at No. 22 has something of the look of a Loire château, and its German neighbour at No. 20 has picturesque neo-gothic turrets.

Now for dinner. It might be worth trying one of the brasseries near here, such as Keyzer at Van Baerlestraat 96, an old-style Dutch restaurant which has been serving its customers sole meunière, Texel lamb and smoked eel since 1903. Popular with conductors and pianists performing at the nearby Concertgebouw (one

SPANJE

24

of the world's great concert halls), it has a warm and bustling atmosphere. Other members of the orchestra tend to head off to De Knijp at Van Baerlestraat 134, a more casual brasserie with a fin-de-siècle decor. The staff are friendly and the portions generous.

Otherwise, we can head back to Leidseplein to eat at Het Swarte Schaep, just off the square at Korte Leidsedwarsstraat 24. The last of the grand restaurants in this neighbourhood, the Swarte Schaep is, as its name suggests, something of a black sheep. The restaurant occupies a building from 1687 with an interior that has everything we might have hoped for, including heavy dark furniture and polished brass utensils, together with some features we might prefer to do without, such as a steep flight of stairs. The cooking is solidly French, featuring steaks, duck and game cooked to perfection. Perhaps not the most exciting food in Amsterdam, but the service is good and the setting just right after a day looking at Dutch interiors.

Amsterdam Explored Further

PROFIL VAN DE KERK

PLATTEGROND DES KER

Amsterdam Explored Further

We have now seen the main sights, wandered along the most important canals, and lingered over coffee in some of the best cafés. That may be all we need to do, but for those with time to spare there are many other interesting quarters of Amsterdam left to explore. These districts tend to be out of the centre, so that it will be necessary to take a tram or rent a bicycle to reach them. The first short excursion takes us into the Jewish Quarter, where we find melancholy reminders of the Jewish community alongside optimistic modern Dutch architecture. The second walk takes us to the Western Islands, a well-preserved old maritime quarter, while the last itinerary goes in search of the eccentric architecture of the Amsterdam School. Each excursion is likely to take up half a day.

I. The Jewish Quarter. The most evocative part of this walk will be the gutted roofless shell at Plantage Middenlaan 24, all that remains of the Hollands Schouwburg. This quiet, forgotten ruin, which few tourists ever visit, was once a 19th-century Jewish cabaret theatre; here thousands of Jews were held before being deported to the concentration camps. A memorial plaque is attached to the outside of the building, and a monument has been put up on the site of the auditorium. It is one of the most moving relics of a community that, before the Second World War, made up one tenth of the population of Amsterdam.

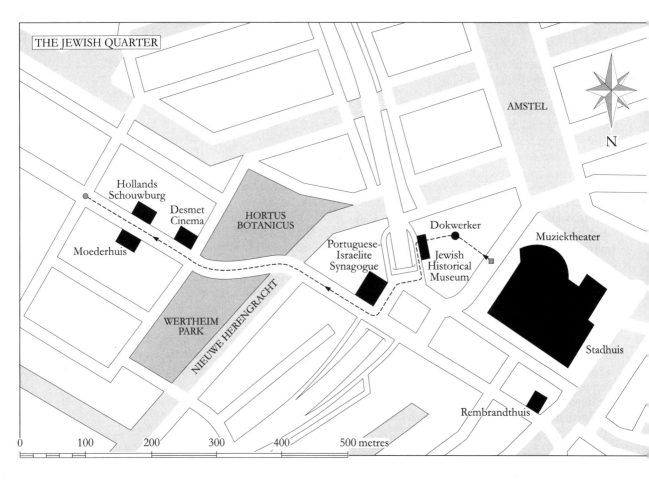

THE JEWISH QUARTER

Hollands
Schouwburg

Desmet
Cinema

Moederhuis

HORTUS
BOTANICUS

Portuguese-
Israelite
Synagogue

Dokwerker

Jewish
Historical
Museum

AMSTEL

N

Muziektheater

WERTHEIM
PARK

NIEUWE HERENGRACHT

Stadhuis

Rembrandthuis

0   100   200   300   400   500 metres

Jewish refugees from Spain and Portugal began settling in Amsterdam in the 1580's, drawn by the promise of religious toleration enshrined in the Union of Utrecht. The Sephardic Jews, who spoke Ladino and dressed flamboyantly, brought an exotic elegance to the eastern districts of the city. They were followed in the 17th century by Ashkenazi Jews, driven out of Germany and Poland by the Thirty Years' War, who spoke Yiddish. A Jewish district - it was never a ghetto - grew up around the Waterlooplein, where Jews ran a boisterous street market. The war put an end to all that, and left the district desolate for decades. Eventually, the city redeveloped it, building a metro line, apartment blocks and a new town hall and opera house. For all this, the neighbourhood still has a tragic undertone.

We begin this walk outside the town hall on Waterlooplein (reached by trams 9 or 14). If we cross the road where the trams run, we will reach the Jewish Historical Museum, at Jonas Daniel Meijerplein 2. This striking modern museum occupies a complex of four synagogues built by the German Jews in the 17th and 18th centuries.

The collection is limited, as most of the Jewish treasures were plundered during the war, but it is well worth visiting for the interior alone. A fascinating exhibition is devoted to businesses established by Jews in the Netherlands, such as diamond cutting, the Unox meat packing factory and Hema stores, where everything originally cost less than 50 cents. The museum café occupies a small synagogue known as the Obbene Shul, where kosher delicacies such as cheesecake are served.

On leaving the museum, we cross the road to reach Jonas Daniel Meijerplein, now a windswept square but once a popular place to stroll. The synagogue with the dome is the Neie Shul, built in 1752. The older, more sombre, synagogue to the right is the Grote Shul, built by Daniel Stalpaert in 1671. The square is now almost deserted, apart from the impressive bronze statue of the Dokwerker by Mari Andriessen. Unveiled in 1952, it commemorates the strike by harbour workers in the winter of 1941, called in protest at the arrest of several hundred Jews following an attack on a policeman in an ice cream shop.

The massive Portuguese-Israelite Synagogue (seen *c.* 1675 on page 262) stands just beyond the statue. This solid square building was designed by Elias Bouwman in the 1670's for the flamboyant Portuguese Jews. We can look inside the lofty interior, which is open most days, apart from Saturdays; male visitors, out of respect, should borrow a black cap to cover their head.

On leaving the synagogue, we return to the square with the Dokwerker and walk alongside the church. This brings us to Nieuwe Herengracht, the eastern continuation of Herengracht. The greenhouses on the opposite side of the canal belong to the Hortus Botanicus, a tiny botanical garden established in 1682 for the cultivation of medicinal herbs and exotic plants shipped back from the Dutch East Indies. Some of the species were presented by Joan Huydecoper, the East India Company director whose portrait we saw in the Amsterdam Historical Museum, and whose mansion may one day be reconstructed on the Bloemgracht. The small garden is carefully landscaped with ornamental ponds and rare trees, and the palm houses are particularly romantic in torrential rain.

If we turn right at the next bridge, we will pass the entrance to Hortus at Plantage Middenlaan 2. Across the road, the gate of the romantic 19th-century Wertheimpark is guarded by two curious sphinxes with lanterns balanced on their heads. Continuing down Plantage Middenlaan, we come to Desmet at No. 4, a small Art Deco cinema located in a former Jewish cabaret theatre. The two screens show a mixture of classics, gay movies and, to pay the bills, the occasional Hollywood hit.

The Hollands Schouwburg is only a few doors further down, at No. 24. Plans to turn it into a cinema raised such a storm of protest that it was finally left as a ruin. A small museum contains Jewish mementos including items of clothing and a battered satchel which belonged to one of those deported. Outside, in the courtyard, an eternal flame burns near three tombstones symbolising a father, mother and child.

A building on the opposite side of the street catches our attention. The Moederhuis at No. 33 was built by Aldo van Eyck in 1978 as a home for single mothers. The bright primary colours on the façade seem like a cry of joy in this melancholy neighbourhood.

II. The western islands. A forgotten area of three islands lies to the north of the Haarlemmerstraat. Cut off from the centre by the main railway line, this corner of the old city retains a sleepy, maritime atmosphere. Florisz's map shows the three islands in 1625, soon after they were built to provide land for shipyards, tanneries, timber yards and warehouses. We still find crumbling brick warehouses (now converted into apartments) and small boat yards where sailing ships are overhauled. We also pass a small urban zoo, a row of splendid merchant's houses and an artist's studio where George Breitner briefly worked. An hour is sufficient for this walk.

The first problem is to find the islands. We have to get under the railway line, which we do by walking down Brouwersgracht and turning right where it joins Prinsengracht, down Korte Prinsengracht. On reaching Haarlemmerstraat, we cross the Eenhoornsluis bridge, then continue

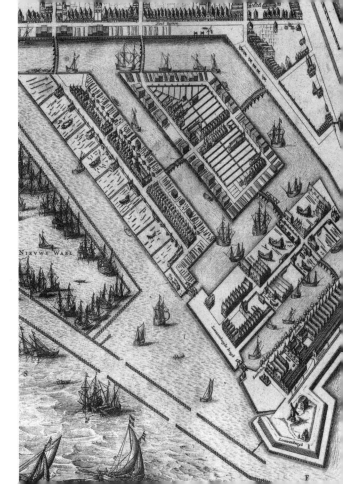

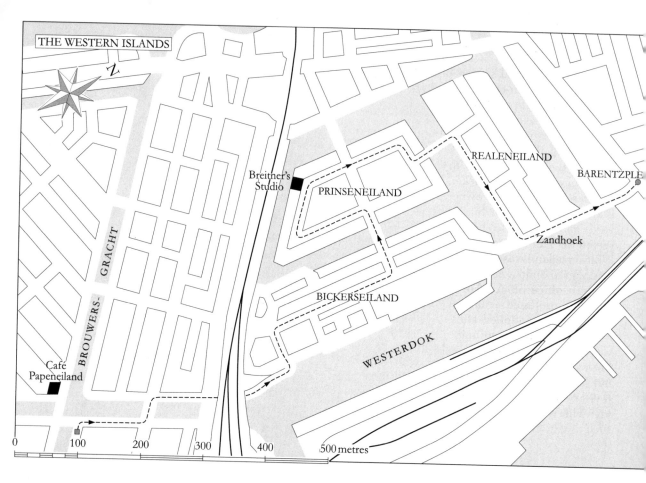

THE WESTERN ISLANDS

N

Breitner's
Studio

PRINSENEILAND

REALENEILAND

BARENTZPLE

Zandhoek

BICKERSEILAND

BROUWERS- GRACHT

Café
Papeneiland

WESTERDOK

0   100   200   300   400   500 metres

right down the final stretch of Korte Prinsengracht, past a 17th-century warehouse, at No. 14, decorated with a stone tablet to identify it as 'The warehouse of the Gilded Coach.' We follow the footpath under the railway bridge, past Squash City, then keep to the waterfront. We are now on Bickerseiland, a 17th-century artificial island named after Jan Bicker. He was a powerful merchant and ship owner who bought the island from the city in 1631, building new shipyards and warehouses here alongside those we see on the Florisz. map.

Bickerseiland was nearly destroyed by a postwar plan to build a new fast highway lined with modern office blocks. Fortunately for us, the islanders protested against the scheme, which was finally abandoned after only two solitary office blocks had been built on the Westerdok waterfront - De Walvis (the whale) and De Narwal (the narwhal). The modern apartments we see on our left were designed by Paul de Ley under a revised plan in which priority was given to housing. The residents have added folksy touches such as garden gnomes and a wishing well. We turn left down Zeilmakersstraat, right on Grote Bickersstraat and then left down Minnemoersstraat. This brings us to the leafy Bickersgracht, where we turn right, past modest houses with wisteria and climbing roses clinging to the bricks. The Florisz map shows timber yards along this stretch of waterfront, which is now occupied by a small urban farmyard with a loud crowing cock.

We turn left to cross the wooden bridge, pausing to look at the rusting barges and wooden sailing boats moored in the cluttered boatyard. The bridge takes us onto Prinseneiland, which was barely developed at the time of Florisz's map, but is now tightly packed with tall brick warehouses. These crumbling hulks were converted into apartments long ago. If we then turn left and follow the road around, we come upon two curious wooden buildings on the waterfront at Prinseneiland 24A and 24B, built by a local carpenter in the 1890's as artists' studios. The studio at 24A was originally rented to George Breitner while 24B was occupied by the carpenter's son, an aspiring artist called Cornelis Maks.

Breitner was offered the place at a low rent on the understanding that he would teach the son to paint, but the arrangement does not seem to have been a great success. The studios were bitterly cold in winter and unbearably hot in the summer. Maks failed as an artist and Breitner moved out in 1914, having produced a few impressionist paintings of the Nieuwe Teertuinen opposite (one of which now hangs in the Amsterdam Historical Museum).

Continuing round the corner, we pass a warehouse called Vrede (peace) and another, perhaps to even the score, named after Mars. Around the next corner is another white wooden drawbridge looking very like the one drawn on the Florisz map. Its name, the Drieharingenbrug (Three Herring Bridge), refers to carving above the door of the little house on the opposite side (left of the bridge). Three Herring Bridge was built in 1780 by a ship's carpenter called Haring Booy, clearly someone who enjoyed a good pun.

The wooden drawbridge takes us onto Realeneiland, the most northerly of the three islands. It was named after Reynier Real, a wealthy 17th-century merchant and politician who owned a large part of it. The Florisz. map shows only a few shipyards and a cluster of houses towards the northern end, but the island is now densely developed. If we turn right along the Zoutkeetsgracht, and left at the end, we come to an unexpected row of well-preserved merchants' houses on the Zandhoek waterfront. This attractive quay is named after the sand market established here in the 1630's where ships unloaded the sand they used as ballast, which was much in demand for laying the foundations of the 17th-century city. Some of the houses along the quay appear on the Florisz. map, but others were not built until the 1660's. Most of the buildings still have large 18th-century windows and colourful stone tablets illustrating names such as D'Eendracht (unity), Noach's Ark (Noah's Ark) and In den Gouden Reael, which is decorated with a Spanish golden *real* coin embossed with the bust of Charles V.

The front doors are reached by flights of wooden steps dating from the time when this quay was prone to flooding. We can even see one

house (No. 12) with a section cut out of the steps so that a wooden board could be hastily inserted if water started to lap at the door. The 19th-century photographer Jacob Olie lived at No. 10, occasionally photographing his family posed on the wooden steps, or the brown-sailed ships moored along the quayside.

Olie must have set up his tripod opposite the house at No. 3 to take the photograph on page 271. We can see a woman standing on the steps of Noah's Ark, No. 4, and a shop sign announcing a bakery at No. 6. Olie's own house is beyond the Holland sign, and the last in the row, the Gouden Reael, was then a rough seamen's café; now it is a smart restaurant.

We now walk to the end of Zandhoek and cross the canal by an iron drawbridge which replaced the wooden bridge we see on the Florisz map. The quay on the opposite side was marked Soutketen (salt works) by Florisz, but was renamed Bokkinghangen (herring racks) when herring smoke houses were built here in the 1650's. The smoke houses had not yet been built when Rembrandt came out here early one morn-

ing in the mid-1650's to draw the wooden windmill which stood on a nearby Leeuwenburgh bastion. Rembrandt must have stood near the Lynbanen (rope walks) marked on Florisz's map, looking north.

He did several drawings of the mill, perhaps because it reminded him of his father's windmill on the western ramparts of Leiden. This drawing dates from the period soon after Saskia died, when Rembrandt wandered in search of lonely spots on the edge of the city. The windmill has gone and Barentszplein, where it once stood, is now occupied by a children's playground. A huge abandoned grain elevator stands near here on the IJ waterfront. Known as Silo, it is now used for raves and parties, though it may soon be converted into apartments.

We have now explored the islands, and all that remains is to get back to the centre. We can pick up tram 3 at the far end of Zoutkeetsgracht, the canal we crossed a few minutes ago, or retrace our steps to the Zandhoek, cross the bridge straight ahead and continue down Grote Bickersstraat. This way takes us past a concrete office

block called De Walvis at Grote Bickersstraat 72, which gives us an idea of the direction architects were taking in the 1970's, before local residents took to the streets to protest.

If we turn left down Touwslagersstraat, we will find a path that leads back under the railway underpass. We might then take a different route back to the centre by turning left along Haarlemmerstraat, a lively shopping street with the occasional interesting buildings such as the Posthoornkerk, a 19th-century Catholic church built by P. J. H. Cuypers in his favourite gothic style, but now, like most of his churches, converted into something else (in this case an art gallery).

III. Amsterdam School Architecture. We

have already come across several Amsterdam School buildings, such as the Scheepvaarthuis on Walk 4 and the bridge over Keizersgracht illustrated on page 209, but we have to go out to the suburbs to find the large-scale housing projects designed by Michel de Klerk in the 1920's. For ten years, this strange, dreamy style held sway in the Amsterdam town hall, leading to a remarkable series of Expressionist bridges, lamp-posts and electricity substations. The style fell out of favour towards the end of the 1920's when the Modern Movement came along with its promise of cheap concrete and glass buildings. This tour is best done by tram and bus, beginning at Centraal Station. It takes two to three hours to complete, so we will need to stamp our ticket several times. A good map of the city might prove a useful buy before we leave.

We begin by taking bus 22 from Centraal Station to the Zaanstraat stop, where we step off next to a striking brick apartment block with a distinctive brick spire. Known as Het Schip (The Ship), this complex was built in 1917 by Michel de Klerk to provide workers' housing, a post office and a community centre. It has mediaeval-looking turrets, curvaceous brickwork and narrow wooden windows. Every detail is carefully crafted, including the chunky lettering, the strange doorways and the arched post office window seen here. The building may look vaguely like a ship from the outside, but the inner courtyard, entered through an arch in Oostzaanstraat, suggests a village square. The building in the centre is a local community hall, though it looks more like a country church.

If we walk east along Zaanstraat, we come to a square, Spaarndammerplantsoen, where Michel de Klerk worked on two earlier projects. The housing on the north side dates from 1914, while the dramatic row of houses on the other side was built in 1916 for the Eigen Haard housing association. The houses on the south side are decorated with curious brick details such as staircases in the form of seashells, and entrances with eccentric stair windows like the one here.

We now take bus 22 back to the Haarlemmerplein, where we change onto tram 3 (taking it in the direction of the Muiderpoort). We leave at the Roelof Hartplein halt, where we can stop for coffee in the nostalgic Café Wildschut at No. 1. Decorated with fittings salvaged from abandoned cinemas, the interior is reminiscent of an Edward Hopper painting. The Art Deco lamps shed dim pools of yellowish light on ancient cinema chairs, while languid vocalists sing husky 1930's songs

in the background. If we sit near the plate-glass window, we can admire the Amsterdam School architecture outside, built in the late 1920's to create a monumental entrance to the new Zuid district.

Fortified with a strong espresso, we can leave the café and cross the square, then wander down Johann Coenenstraat, where J. F. Staal built the block on the right in 1924. Again, it is the details that are worth noticing, such as the doorways, letter-boxes, hoist beams and house numbers. If we now turn left into the secluded courtyard Harmoniehof, we find another Amsterdam School complex dating from 1926, though most of the brick details are now overgrown with ivy.

We now go back to Roelof Hartplein, and take the next tram 12 that is heading in the direction of Amstelstation, and get off at Cornelis Troostplein. We then walk down Lutmastraat until we reach the small square Hendrick de Keyserplein, where we turn right down Burgemeester Tellegenstraat. This brings us to the monumental De Dageraad (The Dawn) housing complex on P. L. Takstraat, built in 1922 by Pieter Kramer. As

the name suggests, this complex was seen as a new dawn in workers' housing, a fresh start after the horrors of the First World War. The two rounded corner buildings present an extraordinary sight, while the details to look out for include unusual hoist beams, heavy doorways and strange beasts carved by Hildo Krop.

There are two secluded squares of Amsterdam School housing on either side of P. L. Takstraat, though as they are identical we need only look at one. If we walk to the end of the street and turn left along the canal Jozef Israelskade, then left again up Paletstraat, we reach the secluded Henriette Ronnerplein, where Michel de Klerk built a series of small apartment blocks in 1922 for De Dageraad housing association. Modelled on Dutch country villas, each block in fact contained eight apartments.

From here, we wind our way back to the tram, leaving the square on the north side along Henriette Ronnerstraat, turning right on Talmastraat, left on Mauvestraat and right on Lutmastraat. Tram 4, which will take us back to Centraal Station, stops on Van Woustraat, though we might first take a brief look at the Cinétol at Lutmastraat 154. This impressive modern building was designed in 1926 by Brinkman and Van der Vlugt. It was originally a theosophical society meeting hall, then a cinema, and is now a local public library. One of the first buildings in the Dutch Modernist style, it marked the beginnings of a brave new movement that would soon replace the Amsterdam School. Michel de Kerk died in 1923 at the age of 39, and the style he shaped was abandoned by about 1928. After perhaps glancing inside the Cinétol library, we can take tram 4 back to Centraal Station.

Trips by bicycle. We cannot help admiring Amsterdammers as they pedal through the traffic on their sturdy black bicycles, sometimes with a beaming child perched on the handlebars, a crate of Grolsch strapped to the rear pannier and perhaps even a dog on a lead trotting alongside. After we have walked the canals, we might feel tempted to join them for a day, picking up a rented bike at Centraal Station or, better still, one of the smaller shops such as

MacBike (Nieuwe Uilenburgerstraat 116), Bike City (Bloemgracht 70) or Frédéric (Brouwersgracht 78). The smaller shops are more likely to take time to explain the basic mechanics, such as the brakes which are on most bicycles operated by pedalling backwards. It makes sense to take a few minutes getting used to the bike before setting off into the traffic, bearing in mind that a *fietspad* is a cycle lane, a one-way street can be used in both directions if the sign says *m.u.v. fietsen* and that bicycles are obliged to stop at red lights, even if in practice they seldom do so.

Once we have mastered the basics, we can head off to explore the Dutch countryside. Thanks to Amsterdam's compact size, we can get beyond the last apartment block in about thirty minutes, reaching placid Dutch fields with grazing cows and splashing wildfowl. There are two easy routes to take, one that follows the meandering Amstel and another that goes north to the Waterland. Both can be done in about half a day.

IV. The Amstel. On Sunday afternoons, Amsterdam families set off down the Amstel with mother and father in front, the children wobbling behind and perhaps the grandparents bringing up the rear with folding chairs strapped to their bikes. This route takes us past some of the places where Rembrandt went on lonely walks after the death of Saskia, sketching the landscape with a simplicity that seems more Japanese than European.

We begin at the Blauwbrug, a grand 19th-century bridge modelled on the Pont Alexandre III in Paris. Watching out for trams, we head down the left side of the Amstel, crossing the graceful arched bridges over Herengracht, Keizersgracht and Prinsengracht, and passing the wooden Magere Brug on our right. We soon reach Sarphatistraat, where a degree of care is required to cross the tram tracks. We then turn left and first right to pass behind the Amstel Hotel, a 19th-century grand hotel on the waterfront. After steering around the parked limousines, we go through an underpass which brings us out on a quiet stretch of the river. We now cycle past flamboyant 19th-century houses and the ornate neo-baroque theatre called De

IJsbreker at Weesperzijde 23. The theatre café has preserved its 19th-century eclectic grandeur, complete with mirrors, murals of languid maidens and fanciful Art Nouveau lamps.

We might stop here, or wait until we have pedalled further before we take a break. Our route continues down the Amstel until we come to the next main road, where we turn right to cross the river by the Berlagebrug, with its distinctive red and black lampposts. We then turn left and continue down the right side of the Amstel, leaving the main road just beyond the Rivierstaete building and turning left where the red cycle-route sign points to Ouderkerk. This quiet tree-lined road follows the Amstel all the way to the village of Ouderkerk, so we can put away our map and enjoy the scenery.

The road passes Zorgvlied cemetery and the Amstelpark. Cycling is prohibited in the park, but there is nothing to stop us locking up our bicycles and strolling in the park, perhaps to look at an exhibition in the Glazen Huis art gallery, wander in the rosarium or lose ourselves in the maze. We shouldn't stop too long, however, but

press on past a windmill and, nearby, a statue of Rembrandt sketching this bend in the river. Rembrandt drew many windmills around Amsterdam (such as the one on page 273), but he never set eyes on this particular one, which was moved here only recently.

We then pass the old café Kleine Kalfje, where some cyclists lose their willpower, and settle down with a glass of beer; we, of course, will press on to Ouderkerk, which we reach in about ten minutes, and where we turn left across the Amstel, then right and right again down Kerkstraat. We soon pass the entrance to the Portugees Israelitische Begraafplaats, a romantic ruined Jewish cemetery where the Portuguese Jews living in Amsterdam were buried under flamboyant tombs. (Male visitors should, out of courtesy, borrow a skull cap from the cemetery office at Kerkstraat 7.) This cemetery appears in a painting by Jacob van Ruisdael of about 1660, and now in Dresden, reproduced here. If we wander among the overgrown tombs carved with Hebrew and Portuguese inscriptions, we should find the actual three tombs painted by Ruisdael, though we will see nothing of the waterfall or the ruined castle. This is the painting that stirred Goethe to write: 'Even the tombs in their ruined state point to a past that is older than the past: they are tombs of themselves.'

Leaving the cemetery, we now cycle into the village to look for a café. There are several attractive places on the Amstel waterfront where we can sit down for a coffee and apple cake before pedalling back to Amsterdam.

V. Waterland. A protected area of placid watery landscape lies just north of Amsterdam. Twenty minutes of pedalling through the suburbs brings us to the ring road, beyond which lies unspoilt countryside. Here we find the typical features of Golden Age Dutch landscape paintings - flat fields, distant church spires and a vast sky. The one thing to remember, of course, is that the weather can change. We can set off under blue sky and find ourselves an hour later stranded in the open fields as lightening cracks all around.

We set off from Centraal Station, where we might be wise to heed the wind vane on the south tower, as we can often be carried along by a following wind, which we then have to battle against on the homeward journey. We cycle under the railway viaduct, using the tunnel to the north of the station, then turn left on the busy De Ruijterkade. This brings us to the free ferry across the IJ, which we took on our tour of the old harbour. It will leave within a few minutes, taking us across to the Buiksloterweg. We follow the other cyclists along this road, but turn right at the café Trefpunt. A quiet, bumpy road take us along the North Holland Canal. At the first bridge, we turn right across the canal and main road, taking care here as the traffic can be dangerous. After cycling down Havikslaan, we turn left onto Meeuwenlaan, and follow it to the next round-about, where we turn right onto the Nieuwen-dammerdijk, an ancient dike lined with old wooden houses. We can relax now, as only local cars use this road. We can even dispense with a map, as the brick-paved skirts the foot of a sturdy dike built to protect the farmland from flooding. The name changes to the Schellingwouderdijk and then the Durgerdammerdijk, which leads us eventually to the former fishing village of Durgerdam, where painted wooden houses line the waterfront.

Beyond Durgerdam, the dike road follows a pleasant meandering route to the village of Uitdam. This might be as far as we want to go; if not, we can pedal on to Monnickendam, a sleepy town with narrow canals and neat brick houses. The enclosure of the Zuyder Zee destroyed the local fishing industry, though the smell of smoked eel still wafts through the back lanes near the harbour. If we are ready to stop, we can sample delicious smoked fish in Nieuw Stuttenburgh at Haringburgwal 4, a jaunty restaurant furnished in an engagingly eccentric style with mechanical musical instruments, a stuffed alligator and a chirpy canary. The dishes to try are *gerookte IJsselmeer paling* (smoked IJsselmeer eel) and *Monnickendammer twaalf uurtje* (a lunch platter of three types of local smoked fish).

The pretty town of Edam, famous for its round red cheeses, is not far beyond here, though it may be wise to head back now, saving time by taking the cycle path along the tree-lined N247. This leads us through the prim lakeside village of Broek in Waterland, famous in the 18th century for the meticulous cleanliness of its inhabitants, who would sometimes be seen scrubbing the trees. All but the most self-disciplined of cyclists call at the café De Witte Swaene at Dorpstraat 11 for a pancake or a beer before pedalling the final few kilometres back to Amsterdam.

To avoid returning by the main road, we can go through the underpass at Broek, then follow the quiet road to Zunderdorp. Not far beyond here, we come to the ring road. On one side of it are the peaceful green fields of Waterland; on the other the urban streets of Amsterdam. Once under the road, we cycle straight ahead, remembering that cars coming from the right may have priority over us. We eventually ascend to the Nieuwendammerdijk, where we turn right, then left at the roundabout. All we need do now is to retrace our route along Meeuwenlaan, turning right along Havikslaan and then left once we have crossed the canal. Five minutes later, we will be chugging back across the IJ on the ferry, looking forward to a beer in our favourite café.

Appendices

Tourist Information

I. Tourist offices. The main tourist office in Amsterdam is located opposite Centraal Station, at Stationsplein 10. It is open from Easter to September every day 9 am-11 pm (closing at 9 pm on Sundays in September); from October to Easter it is open Monday to Friday 9 am-6 pm, and on Saturday and Sunday 9 am-5 pm. You can phone for information on 06-34.03.40.66, but the lines are often busy. It is often simpler to write for information to: Postbus 3901, 1001 AS Amsterdam. Or contact the Dutch tourist office in London, at 12 Buckingham Gate, London SW1E 6LD (letters to P. O. Box 523, London SW1E 6NT; telephone 0171-828 7900); or in New York at 355 Lexington Avenue, 21st Floor, New York, NY 10017 (telephone 212-370 7360). Dutch tourist offices sell the *Museumjaarkaart*, an annual museum ticket valid for most Dutch museums, worth buying if you intend to visit six or more museums (passport photograph required).

II. Opening hours.
Museums: The **Rijksmuseum** (telephone 673.21.21) and the **Van Gogh Museum** (telephone 570.52.00) are open every day 10 am-5 pm. The **Stedelijk Museum** (telephone 573.29.11) is open every day 11 am-7 pm. The **Anne Frank House** (telephone 556.71.00) is open Monday to Saturday 9 am-7 pm and Sunday 10 am-7 pm. The **Amsterdam Historical Museum** (telephone 523.17.43) is open Monday to Friday 10 am-5 pm and Saturday and Sunday 11 am-5 pm. The **Dutch Maritime Museum** (telephone 523.23.11) is open Monday to Saturday 10 am-5 pm and on Sundays and public holidays 12 am-5 pm. The **Museum Amstelkring** (telephone 624.66.04) and the **Rembrandt House** (telephone 624.94.86) are open Monday to Saturday 10 am-5 pm, Sundays and public holidays 1 pm-5 pm. The **Museum van Loon** (telephone 624.52.55) is open Sundays 1 pm-5 pm, Mondays

and Tuesdays 11 am-5 pm. The **Jewish Historical Museum** (telephone 625.42.29) is open every day 11 am-5 pm, but closes on Yom Kippur. The **Beurs van Berlage Museum** (telephone 626.89.36) is open every day 11 am-5 pm. The **Hollands Schouwburg** (telephone 626.99.45) is open every day 11 am-4 pm. The **Royal Palace** (telephone 624.86.98) is open in the summer on most days 12.30 pm-5 pm. The precise opening times are listed on a small notice at the main entrance on Dam. The **Hortus Botanicus** (telephone 625.84.11) is open every day 9 am-5 pm. The **Tropenmuseum** (telephone 568.82.00) is open Monday to Friday 10 am-5 pm and on Saturday, Sunday and public holidays from 12 pm-5 pm. **Artis** (telephone 523.34.00) is open every day 9 am-5 pm.

Churches: The **Oude Kerk** (telephone 624.91.83) is open Monday to Saturday 11 am-5 pm and Sunday 1.30 pm-5 pm. The **Nieuwe Kerk** (telephone 638.69.09) is open every day 10 am-6 pm. The **Zuiderkerk** (telephone 622.29.62) is open Monday to Friday 12 pm-5 pm, and stays open until 8 pm on Thursdays.

Shops: Most shops are closed on Sundays and Monday mornings. Large shops tend to be open 9 am-6 pm, but small boutiques and specialised shops may not open until 10 am or even later.

Dutch public holidays: Banks, shops and some museums are closed on January 1, Good Friday (though some shops open in the morning), Easter Monday, April 30 (the Queen's Birthday), Ascension Day, Whit Monday, December 25 and December 26.

III. The tram network. You may need to use a tram to reach the suburbs, so it is worth being aware of the Dutch ticket system. Journeys are paid for with a *strippenkaart*, sold at the transport office next to the tourist office on Stationsplein and in most tobacconists. This strip ticket is valid on trams, metros and buses throughout the Netherlands. Once stamped in a machine, the ticket is valid in the relevant zones for an hour from the time indicated. Most journeys in Amsterdam are within one zone, which means stamping two strips. Outside the central zone, you add one additional strip for each zone. Once you understand the strippenkaart, you simply have to study the public transport map displayed in tram shelters. If in doubt, ask the driver for assistance.

III. The Dutch language. Ten years ago, most English-speakers would have considered learning Dutch a needless pursuit, but it is now quite useful to have at least a casual knowledge of the language. How else can you ever hope to pronounce the names of cafés such as De Engel-bewaarder, or understand the Opland cartoons in *De Volkskrant*, not to mention asking directions to the Oudezijds Voorburgwal?

One of the rewards of learning Dutch is to uncover a hoard of wonderful words such as *handschoen* (gloves, literally 'hand-shoes') and *kinderhoofdjes* (cobblestones, literally 'children's heads'). The Dutch language is also full of pithy local proverbs, such as *oude koeien uit de sloot halen* (to heave old cows out of the canal) and *hij heeft een klap van de molen gehad* (he has been walloped by a windmill).

On first impression, many Dutch words look as though they were written by someone who had had *een klap van de molen*. The secret is to split them into component parts, as in *hand* and *schoen*, when the striking similarity with English will often leap out. Sometimes a slight reshuffling occurs, so that the English *the* becomes *het* in Dutch.

To add to the confusion, there are some curious typographical conventions. The names of cafés and restaurants sometimes begin with *'t*, an abbreviation of *het*, as in 't Smalle or 'tSmackzeyl. People's names can also sometimes seem quite odd in Dutch, such as *Florisz.* which is a shortened version of Floriszoon (son of Floris).

Pronunciation is not as big a problem as it might seem. The letter *g* is the hardest to master. Text books tend to tell you say it like the *ch* in loch, but many people find loch difficult enough to say. Other tips are to say *oo* in words like *brood* (bread) like the *oa* in toad. It will be a long slog before we can hope to discuss Dutch politics *in het Nederlands*, but surprisingly little effort is needed to make it sound less like Double Dutch.

APPENDIX B

Finding a hotel

You can spend the night in a 17th-century merchants' house, or aboard a gently-rocking houseboat moored on the Amstel. Some hotel bedrooms have wooden beams and others look out on canals. There is a Philosophers' Hotel, a Bicycle Hotel, a hotel in a converted bank and another in a former city hall.

So the problem is not finding the hotel, but the room. You might begin by telephoning the Dutch tourist office for the latest copy of their hotel guide. This contains all the information you need on prices and facilities. You can ask a travel agent to make a booking, or telephone or fax the hotel direct (adding 31-20, the international code for the Netherlands and the town code for Amsterdam, before the numbers given here). It makes sense to book ahead in the summer months to get a decent room at a moderate price. If you leave it to the last minute, there is likely to be little choice.

Acro, Jan Luykenstraat 44. Tel. 662.05.26. Tram 2, 3, 5 or 12 to Van Baerlestraat. One of the best budget hotels in town. Located in a leafy 19th-century street close to the Van Gogh Museum, Acro has an elegant lobby and a small bar serving espressos and beers. The bedrooms are bright and spacious, with stylish modern furniture and bright bathrooms. Not the cheapest hotel, but it is worth paying those few extra guilders for a hotel that is comfortable and friendly. (46 rooms)

Agora, Singel 462. Tel. 627.22.00. A cheerful small hotel in a narrow 18th-century house overlooking an attractive stretch of Singel a few steps from the flower market. The bedrooms are pleasant and bright, with a few antiques dotted around. The front rooms overlooking the canal cost slightly more. (14 rooms)

Ambassade, Herengracht 335-353. Tel. 626.23.33. One of my favourite hotels. Located in a row of ten historic houses dating from the

17th and 18th centuries, this hotel offers you a rare opportunity to spend a few nights on the most elegant canal in Amsterdam. The bedrooms are furnished in a tasteful 18th-century French style, with a splendid collection of antique clocks, chairs and paintings. Breakfast is served in a bright dining room with tall 18th-century windows looking out on the canal. Service is polite and efficient, and the only possible drawback I can imagine is that there is nowhere, absolutely nowhere, to park a car. (46 rooms)

American, Leidsekade 97. Tel. 624.53.22. This is a hotel for those who enjoy the bustle and brights lights of a big city. The spectacular Art Nouveau building was designed in 1902 by Willem Kromhout., and though modernised in the 1980's, the interior still reflects the original style. The café is a architectural gem. The location is perfect for cinemas, cafés and bars. (185 rooms)

Amstel, Professor Tulpplein 1. Tel. 622.60.60 This grand palace hotel was built on the banks of the Amstel in 1867 by the entrepreneur Samuel Sarphati. It is by far the most stylish hotel in Amsterdam, with its lofty entrance hall, lavish floral displays and attentive staff. The building was totally restored a few years ago to ensure the continuing loyalty of royalty, pop singers and movie stars. It is, of course, impossibly expensive. (79 rooms)

Canal House, Keizersgracht 148. Tel. 622.51.82. A charming small hotel located in two merchants' houses close to the Westerkerk. Len and Jane Irwin, an American couple, have spent years getting their hotel just right, furnishing each room with antiques and paintings to recreate the mellow mood of the Dutch Golden Age. Ten years ago, when I first visited this hotel, there were no telephones or televisions in the bedrooms, but the Irwins have slowly surrendered to modern demands, admitting telephones and now even hair dryers, though they are still holding out against televisions. The rooms at the front look across the canal to a splendid row of 18th-century houses, while those at the back overlook a peaceful garden illuminated at night. My favourite room is No. 18, which is spacious and overlooks the garden, though the attic rooms are also alluring for anyone who likes to sleep under ancient wooden beams. The staff are very friendly and breakfast is served in a grand garden room with a piano. (26 rooms)

De Filosoof, Anna Vondelstraat 6. Tel. 683.30.13. Ida Jongsma studied philosophy before opening this small hotel in a quiet 19th-century street near the Vondelpark. The rooms are simply decorated, with the occasional quote from Goethe's *Faust* or Heraclitus for guests to ponder upon. The hotel has a friendly, bohemian air, and prices are reasonable, making it popular with students, writers and thinkers. Every Wednesday evening, members of the Dutch Association of Consultant Philosophers congregate in the bar to ponder the deeper questions of life. (25 rooms)

Doelen, Nieuwe Doelenstraat 24. Tel. 622.10.84. The ideal hotel from which to explore Rembrandt's Amsterdam. Indeed, Rembrandt's *Night Watch* originally hung in a banqeting hall on the site of the hotel. The figures of Frans Banning Cocq and Lieutenant van Ruytenburch decorate the east wall while, concealed in the depths of the hotel, is a fragment of the wall on which the painting once hung (now preserved as an historic monument). The bedrooms retain a 19th-century grandeur, and the dark browns and golds of the furnishings evoke the mellow mood of Rembrandt's paintings. Suite 515 enjoys a superb view down Kloveniersburgwal, where Rembrandt found many of his clients. (86 rooms)

De l'Europe, Nieuwe Doelenstraat 2-8. Tel. 531.17.77. A grand hotel built in 1896 on the banks of the Amstel, opposite the flower market. The exterior is a merry bustle of Dutch Renaissance details, but the interior has a more elegant Neoclassical tone, with pale yellow walls and Empire furnishings. The rooms are lofty and elegant. Most look out on the Amstel, and some have the added attraction of a view of the Munttoren, or even a balcony to catch the afternoon sun. (100 rooms)

Piet Hein, Vossiusstraat 53. Tel. 662.72.05. A small, friendly hotel in a quiet 19th-century street next to the Vondelpark. The bedrooms are bright and comfortable, decorated with modern prints and a vase of Dutch flowers. The best rooms have a view of the park, but there are cheaper rooms in the annexe. (27 rooms)

Pulitzer, Prinsengracht 315-311. Tel. 523.52.35. This remarkable hotel occupies a block of 24 merchants' houses and warehouses on Prinsengracht and Keizersgracht. Designed in the 1970's by architect Bart de Keyser, the hotel retains most of the original details, including bare brick walls, oak beams and mezzanine floors, so that guests have the rare opportunity of living briefly in the style a 17th-century merchant. The rooms are all different and the hotel tries to allocate regular guests their favourite. You might opt from a room on Keizersgracht to enjoy the urban setting, or a room overlooking the rambling inner garden to wake up to the sound of birdsong and the distant chimes of the Westerkerk. The hotel has an art gallery, a bar, a café and a restaurant. The location is a short stroll from the Anne Frank House and the bohemian Jordaan. (241 rooms)

Rho, Nes 11-23. Tel. 620.73.71. This hotel was originally a 19th-century Amsterdam music hall, but in 1912 was turned into a bank by a gold dealer whose name still appears above the entrance. It became a hotel a few years ago, and the former music hall now serves as a splendid breakfast room. The bedrooms come in various shapes and sizes, but all are elegantly decorated with contemporary furniture and fabrics. The rooms are not too expensive and the location just off Dam is ideal. (80 rooms)

SAS, Rusland 17. Tel. 623.12131. This striking modern hotel occupies a row of restored 18th-century houses on one side of a street and a former bible printing works opposite. The conversion has been done with enormous flair, combining the traditional façades with a seven-floor glass atrium filled with greenery and an artificial waterfall. The main building stands on the site of an old church and is linked to the annexe by a tunnel. Guests are offered the choice of three styles of bedroom. I favour the traditional Dutch rooms, with their oak-beamed ceilings and heavy wooden furniture, though some may prefer the modern Scandinavian rooms or even the exotic Oriental decor. It's worth asking for a room at the top for a view of the canals. (247 rooms)

Victoria, Damrak 1. Tel. 623.42.55. The handsome Victoria Hotel is a relic of the late 19th-century conveniently located across the water from Centraal Station. Now owned by a Swedish group, the hotel has been diligently restored, modernised and expanded. The Victoria Wing retains the original 19th-century rooms with lofty ceilings and large windows, but the furniture is modern and the mattresses made according to exacting Scandinavian standards. The day begins with a generous buffet breakfast that features seven types of cereal and six types of bread, and ends, if you wish, with a dip in the pool or a steamy sauna. (321 rooms)

Seven Bridges, Reguliersgracht 31. Tel. 623.13.29. The sort of hotel popular with young North Americans on tight budgets. The rooms are basic, but the friendly laid-back atmosphere hits the right spot. I particularly like the garden room, or any of the rooms overlooking the canal. The hotel is named after the seven bridges that can be counted from a nearby spot.

Toro, Koningslaan 64. Tel. 673.72.23. A good hotel for those looking for peace and quiet. Located in a bright, elegant 19th-century villa filled with plants and flowers, Toro has something of the atmosphere of an English country house.

The bedrooms are spacious and comfortable, some looking out on the Vondelpark. Breakfast is served in an airy room furnished with antiques and family portraits. (22 rooms)

Wiechmann, Prinsengracht 328-330. Tel. 626.33.21. This hotel enjoys an enviable location on the lively Prinsengracht. The bedrooms are simple and modern, while the lobby and breakfast room are enlivened with a few antiques, including an impressive suit of armour standing sentinel at the entrance. (36 rooms)

Wijnnobel, Vossiusstraat 9. Tel. 662.22.98. This small family-run hotel is ideal for those looking for a cheap room near the main museums. The bedrooms are bright, clean and generally large. Those at the front look out on the Vondelpark and the distant winking neon lights of Leidseplein. The location is perfect for getting to the Rijksmuseum or strolling in the park. The one problem is that there are no private bathrooms or breakfast room. For those who can survive without such luxuries, this is one of the best cheap hotels in the city.

APPENDIX C

Food and Drink

The Dutch are odd about food. We often see 17th-century paintings, such as the still life opposite by Abraham van Beyeren, in which tables are laden with bowls of fruit, glasses of wine and crumbling Dutch cheeses. This may look like a tempting feast, but a 17th-century Dutch person would have interpreted such luxury as a warning about decay and decadence. The juicy peeled lemon symbolised the deceptive sparkle of life; the toppled wine goblet spelt out death as clearly as a gaping skull. Anyone who enjoyed a rich meal in the Dutch Republic was obviously courting disaster. Even now, an educated Dutch person can hardly look at a crumbling lump of Old Gouda without briefly reflecting on mortality.

So we must not expect too much of Dutch cooking, which is, at its best, simple and straightforward. Vermeer's *Kitchen Maid*, with its jug of cold milk and crusty bread, reveals a profound Dutch desire for simplicity. In Amsterdam, we can look forward to such simple pleasures as sampling a maatjes herring at a canalside stall, eating a hunk of moist apple cake in a brown café, or perhaps sipping a Dutch gin in a traditional 17th-century tasting house. We might also enjoy investigating the various types of cheese produced by the dairy farms of the northern Netherlands. These are consumed in prodigious quantities by the Dutch, who tend to eat Gouda for breakfast, lunch and perhaps even dinner. We may find that too much, but we ought at least to become acquainted with the various ages of Gouda (young, mature and old).

The seafaring Dutch are also strongly attached to herring, which they often eat standing up at a jaunty little stalls decorated with Dutch flags. They are particularly fond of maatjes - young herring lightly cured in brine and eaten with finely-chopped raw onion. Word goes out when the first catch of maatjes is landed in May, and the Dutch rush to their favourite fish stall to sample the new fish, eating the herring by holding it by the tail and swallowing it whole.

The 17th-century voyages of discovery led to some changes in the traditional Dutch diet, as the ships of the East India Company returned with exotic spices never used before by Dutch housewives. Several new cheeses were concocted using the imported ingredients, such as *Leidse Kaas*, a cheese spiced with cumin, and the elusive *Fries nagelkaas*, a delicious Frisian cheese flavoured with cloves. The Dutch colonialists returned later with a taste for the traditional spicy cuisine of Indonesia. Most Dutch towns now have at least one Indonesian (or Chinese-Indonesian) restaurant, where customers sit down to an enormous *rijsttafel* featuring a spread of perhaps twenty different dishes. The ingredients vary, but we can expect to find a large bowl of *nasi* (white rice), a bowl of *kroepoek* (prawn crackers), several bowls of spicy meats (some of them very hot), a cooked vegetable salad, peanuts, coconut, a bowl of fruit and some little pots of spices. The main types of Indonesian cooking are

Javanese (fairly mild), Balinese (hot) and Sumatran (extremely hot). The word *pikant* (spicy) is not to be taken lightly.

Where to eat

Restaurants in the centre of Amsterdam tend to be small and constantly busy. It is worth phoning in advance to book a table.

Belhamel, Brouwersgracht 60. Tel. 622.10.95. An intimate candlelit restaurant at the quiet, lived-in end of Herengracht. The staff are utterly attentive, the menu interesting and the prices reasonable. The perfect place for a romantic evening, after which you can linger on the bridge over Brouwersgracht looking at the lights reflected in the water.

Bols Taverne, Rozengracht 106. Tel. 624.57.52. Closed on Sunday, and from mid-July to mid-August. An attractive Old Dutch restaurant located in a 17th-century merchants' house. A series of small rooms are decorated with 19th-century marine paintings and traditional North Holland furniture. A small glass of Bols liqueur is served with the coffee.

Christophe, Leliegracht 46. Tel. 625.08.07. Closed on Sunday and in early January. Christophe Royer has set new standards in canalside dining with his exquisite cooking based on traditional Mediterranean recipes. Christophe is particularly adept at using exotic ingredients such as saffron, figs and truffles to reinvent classic French and North African dishes. The interior was originally as creative as the cooking, but the fashionably bare style proved too much for some of the customers, and it has now been redecorated in a more traditional style featuring light wood and Art Deco lamps.

Dynasty, Reguliersdwarsstraat 30. Tel. 626.84.00. Closed on Tuesday and in January. An exotic Oriental restaurant decorated with silk wall hangings and upturned parasols suspended from the ceiling. The menu lists mysterious Thai and Cantonese dishes such as The Sixth Happiness and the Offering of the Emperor. The garden is idyllic in the summer.

L'Entrecôte, P. C. Hooftstraat 70. Tel. 673.77.76. Closed on Sunday and Monday. A useful restaurant in the Rijksmuseum neighbourhood,

L'Entrecôte follows a simple formula that has proved highly successful in France. Diners have a choice of veal or steak, served in French brasserie style with French fries and salad, and accompanied by a house wine. This simple approach ensures rapid service, though we can, if we want, linger over dessert and coffee.

Fong Lie, P. C. Hooftstraat 80. Tel. 671.64.04. Closed on Monday and for several weeks in July. An intimate Chinese restaurant near the Rijksmuseum offering various tempting dishes such as 'fried butterflies.' The waitresses are friendly and the food is brought to the table in the twinkling of an eye.

Kantijl & De Tijger, Spuistraat 291. Tel. 620.09.94. Open until 11 pm. The original Kantijl & De Tijger opened in The Hague a few years ago. Offering Indonesian cooking in a brasserie setting, it proved immensely successful, prompting the owners to open a branch in Amsterdam. Located just off Spui, this is the perfect place to sample Indonesian specialities. The menu is entirely in Indonesian, but the waiters are well versed in the English versions.

Keyser, Van Baerlestraat 96. Tel. 671.14.41.Closed on Sunday. This traditional Dutch restaurant has been in business since 1903. It is famous for its sole meunière, but also does good Texel lamb and IJsselmeer eel. Located at the back of a bustling café, Keyer stays open until 11.30 pm, making it popular with musicians performing at the nearby Concertgebouw.

Klaas Compaen, Raamgracht 9. Tel. 623.87.08. Open in evenings only. Closed on Sunday. Named after a 17th-century Dutch seaman, Klaas Compaen is a simple Thai restaurant near the Muziektheater. The cooks conjure up delicious dishes, many featuring coconut, in a tiny kitchen behind the bar. Not a place to linger, but a good bet for a quick bite before a concert.

De Knijp, Van Baerlestraat 134. Tel. 671.42.48. Open for lunch on Monday to Friday and every evening until midnight. A romantic restaurant near the Concertgebouw which is occasionally taken over after concerts by the entire orchestra (minus the conductor, who usually prefers the more conservative Keyzer). The dishes are mainly French, but the portions are solidly Dutch.

Lucius, Spuistraat 247. Tel. 624.18.31. Open in the evening only until 11 pm. Closed Sunday. A fashionably bare fish restaurant with long wooden benches along the walls and the day's specialities chalked up on the blackboard. Depending on the season, expect dishes featuring salmon, oysters, mussels, sea bass and John Dory. The staff are adept at translating the more baffling fish names into half a dozen languages.

Luden, Spuistraat 306. Tel. 622.89.79. Luden first opened in The Hague some years ago, offering interesting Italian and French cooking at inexpensive prices. The Amsterdam branch has copied this successful formula, offering a choice of rapid Italian food in the brasserie section or more elaborate French cooking in the restaurant.

Manchurian, Leidseplein 10A. Tel. 623.13.30. An elegant Oriental restaurant offering rare and exquisite dishes from Canton, Peking, Mongolia, Thailand and Indonesia. Owned by the same family as Dynasty, but not quite so fashionable.

Radèn Mas, Stadhouderskade 6. Tel. 685.40.41. Open until 11 pm. An elegant Indonesian restaurant offering overflowing rijsttafels.

Sauvage, Runstraat 17D. Tel. 627.06.18. Open for dinner only. A popular restaurant squeezed into a small living room. Artistic people like the decor and the innovative cooking, though some may find it too cramped, even by Amsterdam standards.

Sluizer, Utrechtsestraat 43-45. Tel. 622.63.76. Closed for lunch at weekends. The two adjoining Sluizer restaurants combine conviviality and good cooking. One restaurant specialises in plain brasserie food served in a brown café setting, and the other serves fish in an romantic Art Deco interior.

Speciaal, Nieuwe Leliestraat 142. Tel. 624.97.06. Open until 11 pm. An evocative Thai restaurant hidden in a back street of the Jordaan. It looks no larger than a shop, but opens out at the back into an attractive room with bamboo walls and ceiling fans. A tropical heat builds up as the waitresses pile ziggurats of rijsttafel dishes onto the plate warmers.

Het Stuivertje, Hazenstraat 58. Tel. 623.13.49. Open for dinner only. Closed on Monday. A popular Jordaan restaurant in the style of a brown café. The menu lists various types of steaks, which come with generous portions of salad and vegetables. Amsterdammers ask for nothing more.

Het Swarte Schaep, Korte Leidsedwarsstraat 24. Tel. 622.30.21. Open until 11 pm. An elegant restaurant off Leidseplein serving delicious duck and game dishes. The interior is decorated in Old Dutch style with dark wooden furniture and polished brass pots.

Tartufo, Singel 449. Tel. 627.71.75. Closed for lunch at weekends. A friendly Italian restaurant decorated in a cool modern style. Good for a light lunch or a lingering dinner.

Tempo Doeloe, Utrechtsestraat 75. Tel. 625.67.18. Open for dinner only. An elegant restaurant offering authentic Indonesian dishes from Java, Bali and Sumatra. The place to go for hot, spicy cuisine, but watch out for anything labelled *pedis*. It can be very hot indeed.

Tout Court, Runstraat 13. Tel. 625.86.37. Closed first week in January. A popular, bustling restaurant run by John Fagel. He offers creative French provincial cooking, though some of his dishes - featuring kidneys, liver and brains - are not for the timid. The interior is an inspiring modern

design, though the space (as in so many Amsterdam restaurants) is quite limited. Book well in advance.

Treasure, Nieuwezijds Voorburgwal 115. Tel. 626.09.15. Closed on Wednesday. The perfect Chinese restaurant, with gaudy decor, big banqueting tables and a menu that covers almost every dish imaginable. The specialities include squirrel fish, Charlie Chaplin duck and one curious dish listed on the menu as 'indescribable in Western terms.' Good for a ten-course Peking banquet or a modest dim sum lunch.

Witteveen, Ceintuurbaan 256. Tel. 662.43.68. Open until 11 pm. This traditional Dutch restaurant became quite fashionable a few years ago. Perhaps it is the Old Dutch interior with its wood-panelling, red velvet sofas and nostalgic paintings by minor Dutch artists. Or it might be the crisp white tablecloths and waitresses wearing formal black uniforms. People of all ages come here to enjoy unusually good Dutch cooking using the best Texel lamb and North Sea sole. As the evening wears on, the mood can become quite festive.

Amsterdam for Children

If we have come with children, the best area to explore is the Plantage quarter, where Amsterdam's zoo and other childhood haunts are found. We should set off straight after breakfast, taking tram 7, 9 or 14 to Plantage Kerklaan, and aiming to get to Artis soon after the gates open at 9 am. Artis has a policy of giving animals as much space as possible, with the inevitable result that there is not much left over for humans. We can promise our children attractions such as the reptile house, which is landscaped like a steamy jungle; a nocturnal house, where the animals are tricked into thinking day is night; and a large pool where seals glide around behind glass walls. The buildings are sometimes amusingly designed, such as the mock ruin where owls peer through crumbling walls, as in the paintings of Hieronymus Bosch. To those inquiring children who ask why the zoo is called Artis, we should explain that the original name of the zoo when it opened in 1838 was *Natura Artis Magister* - Nature is the Teacher of the Arts. A very intelligent child might reply that it ought therefore to be called Natura.

Our children might be ready for a change of scene by midday, in which case we can walk, or take tram 9, to the nearby Tropenmuseum at Linnaeusstraat 2, pointing out on the way the massive Muiderpoort built in 1771 as one of the city gates. On crossing the former moat, we find a splendid building bristling with turrets and beaver-tailed roofs, which was built from 1916 to 1926 to house the Dutch Colonial Institute. The lofty main hall with its cool arcades and colourful majolica friezes decorated with plants brings a certain tropical allure to this quarter of Amsterdam, particularly when the sounds of Andean flutes or a gamelan concert echo through the building.

The museum was originally founded to proclaim the achievements of Dutch colonialism, but it was purged of its much of its old collection in the 1970's, leading one woman to scrawl in the visitors' book: 'It's a nightmare. All the lovely old objects have gone.' One colonial feature survived, though not many people spot it. If we look at the columns in the main hall, we can see that they are carved with scenes from Dutch colonial history.

None of this may interest children, who will probably want to run up the stairs and explore the reconstructed village huts and streets scenes from Asia and Africa. They can also put on headphones to listen to music from far-off places, or peer into dark, dusty Indian village shops. The museum is constantly buzzing with exhibitions and activities aimed at children; it also has a restaurant that serves the sort of food that Dutch children wolf down.

That may be enough of museums for one day, though the maritime museum (described on pages 149-153) is not far from here. It is perhaps wise, though, to head for a café, where our childen may sample a *chocomel*, chocolate milk, or *warme chocolade*, hot chocolate, perhaps served with a slice of apple cake.

We won't find many good parks for children in Amsterdam. The best is the Amstelpark, which in the summer has a miniature train, pony rides, a farmyard and a pancake house. The main drawback is that we have to take tram 4 to RAI, then hunt for the park entrance just beyond the Novotel. A better bet, pehaps, is to let the children climb to the top of the Westerkerk tower, or run around the courtyards of the Amsterdam Historical Museum. As a last resort, we can take them on a canal boat, seeing if they can spot odd details like herons perched on houseboats or statues on the roofs of houses. We could also plan an energetic excursion after dark to look at the illuminated bridges along Reguliersgracht and Leidsegracht, ending up on Leidseplein listening to the buskers.

Further pleasures

I. Cafés. Amsterdam's brown cafés are places to linger over a coffee as we read the newspaper or write a few postcards home. The cosy, fuggy interiors tend to be decorated with an assortment of brown wooden furniture, while the smoke-stained walls are plastered with theatre posters. Some of these cafés date back to Rembrandt's day, such as Karpershoek at Martelaarsgracht 2 which, if the sign in flourishing calligraphy is to be trusted, opened in 1629. The Hoppe at Spui 20 is almost as ancient, as its sawdust-strewn floor suggests. The Smalle at Egelantiersgracht 12 is another long-established tavern where Pieter Hoppe once sold gin. Now restored, the interior recalls the 17th-century taverns painted by Jan Steen.

Other brown cafés are not that old, but manage to convince us of their antiquity. The Molenpad at Prinsengracht 653 and De Doffer at Runstraat 12 are popular student cafés where the candles flicker into the early hours. The Luxembourg at Spui 22 is a more recent arrival; it is one of the few brown cafés where waiters and waitresses serve at the tables. If we find ourselves on Leidseplein, a beer can be had in Eijlders at Korte Leidsedwarsstraat 47, a favourite haunt of Dutch writers and poets, or Reijnders at Leidseplein 6, a cheerful, mildly scruffy bar where the billiard players are prone to burst into sentimental song at the slightest excuse.

A new breed of white café came along in the early 1970's, with white walls and shiny metal tables. One of the first of the new cafés was Land van Walem at Keizersgracht 449. Decorated in a style that recalled the architecture of Gerrit Rietveld, it quickly became popular with graphic designers, fashion models and successful artists. It was joined by Morlang at Keizersgracht 451 and several others, some of which have gone bust in the meantime.

Now we have grand cafés, which hark back nostalgically to the establishments listed a century ago in Karl Baedeker's guidebooks. The American on Leidseplein is the most impressive survival of this age. It has been joined by the reopened De Kroon on Rembrandtsplein, a wonderful relic from the late 19th-century, and the striking De Jaren at Nieuwe Doelenstraat 22, a vast modern café on several levels with a water-front terrace.

Many cafés have small kitchens where a chef prepares basic Dutch dishes such as steaks, fish and *uitsmijters* (ham and egg served on bread). These *eetcafés* are cheaper than restaurants and the food is often excellent. I can recommend De Jaren, Frascati, Walem, Het Molenpad, Luxembourg, Ovidius and the outstanding Van Puffelen.

II. Gin tasting houses. The distilleries of Schiedam, Amsterdam and other Dutch cities produce a remarkable variety of gins (*jenevers*). The key distinction is between old (*oude jenever*) and young (*jonge jenever*), though Dutch distillers like to concoct various exotic brands by adding herbs and spices. Specialities include *bessen jenever* (flavoured with berrries), *korenwijn* (jenever distilled with the oils of juniper berries) and *Beerenburg* (a herbal bitter invented by the Amsterdam spice dealer Hendrick van Beerenburg). Other jenevers are served on special occasions, such as *Bruidstranen* ('bride's tears', served at weddings) and *Boerenjongen* ('farmer boy', a mild jenever given to boys). Many Dutch cities still have traditional 18th-century tasting houses known as *proeflokalen* where jenevers are served in tiny tulip glasses. The opening hours of the proeflokaal are more like those of a shop than a pub, opening at about 11 am and chasing the last customers out soon after 8 pm.

III. Canal boats. It is worth taking a one-hour canal boat tour, if only to see the city from the water, though the dull commentary, repeated in four languages, can be dispiriting. The most interesting tours are run by the Rederij Noord-Zuid, beginning near the Rijksmuseum, opposite

Stadhouderskade 25. They use boats with open decks at the back, rather than the more common enclosed glass vessels. It can also be enjoyable buying a day ticket for the Museumboot, which allows you to hop off at various stops along the route, generally close to the major museums.

IV. Small shops and street markets. The best shops in Amsterdam tend to be tiny, cramped boutiques with low ceilings and treacherous staircases, where you find a thousand types of buttons, an erudite selection of cookbooks or a unique range of tin toys. The most interesting shopping streets are those that cross the main canals, such as Utrechtsestraat, Runstraat, Berenstraat, Wolvenstraat and Prinsenstraat. The Jordaan is also dotted with intriguing little shops.

V. Concerts. The Dutch take classical music seriously. We will find concerts being performed in historic churches, the Pianola Museum and even occasionally Cristofori's piano shop at Prinsengracht 583. If we are serious about music, we should try to get tickets in advance for the Concertgebouw, where the famous Concertgebouw Orchestra performs.

Be sure to check the date. If it is near the end of August, we might catch the Pulitzer Concert, when a chamber orchestra performs classical music after dark on a barge moored outside the Pulitzer Hotel. Music lovers crowd onto the quays and bridges, or listen from little boats bobbing on the water. The event is now televised, but nothing can beat the experience of standing on the canal on a warm summer evening listening to the music.

VI. Jazz bars. Jazz bars are often the friendliest places in a strange city. My favourite jazz dive is Alto, off Leidseplein at Korte Leidsedwarsstraat 115, a small, cosmopolitan place with a relaxed atmosphere. The doors open at 9 pm, but it is rare for anyone to play a note before 10 pm. Those with stamina will go on playing until 3 am on most nights, and even later at the weekend. The String, off Dam at Nes 98, is another relaxed café where folk singers perform until long after the last tram has gone. The more serious jazz musicians perform at the Bimhuis, at Oudeschans 73, but you will have to buy a ticket in advance for a performance. Another address to consider is the IJsbreker, on the right bank of the Amstel at Weesperzijde 23, famous for both experimental music and exceptional hot chocolate.

VII. Carillon concerts. We may notice the bells of a carillon playing as we are wandering along a canal or sitting on a café terrace. Most Dutch towns have a 17th-century carillon, but Amsterdam has four, which hang in the towers of the Oudekerk, Zuiderkerk, Westerkerk and Munttoren. The bells are primed to play a snatch of music - a folk tune or nursery rhyme - every 15 minutes. Once a week, the local carilloneur climbs to the top of the tower, sits down at a wooden keyboard in the draughty belfry, and hammers out a concert lasting an hour or so. The carilloneur rings the bells by banging the keys with the side of the fist, which can be painful, as we will have discovered if we tried out the keyboard in the Amsterdam Historical Museum.

It is worth trying to catch one of the hour-long carillon concerts performed every week. The Westerkerk carillon is played on Tuesdays from noon, the Zuiderkerk on Thursdays from noon, the Munttoren on Fridays from noon, and the Oudekerk on Saturdays from 4 pm to 5 pm. We can listen to the Oudekerk concert on walk 1, the Zuiderkerk on walk 3 and the Westerkerk on walk 8. We can also catch the Westerkerk concert from the café terrace of 't Smalle or De Prins, or, more idyllic still, sitting in the garden of the Pulitzer Hotel.

VIII. Cinemas. Film fans should find something worth watching in the Amsterdam cinemas, even if they do not speak a word of Dutch. Almost all films are screened in the original language with Dutch subtitles, apart from children's cartoons which tend to be dubbed. To add to our pleasure, Amsterdam retains some scintillating old cinemas from the 1920's and 1930's with intact Art Deco and Modernist interiors.

The oldest cinema in town is the Uitkijk at Prinsengracht 452. It was founded in 1913, just as Chaplin's first films began flickering on cinema screens. Occupying a house built in 1902, it is Amsterdam's only canalside cinema. The programme features films that have won awards at the Cannes or Berlin festivals, or any serious movie likely to fill the 158-seat theatre. The grandest cinema is Tuschinski, Reguliersbreestraat 26, whose twin towers look as if they might have come from the set of D.W. Griffith's *Intolerance*. The interior is equally spectacular, with deep peacock carpets and moody Oriental decoration. This dream palace was built in 1921 by Abram Tuschinski, a Jewish emigré from Poland who later died in a concentration camp. The six-screen cinema is now owned by the Cannon group, who have spared no expense in preserving the interior, and generously allow visitors to wander around the lobby without buying a ticket. The cinema organises occasional guided tours in July and August.

The Movies at 161 Haarlemmerdijk 161 was opened on the edge of the Jordaan in 1928. This three-screen complex is decorated in an exotic Egyptian style and illuminated with dim·Art Deco lights. The films screened here tend to be alternative works by Spanish and Italian directors, which are earnestly discussed afterwards in the cinema café. Desmet, Plantage Middenlaan 4A, is another relic of cinema's Art Deco age, where we can watch recent avant-garde movies or forgotten classics.

Several mainstream cinemas are located on Leidseplein, but Cinecenter, just off Leidseplein at Lijnbaansgracht 236, shows more unusual films in its four small theatres. The café in the foyer offers a comfortable place to linger before the film. The Melkweg at Lijnbaansgracht 234 has a small cinema where the most unexpected films are sometimes screened. It has even devoted an entire season to 'road safety films of the 1950's', probably for the horrific crashes rather than the promotion of safety awareness. The Filmmuseum in the Vondelpark, which occupies a grand café built in the 1880's, can be counted on to blow the dust off old reels by forgotten movie geniuses. The museum's passions embrace Visconti, American B movies and Japanese cinema.

IX. Marken. If we are here in July or August, we

had better avoid Marken. It will be too crowded. Even H.V. Morton found Marken impossible, and he travelled there in 1905 when it was necessary to take a steamer to the island. Now that Marken is linked to the mainland by a causeway, it would seem that this little island community is beyond hope.

But perhaps not. If we come out of season, and take time to explore the remote parts of the island (not that anything is particularly remote), we stand a good chance of finding something of the breezy charm that enchanted the 19th-century French artists who flocked here in search of the picturesque. We can still travel to Marken by boat, though we need to plan the trip carefully, taking a bus 115 from Centraal Station to Monnickendam, then catching the Marken ferry from the harbour.

Monnickendam is a sleepy old port where the locals seem to have no interest in luring tourists. Yet it is an attractive town, with several old eel smoke houses near the harbour. If we are not in a rush, we can stop in the café-restaurant Nieuw Stuttenburgh at Haringburgwal 4, a traditional Dutch restaurant described on page 282.

The ferry drops us in the old quarter of Marken, the Havenbuurt, where we get our first glimpse of the island's curious black tarred wooden houses, built on stilts to avoid flooding. Ignoring the tourist shops, we head inland to the Kerkbuurt, the quarter around the church, then follow the signs to the Rozenwerf. We will notice several clusters of houses standing on a low hillocks to avoid flooding. A brisk walk along the dike leads to a solitary lighthouse at the tip of the island.

We can then walk back along the other shore and end our trip in the pleasant café-restaurant De Taanderij at Havenbuurt 1. It is closed on a Monday, which is a pity, as this is the day when the locals launder their gaudy traditional costumes and hang them on the lines to dry.

Books about Amsterdam

I. What to read. Many of the best observations on Amsterdam were made by writers in the 17th century such as John Evelyn, whose diary contains entries he wrote during a journey through the Low Countries in 1641. Evelyn is enthusiastic about the houses of correction and astonished to learn about a Dutch woman on her twenty-fifth husband. William Temple visited the Netherlands on official business, organising a political alliance and arranging a royal marriage, but he nonetheless found the time to write his sharp *Observations upon the Netherlands* (1673), in which he reassured his English readers that the Dutch were prone to gout and scurvy. A century later, Boswell spent a year in Holland in 1763-64, officially to study law but unofficially in pursuit of a suitable wife. His youthful diary entries can be read in *Boswell in Holland* (1952), edited by Frederick A. Pottle. The entry for 26 May 1764, records his visit to an Amsterdam brothel where he 'performed like any common sailor.'

Sacheverell Sitwell's *The Netherlands* (1948, reprinted 1974) is a lively study of Dutch art and society in the 18th century, good on the differences between the English and the Dutch. Adam Hopkin's well-informed *Holland* (1988) explains various characteristic aspects of Dutch culture such as public life, Dutch interiors and the trauma of the Nazi Occupation. It includes a lively account of Rembrandt's Amsterdam, which might be read before embarking on walk 3 in this book. Simon Schama's *The Embarrassment of Riches* (1987) is a feast of a book that explores the nooks and crannies of Dutch culture in the Golden Age. Like all of Schama's books, it is an intriguing cabinet of curiosities to dip into on a long winter evening.

The heroic period in Dutch history is vividly recreated in John Motley's classic three-volume *History of the Dutch Republic* (first published in

1856), a thoroughly readable, if somewhat unreliable, 19th-century account of the Dutch revolt. Some of Motley's mistakes were corrected in Pieter Geyl's *Revolt of the Netherlands* (1958), though history students are now expected to rely on Geoffrey Parker's more recent *Dutch Republic* (1977).

It is worth hunting for a copy of Eugène Fromentin's *The Masters of Past Time* (1948), a French painter's personal account of a journey through the Low Countries in search of Dutch and Flemish art. A similar journey could be done today, at least through Holland, with the help of Christopher Wright's *Amsterdam and The Hague* (1995), a guide to selected paintings in Amsterdam, The Hague, Haarlem and Leiden, including Gerrit Dou's painting of *Rembrandt's mother reading the Bible*, reproduced here, which Wright tells us is not in fact Rembrandt's mother any more than the book is the Bible. One of the most complete studies of Dutch art is R. H. Fuchs' *Dutch Painting* (1978), which begins with the Flemish Primitives and ends with some of the Dutch artists who can now be seen exhibiting in the

Stedelijk Museum. The more limited *Dutch Art and Architecture 1600-1800* by Jakob Rosenberg, Seymour Slive and E. H. ter Kuile (1977), is mainly about paintings but has interesting insights into the architecture of the period. Those who like to know something about the artists' personalities will find this book particularly fascinating. One of the more controversial books of recent years, Svetlana Alpers' *The Art of Describing: Dutch Art in the Seventeenth Century* (1983) argues that Dutch artists were engaged in a scientific recording of the world, not a view that has won much support in the Netherlands.

Kenneth Clark has written a useful little introduction to *Rembrandt* (1978), but Christopher White's biography *Rembrandt* (1984) has more on Rembrandt's links with Amsterdam. It is also worth hunting for a copy of the catalogue of the 1992 Rembrandt exhibition, *Rembrandt: the Master and his Workshop*, which explains the techniques used by the Rembrandt Research Project to discredit many alleged Rembrandt paintings.

Of the many books on Van Gogh, the most thorough is Jan Hulsker's *The Complete Van Gogh* (1980). Van Gogh's desperate pursuit of painting is revealed in *The Letters of Vincent Van Gogh*, selected and edited by Ronald de Leeuw. The catalogue of the 1990 Van Gogh exhibition adds some new insights on the artist. The 1996 Vermeer exhibition has also spawned an impressive catalogue which reveals some of Vermeer's perspective techniques.

One book that hardly needs to be mentioned is Anne Frank's *The Diary of a Young Girl* (1947). Written by Anne Frank while her family were in hiding from the Nazis, it is one of the essential texts of modern literature. The 1995 edition restores lengthy passages that were cut from the original text by Otto Frank, generally because they were about sex but occasionally when they criticised the other people hiding in the secret annexe.

The greatest Dutch novel remains Multatuli's *Max Havelaar* (1860), a biting account of a pompous Dutch coffee dealer's life in the Dutch colonies. Albert Camus' *The Fall* (1957) is set in Amsterdam, where the narrator dwells on wartime morality as he wanders along the dank canals. The war years tend also to preoccupy many modern Dutch writers, including Harry Mulisch, whose novel *The Assault* (1986) deals with the consequences of an attack on a policeman in occupied Haarlem. For a less demanding read, the enjoyable detective novels of Nicholas Freeling are often set in Amsterdam locations.

E. V. Lucas' *A Wanderer in Holland* (1905) is still one of the most readable guidebooks to the Netherlands, with lively descriptions of artists and interiors. A more useful guidebook for the contemporary visitor is *The Time Off Guide to Amsterdam*, compiled by various Dutch writers whose intimate knowledge of the city's nightlife is unrivalled. The architectural details of Amsterdam are discussed in a fascinating little book, *Amsterdam in Detail*, edited by Maarten Kloos (1996) - excellent on pavement bricks, hoist beams and the other tiny features that make Amsterdam unique. Finally, Gillian Riley's *The Dutch Table* (1994) is a delightful study of Dutch cooking written by a food historian.

II. Where to find books. Amsterdam is a book-hunter's paradise. The city has several large bookshops such as Scheltema, Holkema & Vermeulen at Koningsplein 20 and the excellent Athenaeum Boekhandel at Spui 14. The smaller and more serious Allert de Lange at Damrak 62 has a good selection of literature in Dutch, German, French and English. Books in English, along with videotapes and magazines, are found in W.H. Smith at Kalverstraat 152, just off Spui, and in The English Bookshop at Lauriergracht 71. But the pleasure really starts when you begin to explore the specialised bookshops, such as Ciné Qua Non at Staalstraat 14, which specialises in film books, the International Theatre Bookshop at Leidseplein 26, or Architectura & Natura at Leliegracht 44, where architecture and nature books lie around in teetering piles. For those with stamina to spare, there are also numerous second-hand bookshops in which to hunt for elusive books. Best for English books are the Book Exchange at Kloveniersburgwal 58 and Book Traffic at Leliegracht 50.

Index

Cafés and museums are indexed under collective headings

PALLAS GUIDES

LANDSCAPE PEOPLE ART ARCHITECTURE

Uniform with this volume:

FLEMISH CITIES EXPLORED

BRUGES, GHENT, ANTWERP, MECHELEN, LEUVEN, OSTEND

Derek Blyth

The best of all cultural city guides *The Times*

Superbly informative *RA Magazine*

No one should travel to Bruges without a copy of Derek Blyth's excellent book
Val Hennessey in *Daily Mail*

Derek Blyth guides us expertly – contains much that will be unfamiliar
Times Literary Supplement

Well researched and informative *Aberdeen Press and Journal*

An ideal travelling companion *Geographical Magazine*

SECOND REVISED EDITION

PALLAS GUIDES

LANDSCAPE PEOPLE ART ARCHITECTURE

Uniform with this volume:

MADRID OBSERVED

Michael Jacobs

A zestful, beautifully fluent text: the book's particular delight is its profusion of off-beat information *Lookout* Madrid

One of the best current foreign writers on Spain *Time Out*

An engaging, wonderfully informative and ever-surprising companion *Jan Morris*

Jacobs has a gift for finding exotic corners in a familiar city and of resuscitating the forgotten with colourful intensity
Paul Preston in *Times Literary Supplement*

Ruminative, intelligent and exceptionally well informed *The Oldie*

Learned but very funny *Sunday Telegraph*   Richly idiosyncratic *London Magazine*

The ideal companion we all dream of: patient, lively and endlessly generous with his encyclopaedic, cultivated mind *Irish Independent*

PALLAS GUIDES

LANDSCAPE PEOPLE ART ARCHITECTURE

Uniform with this volume:

VENICE FOR PLEASURE

J. G. Links

Not only the best guide-book to that city ever written, but
the best guide-book to *any* city ever written *Bernard Levin* in *The Times*

One of the most delightful and original guides ever written *Jan Morris*

A trusty companion *Ned Sherrin* in *Mail on Sunday*

An absolute must for anyone going to Venice *Evening Standard*

Essential and much loved *Anderson's Travel Companion*

A world authority on Venice *Jeffrey Bernard* in *The Spectator*

Peerless *Saga Magazine*   Quite brilliant *Country Living*   Classic *Country Lifez*

The little classic *Good Book Guide*   Let's do it again, J. G. *Sue Lawley* in *The Daily Telegraph*

NOW IN SIXTH EDITION, WITH COLOUR

PALLAS GUIDES
LANDSCAPE PEOPLE ART ARCHITECTURE

In our Pallas Guide series

POLAND

As detailed a guide as you will find *Perspectives*

This hefty item is a cultural treasure *Polish American Journal*

CZECH AND SLOVAK REPUBLICS

Highly informative and quite admirable *The Art Newspaper*

As carefully thought out as an old Baedeker *Time Out*

WALES

Certainly the best book on the country *New York Times*

A passionate and fabulously detailed book *The Rough Guide*

EAST ANGLIA

A stunningly good guide *Mail on Sunday*

Peter Sager is an unsung genius *Val Hennessey, Daily Mail*

ANDALUCÍA

Michael Jacobs has an idiosyncratic eye which misses little *The Times*

No other book can compare *Cosmopolitan*